MEMOIRS OF A FRUITCAKE

CHRIS EVANS

MEMOIRS OF A FRUITCAKE

The Wilderness Years 2000–2010

(plus a bit before but it
didn't sound as good)

HarperCollins*Publishers*

HarperCollins*Publishers*
77–85 Fulham Palace Road,
Hammersmith, London W6 8JB

www.harpercollins.co.uk

First published by HarperCollins*Publishers* 2010

1 3 5 7 9 10 8 6 4 2

All photographs are courtesy of the author with the exception of the following:

Plate 1: Page 1, middle left: PHOTOGRAPH BY GARRETT BRENNAN/CPI, CAMERA PRESS
LONDON; Page 1, bottom left: PHOTOGRAPH BY GARRETT BRENNAN/CPI, CAMERA
PRESS LONDON; Page 3, above right: © Starstock/Photoshot; Page 5, middle left: courtesy of
Gordon MacGeachy; Page 5, middle right: courtesy of Gordon MacGeachy;
Page 5, bottom right: © Talking Sport/Photoshot

Plate 2: Page 11, below right: Neale Haynes/Contour by Getty Images; Page 12, below:
© Jackie King; Page 10 middle right: Jeff Moore/Jeff Moore/Empics Entertainment;
Page 13, below: © Brian J. Ritchie/Rex Features; Page 15, above left: courtesy of the Radio
Times; Page 15, above right: © The One Show; Page 16, © Rankin

Endpaper photographs © Camera Press/James Peltekian; Getty Images;
Daily Mirror/Mirrorpix; Press Association Images; Starstock/UPPA/Photoshot;
Rex Features; Shutterstock

A catalogue record of this book is
available from the British Library

HB ISBN 978-0-00-7901692

Printed and bound in Spain by
RODESA

Mixed Sources
Product group from well-managed
forests and other controlled sources
www.fsc.org Cert no. SW-COC-001806
© 1996 Forest Stewardship Council
FSC

FSC is a non-profit international organisation established to promote the
responsible management of the world's forests. Products carrying the FSC
label are independently certified to assure consumers that they come
from forests that are managed to meet the social, economic and
ecological needs of present or future generations.

Find out more about HarperCollins and the environment at
www.harpercollins.co.uk/green

DEDICATION

To my mum Minnie, my daughter Jade, my son Noah and most of all to my wife Natasha, who put up with me spending six months in the garage with my past instead of spending six months in the house with the present.

And to my balls, which thankfully I still have after Tash capitulated on her threat to cut them off if I hadn't finished this book before our summer holidays in Portugal, something I failed spectacularly to do.

CONTENTS

PART TWO WHEN BILLIE MET CHRIS

TOP 10 ...

PART THREE THE RETURN OF RADIO BOY – TAKE THREE

TOP 10 ...

INTRODUCTION

TOP 10 HIGHLIGHTS OF MY TALE SO FAR

10 Born with ginger hair and glasses to Mum and Dad (Martin and Minnie) in Warrington in 1966

9 Younger brother to Diane and David

8 Father died of cancer when I was thirteen and life changed – soon afterwards, I obtained my first job in a newsagent's

7 Heard Timmy Mallett on the radio, fell in love with the wireless

6 Secured job at Piccadilly Radio in Manchester, as tea boy

5 Moved down to London, worked at BBC Greater London Radio

4 Was chosen to front *The Big Breakfast* with Gaby Roslin and Zig and Zag

3 Created *Don't Forget Your Toothbrush*, followed by *TFI Friday*, for Channel 4

2 Took up post as host of Radio 1 *Breakfast Show*, walked out after a year (idiot)

1 Bought Virgin Radio from Richard Branson after borrowing £85 million

NOW THERE ARE SHOWBIZ STORIES and then there are stories about showbiz – the latter for me infinitely more interesting and compelling. These are the stories behind the stories if you like, about how the business works and sometimes doesn't work and what kind of people want, or more often need, to be part of such madness.

That's what this book is. It is my story of my madness and my experience in show business. It was always a dream, it's often been a nightmare, but it's never been dull. If my first book was the climb up the mountain to fame, fortune and the life I thought I wanted, this second volume sees me diving head first off a cliff and then trying to figure out why.

In the days when I took over the ownership of Virgin I was a 'live for today' kind of guy. I tended to jump in with both feet, and worry about the consequences later.

It's only recently that I have woken up to the fact that the live for today philosophy, although often liberating and fantastically exciting at the time, can be damaging and destructive to almost everything you hold dear. Of course there's nothing wrong with the pursuit of one's hopes and aspirations but real life must always be taken care of first – or at least very quickly afterwards, because to achieve success at the expense of a single other human being is wholly unacceptable.

While it's admirable to strive with energy and ambition fuelling your tank, this does not serve as an excuse to start hundreds of things off willy-nilly without at least giving some thought to how they might be concluded. This is the number one crime of the irresponsible dream seeker whose lives are littered with false starts, broken middles and a severe lack of happy endings.

It's better to enjoy happiness and a clear conscience by doing the right things by people along the way. The keys to the kingdom of contentment and a good night's sleep are only a few decent decisions away. Talent is not an excuse to use and abuse or take short cuts.

So let's see how little of this I realised when I needed to, shall we? Because, as you will soon see, having bought my radio station for all the right reasons – things would end up going very, very wrong.

Little did I know that in the ensuing years, I would enter the list of the top 500 richest people in Britain whilst simultaneously becoming a lout, a drunk, dangerously unstable, generally out of control, almost completely friendless, full of hubris, and the unhappiest I'd ever been. These darkest of days would also see me plumb the depths of self-destruction, usually the more publicly the better and not care who witnessed me doing it.

Why I didn't take this journey to its mortal conclusion and how the hell I got my life back on track I am as keen to discover as you – so let's go.

Buckle up my friends – this one really is a bumpy ride.

PART ONE
MEMOIRS OF A FRUITCAKE

TOP
10 'TURNS' I HAVE EMPLOYED

10 Chris Moyles
 9 Gaby Roslin
 8 Terry Wogan
 7 Vernon Kay
 6 Danny Baker
 5 Jimmy Tarbuck
 4 Lionel Blair
 3 Melanie Sykes
 2 Terry Venables
 1 Jonathan Ross

SO WHERE WERE WE?

Ah yes, October 1997 and I had launched my breakfast show on Virgin Radio – a great gig, except that Virgin's owner, Richard Branson, was about to sell the station to the Capital Group, whereupon I would be out of a job in just ten weeks; barely enough time to get used to the decor.

That's when the highly precocious ruse occurred in my ludicrously over-ambitious mind; to see if I could buy the station myself. It was the craziest of my not inconsiderable list of crazy ideas to date, but if I wanted to stay on the air then I had no choice. After my disastrously self-indulgent, ego-fuelled departure from Radio 1 only a few months before, my reputation was in tatters, rendering me virtually unemployable.

Astonishingly, with the help of some major financial backers, and with a top team around me, I pulled it off. Two months after joining the station I snapped up the ownership of Virgin Radio from under the noses of the Capital Group, overnight finding myself breakfast DJ and proprietor rolled into one.

I'd been in a few fairly daunting positions before in my rollercoaster career, though nothing quite on this scale. However, my owning Virgin Radio was only ever destined to be a temporary proprietorship. I was always going to have to sell the station to repay the people who had lent me the money in the first place – a story we will get to all in good time.

Meanwhile, I was still presenting *TFI Friday* every week, so my new job of media mogul had to be fitted in between my morning radio programme and the Friday TV show. But hey, I was a young man with vast amounts of energy, limitless enthusiasm and more ideas than I knew what to do with. What could possibly go wrong? I asked myself.

Answer; everything. But not just quite yet.

There I was, king of my own media castle, albeit with the minor inconvenience of owing the banks, my investors and Richard Branson £85 million.

Was I nervous? Not in the least. Not a lot can make you nervous after borrowing £85 million – unless it's the possibility of losing it. But I wasn't going there. I was excited and couldn't wait to get to grips with my new empire.

In the beginning, before I discovered there was also a downside to being the boss, what turned me on most was the freedom I had to be creative. I was now in a similar position to many of my heroes, two in particular, namely Charlie Chaplin and Jim Henson. I have been a fan of both for years.

Chaplin was a truly exceptional man, almost more so for his business acumen than his on-screen genius. As soon as Charlie could afford to, he bought his own studios on La Cienega Boulevard in Los Angeles, where he began to self-fund and self-produce some of his most famous movies. With independence came control and with control came purity and perfection. He could green-light his own projects and make them exactly as he wanted without having to kowtow to any studio egomaniacs.

This situation only served to bolster Charlie's already formidable confidence, and with talent plus creative control equalling power and profitability, before he was thirty the boy from the slums of south London was earning well in excess of $1 million a year – back in the 1920s!

Jim Henson was equally autonomous with his legendary Muppet productions almost half a century later; the beautifully ironic connection being that he bought the old Chaplin studios to use as his base. My favourite part of this story is that whereas in Chaplin's day there was a giant statue of his tramp standing proudly on the roof for all of Tinseltown to see, when Jim moved in he erected a similar-sized statue of Kermit the Frog. And best of all – in homage to the studio's former illustrious owner – Henson also dressed the world's favourite amphibian as Chaplin's tramp, complete with black suit, funny shoes, cane and bowler hat. This cleverest of tributes can still be seen atop the studio roof today.

With thoughts like these racing through my mind, I couldn't help feeling inspired by the massive opportunities that lay ahead of me. I too owned my own company, the Ginger Media Group, consisting now of a television production arm – Ginger Productions, which made *TFI Friday* – and a radio station. I also had a five-year lease on my own television studio, and I was surrounded by producers, writers and people who could make things happen at a moment's notice.

Almost straight away I decided to take advantage of my new-found freedom.

It was a Saturday morning and I'd just been for a run. Having returned home a little sweaty I decided to treat myself to a few bubbles and a good old soak – I love the lure of the lather. I lay there luxuriating and listening to one of our competitors, broadcasting that it was the first day of the footy season and how we should all be lapping it up.

The presenter and his various contributors sounded progressively more ebullient, and as the show went on, the more I felt we were missing out as my station had little if anything to do with football. This was a big day for millions of people and we were not part of it.

'Hang on a minute, I don't need to feel like this anymore,' I thought. 'I own the damn radio station, I can do anything I want and I don't have to ask anyone's permission.'

I jumped out of the bath, rang the studio and told the DJ who was currently on air to inform the guy who followed him that he could have the afternoon off. I was on my way in and I would be presenting our new Saturday afternoon sports and music show.

'Really, what shall I say it's called?' he asked.

'Oh, er – hang on a sec, I'll ring you back with that.'

I hadn't considered a title. Two minutes later I was back on the phone.

'Tell him – and the listeners whilst you're at it – that the new show is called *Rock and Roll Football*. Music and footy all the way till final score. It does exactly what it says on the tin.'

After making a quick cup of tea and throwing on some clothes, I began a ring round of the biggest footie heads I knew and asked them to come and help me. To a man they obliged, although they had little idea as to what exactly they might be helping me with.

That afternoon we launched one of the most straightforward shows I have ever been involved in. All we did was play music whilst watching Sky Sports *Soccer Saturday* with the sound down. Every time there was a goal we let our listeners know where it had occurred and who had scored it, then it was back to the music. At half-time we would have a quick 'round the grounds' catch-up, also featuring different half-time treats from different clubs; curries, kebabs, pork pies, pasties and whatever else fans were munching on.

Come five o'clock we presented our own slapdash version of the classified results, followed by any breaking footie stories, followed by half an hour of going-out music, which was exactly what we had intended to do the second the original programme had come off air.

Rock and Roll Football remained on air every Saturday afternoon during the football season until 2008 – almost a decade after I had left the radio station, picking up some pretty hefty sponsors along the way. And all because of a sweaty jog resulting in me needing a bath and a few bubbles.

As my reign as boss continued, my creative freedom quickly extended to hiring new talent that I thought might strengthen our line-up. My first top-three signings were ex-England football manager Terry Venables, BRMB's Harriet Scott and the über-famous Jonathan Ross.

Because *Rock and Roll Football* had been an instant hit, I decided to start the sporting theme earlier on in the schedule and asked El Tel to co-host a football phone-in at midday on Saturday.

Terry was another hero of mine who had since become a pal. We first met in a local wine bar, when he let me into the secret of how he set about organising the England team to trounce Holland 4–1 at Wembley during Euro 96. He swore me to secrecy, so all I can say is it was simple but genius. Now I wanted *that* genius on the radio. Thankfully, he agreed and our footy phone-in was born.

Hiring Harriet Scott, my first female signing, was the result of listening to a good old-fashioned demo-tape that someone played me one morning. She had clearly racked up a lot of hours on the wireless, sounding warm and at ease, her style flowing effortlessly thanks to all those little tricks of the trade without which a radio show can sound so terribly clunky.

We called her agent and offered her a gig straight away. She accepted and a few weeks later moved down from Birmingham to London to become the new host of our afternoon show.

However, there was more to Harriet than first met the eye. She was a young lady who'd had her own fair share of headlines in the past – front pages of the tabloids, no less.

'Oh, I remember now,' I exclaimed one night in the pub when she mentioned the incident in question. The story was all about a to-do she'd had with the husband of a famous female television presenter with whom it was alleged she was having a secret liaison. Apparently during one of their dates she'd whacked him one and given him a black eye in the process. The tabloids subsequently splashed the picture of the bloke and his shiner all over their front pages.

'Feisty little Harriet,' I thought.

'And yet you seem so calm and gentle and … small,' I said to her.

'Yeah, well you just watch it matey, there's plenty more where that came from,' she giggled. At least I think she giggled.

Several years later, when I was no longer her boss, Harriet and I dated for a while – a most enjoyable experience from beginning to end I'm glad to say, and one from which I emerged entirely injury-free. Goodness only knows what the other fellow had done to incur her wrath.

Jonathan Ross was the next name on my hit list, and oh what twists and turns our relationship would come to experience. Jonathan has been a recurring theme throughout my career for reasons that will become evident as the pages of this story unfold, but I initially encountered him in my very first job after I'd moved down to London.

I was a wet-behind-the-ears twenty-three-year-old from Manchester's Piccadilly Radio and had managed to blag a job as a production assistant on a new night-time station called Radio Radio.

Jonathan was quickly becoming the hottest new face on television with his Channel 4 chat show *The Last Resort* and had agreed to present a one-hour radio show twice a week for the fledgling network in return for a squillion pounds. Unfortunately for everyone involved none of this lasted very long, with the company folding only a few months later under spiralling costs and practically zero advertising revenue.

Following Radio Radio, our paths had crossed several times since, as I had now become a recognisable face in my own right and had appeared as a guest on his *Saturday Zoo* show, as well as attempting to collaborate with him in an effort to get him back on television when he'd lost his way a bit.

[Adopt Michael Caine voice here] Now not a lot of people know this but I actually wrote *TFI Friday* for Jonathan. I was going to produce it with him as the presenter.

I'd asked him over to my flat in north London for a cup of tea, where the two of us lay on the grass in my garden, chewing the television fat. I remember it vividly, second only to the day I asked Jools Holland (my ultimate TV hero) to be musical director on *Don't Forget Your Toothbrush*, another red-letter day for the Evans boy.

My initial idea for Jonathan was for a Sunday show based in a church, with Jonathan as the preacher/host, the congregation/audience in the pews, guests in the confessional and music from the choir area.

The Sunday Joint, as I had titled it, slowly evolved into *TFI Friday* after I came to the conclusion it was probably better to piggyback on the natural positive energy of a Friday evening than try to manufacture similar energy on a Sunday.

The main man at Channel 4 at the time liked the idea for the show but when I declared Jonathan as my first-choice host, replied with these exact words:

'Everyone knows Jonathan is yesterday's man.'

This didn't stop the same exec trying to rehire him a few years later when he was back on top.

As Jonathan's brother Paul always says, 'Form is temporary – class is permanent.' Bravo Paul and bravo Jonathan, for now at least.

After I eventually took up the mantle of *TFI Friday*, Jonathan's career continued to founder but I was always wondering how I could get to work with him. Now I owned my own radio station I could simply offer him a job.

Our Saturday line-up was becoming an unexpected highlight of the week, with Terry at lunchtime, *Rock and Roll Football* in the afternoon, and Johnny Boy Revell and his *Wheels of Steel* ushering us into Saturday night. If Wossy was at a loose end, he could do a lot worse than kick off our Saturdays with a mid-morning music/interview show ...

For me he is the most natural talker in British broadcasting. He isn't just blessed with a sharp mind and a quick jaw; it's almost as if Jonathan needs to talk to stay alive.

The only other person I've seen blessed/blighted with this condition is the great Danny Baker, who runs JR pretty close when it comes to the art of rabbiting. I once went out for lunch with both of them. I don't think I said more than fifteen words for the duration of the whole meal, as Jonathan and Danny went head to head in a conversational clash of the titans. They talked continuously and – for the most part – at the same time. I was sure that neither of them listened to a single word the other one had to say.

When I made the call to JR about coming to work for me it was a really big deal. I felt almost audacious as I sat in my recently purchased, stupidly big, green Bentley parked spookily enough in Great Portland Street, right outside what is now Radio 2. Of course little did any of us know at the time how important that building would become to both our stories in a decade's time.

As I dialled his number on my car phone, I continued to rehearse my pitch to him as to why he might want to join the wonderful world of the wireless. After no more than a couple of rings he picked up and I launched straight in.

'What do you have to lose?' I concluded after I was done.

'Chris, I'm not so sure you know, radio's what you do, I'm a telly man, always have been, and that's where I want to be.'

I suspected this was how the conversation might go and I could understand Jonathan's concerns. Some television people – in those days, especially – may have seen radio as a step down, but I had prepared my little spiel. I told Jonathan that radio was the best 'shop window' in our business bar none; the perfect advert for a broadcaster's talent. I explained to him that because he was so natural he had nothing to fear. I added that radio also has a knack of easing a broadcaster back into people's consciousness, whilst also affording them a more intimate relationship with a much more discerning and receptive audience.

This – and whatever else I said during the course of our brief chat – must have struck a chord, as Jonathan called me back a couple of days later, saying he was up for it. He was on air within a fortnight and quickly settled in to become another quality cannon to add to our weekend arsenal of radio fire power.

We gave him a show that ran from ten till one on a Saturday morning. It was precisely the time my old Greater London Radio show had aired almost a decade before, not the only thing the two shows had in common. I called in my old colleague Andy Davies to produce Jonathan. Andy had done exactly the same for me at GLR, so I thought he would be the perfect person to hold Jonathan's hand – and I'm glad to say I was right.

The happy couple were still together ten years later, doing an almost identical show for the mighty Radio 2 and winning countless awards in the process. The shop-window theory worked a treat; within a year of joining us, the BBC came for Jonathan in a big way, transferring his show lock, stock and barrel to Saturday mornings on their national FM network.

With the power of Radio 2 behind him, Jonathan was firmly back on the entertainment map and it was only a matter of time before the clarion call of television could be heard. The birth of his Friday night BBC 1 talk show followed in 2001 and in no time at all Jonathan was back on top, where he would remain for the best part of the next decade.

The irony was that Jonathan wrote to me asking if I would be a guest on that first series of his talk show, some three years after I had employed him at the radio station and approximately a year after I had gone slightly cuckoo and off into my wilderness years. In many ways, Jonathan and I had effectively swapped places, but the last thing I wanted to do at that point was jump back on the bus. I replied to him by letter saying, 'Thanks old boy, deeply flattered, good luck with your new venture but I'm not really "at it" anymore.'

I meant every word at the time and in truth never expected to be 'at it' again – least of all with him, on the very same show, nine years later, which is exactly what happened.

I did eventually appear on *Friday Night with Jonathan Ross* in October 2009 to promote my first book, *It's Not What You Think*.

However, as you will come to learn, this was a book that only came about as a result of Jonathan's infamous appearance on Russell Brand's radio show. I can assure you that if Jonathan and Russell had not made *that* phone call to Andrew Sachs, neither of my two books would ever have come into being, but that is a story I will return to later on.

TOP 10

THINGS A PROPRIETOR SHOULD NEVER DO

10 Get drunk with the staff

9 Think an employee is ever having a natural conversation with them

8 Park a big posh car right outside the building

7 Have more meetings

6 Become involved in personal issues

5 Trust anyone

4 Be swayed from your core beliefs

3 Employ pals

2 Employ beautiful secretaries

1 Incentivise the workforce: reward – yes; dangle carrot – no. One day you will run out of carrots

WITH THE PURCHASE OF VIRGIN RADIO, unbeknown to me, the seeds of what was to become a lonely and almost fatal madness had also been sown. The aforementioned artistic freedom was there, for sure, but this came hand in hand with corporate responsibility, and these two components, yoked together, were never going to happily coexist. Something I would unfortunately have to discover the hard way.

I should have spotted the signs. I remember turning up for work at Golden Square in Soho one morning, no more than a month into my tenure. It was the middle of winter, when early mornings are painful to the touch. No sooner had I entered the building than I was confronted with what must have been fifty or sixty boxes piled on the ground floor, taking up so much room they almost made the corridor

15

impassable. Upon inspection I discovered that inside each of these boxes was a brand new computer.

'What do we need all these computers for?' I remember asking myself. 'What's wrong with the ones we already have? Who is cleared to sign cheques for such large orders and shouldn't I know about purchases of such bulk?'

Not the most colourful of thoughts with which to start one's day.

For ownership – see headaches. Lord, why did I not realise? Lots of people (OK, men, mostly) like the idea of owning their local pub, or golf course, or restaurant, but it's far better just to go there, have some fun, pay the bill and leave the mowing of the fairways and cleaning of the dirty pots to someone else.

Worse than managing things, though, is managing people.

I will never forget my first encounter with a group of my new employees, when I organised for all the DJs to meet up at the local pub for a bonding session. I thought they would be a like-minded bunch to start with; my fellow presenters in a world full of padded walls, soundproof glass and overblown egos. In contrast to other stations – where off air, the DJs barely ever see or speak to each other – I was determined that at my radio station things would be different. We would be one big happy family, like the Monkees on telly, or the Beatles in *A Hard Day's Night*. I thought a regular get together would give my guys a voice, a feeling of inclusiveness – nothing too cute or touchy-feely, merely a line of communication to each other and to me, their boss. I thought the best plan would be to organise a lunchtime meeting in a pub round the corner from the studio.

Wrong!

The morning meeting I had across town that day overran and, as a result, I found myself having to sprint the mile or so back to base to make it on time for our DJ summit. I eventually arrived at the pub a few minutes after one o'clock, puffed out and red in the face but nonetheless excited about the prospect of meeting my elite guard all together for the first time. I was looking forward to a few beers and getting down to the business of encouraging the guys to spring forth their opinions and visions for our future together.

Wrong! Again.

There they were, my all-star line-up, stood somewhat lacklustre to say the least, at the bar, barely saying a word to each other.

What on earth were they thinking? Did they have it in their minds that I was going to fire them on the spot?

Looking back, perhaps they did. Perhaps it was exactly that, their lack of cheery chat may well have been terror-induced, but they were not to know my motive was one of unification, not suppression.

Already I could sense that this wasn't going to plan and they were getting the wrong end of the stick. I was definitely one of them but in danger now of being perceived as a potential enemy – as having crossed over to the dark side.

Sure DJs did fall by the wayside as a result of my proprietorship. The management of people is a huge and complicated task and one that takes a very special talent, a talent not to be underrated.

'Show me the money,' Tom Cruise famously said in *Jerry Maguire*. Tom, you were wrong.

'Show me the manager,' any day of the week.

TOP 10 CRAZY THINGS TO DO WITH YOUR MONEY

10 Spend it on people you have never met before
9   Spend it on people you don't like
8   Spend it on people you suspect don't like you
7   Spend it on really expensive wine, when everyone is too far gone to appreciate it
6   Spend it on holidays you don't want to go on
5   Lend it to idiots
4   Invest in businesses run by idiots
3   Play the stock market (the big boys have the rest of us by the balls)
2   Think for one second it can ever buy you happiness
1   Forget how hard you worked to earn it

ULTIMATELY, MY OWNERSHIP OF THE GINGER MEDIA GROUP (GMG) would last no longer than two years, thank God, after which my brief and bizarre run as a rookie media mogul would morph into my becoming a multi-millionaire part-time DJ, with too much time on his hands and a bank account burning a hole in his pocket ...

Sounds fabulous, doesn't it?

So why, then, is such coveted good fortune all too often the downfall of the people who come to experience it?

Perhaps it's something to do with the paradise syndrome – a recognised psychological condition in which people imagine things are too good to be true, and so end up sabotaging them until they return once again to the shitty bad old days.

Was this what happened to me? I suspect it was. But before I get to the part where it all went wrong, let me cut to the chase and tell you how all this money ended up coming my way in the first place.

It was my job as proprietor of GMG, along with my CEO, David Campbell – DC, as I've always known him – and my agent Michael, to grow our new business from day one, just as we had promised our investors we would do. We had claimed to be able to at least double the £87 million we had originally paid, within three to five years. If and when this was achieved, we had agreed to sell it again and all retire to the Bahamas – or as it turned out in my case, Guildford.

Our initial plan for the 'growing' part was based around building up our already established television and radio business, whilst at the same time diversifying into becoming a more broad-based media company. The internet had just been born, and digital television and radio-broadcast platforms were taking their first steps as toddlers. In short, we were witnessing the beginnings of a communications and technological revolution, and rarely, if ever, had there been a better time for expansion.

GMG's growth was, however, about to be stunted.

There was a problem, you see, a very simple problem – we were too successful, too quickly, without really doing very much at all. The ratings and revenue from the radio station increased at such an unexpected rate after we had taken over that the business almost immediately doubled and then almost tripled in value. Suddenly there was very little for us to do, over and above turning up for work every day. There was no need to push ourselves, there was no need to look for new opportunities and, most importantly of all, there was no need for us to take any risks.

So what was the problem, you may ask?

Well, it was like this. I had a very ambitious management team consisting of several natural entrepreneurs whose very DNA dictated they had to take any money-making heat they could get their hands on and turn it into a full-blown volcano – whether it was needed or not. Unfortunately at this juncture, because of our premature success in reaching and exceeding all our financial targets, these same guys soon found themselves at direct loggerheads with the boys and girls in our boardroom.

The management wanted to stick to the original brief of expansion, whereas our investors only cared about extracting the added value. As this point had already been reached, the investors understandably didn't want any further and unnecessary throws of the dice.

Here's what happened next:

Everyone knew we were worth millions more than just a few months before, maybe even as much as a hundred million more, maybe even more than that. In short, we were very good for credit, almost fireproof. Not surprisingly the management team decided the time was ripe for taking on bigger challenges – like buying a national newspaper for example, specifically the *Daily Star*.

If you want to make money, never buy a gleaming champion for sale at the top of the market, go instead for a leaky old boat that no one wants or cares about anymore.

The *Daily Star* was that boat; it was losing money hand over fist, had problems with its printing and distribution, and had become a predictable one-trick pony of gossip, girls and sport done on the cheap. However it was still also enjoying half-decent circulation figures and, with a little love and affection both behind the scenes and on the page, my trusty CEO, DC, reckoned it could be polished up and be back in the black within a year. He had investigated alternative ways of printing and the sharing of distribution facilities to help cut costs, and he and I had even had a clandestine lunch with Piers Morgan who, in principle, had agreed to be our editor.

Our thinking was something along the lines of radio stations being very similar to newspapers in so many ways. Why couldn't our millions of new listeners become millions of new readers, and vice versa?

As momentum around Project Star gathered pace, the frisson of our second big deal was well and truly in the air – especially when we discovered we could snap up this ailing daily for the knock-down price of just £25 million, a snip at the time for a UK national newspaper title.

Alas, though, it was not to be.

The board rejected our request for permission to buy the *Daily Star* hands down. We had the deal in the bag, but they were insistent we didn't need it. Their exact phrase was 'Why do we need to bet the ranch anymore?'

The board left us in no doubt that they were more than happy with things as they stood. My management team, on the other hand, could not have been less satisfied with the situation. In fact they were about to throw their toys, along with their immense talent, right out of our company pram.

As soon as they were informed of the board's decision, all three of them – the chief executive officer, the financial officer and the managing director – walked straight out of the building.

I couldn't believe it.

Here was I, a radio DJ, former newsagent, kiss-o-gram and forklift-truck driver, now alone at the head of a £200 million company with close to two hundred employees and hundreds of thousands of pounds flowing in and out of our accounts on a daily basis.

I needed my boys back and I needed them back bloody quickly. I summoned the board to an emergency meeting scheduled for the second I came off the air the next day.

'The management feel they can no longer work with you and have left,' I offered up as a starter.

'They have what?' said one of the board.

'They've gone, they're no longer here, I am on my own and I am just a DJ, I have no idea what really goes on here and we need to get them back.'

'Oh dear,' said another member of the board.

'Precisely,' I concurred.

'Well, this is not good, not good at all,' said a third.

'I agree wholeheartedly,' I whimpered. By now they could see I was distressed.

'What exactly is their issue?' said the guy who had spoken first.

'Growing the company is what they do, they identified a perfectly valid opportunity and you have refused point blank to support them.'

The board were sympathetic to their case but immovable when it came to taking any risk. I have to say they had a perfectly sound argument and one with which I was finding it very difficult to disagree. However, I still had a problem.

'That may be the case,' I bleated, increasingly desperate, 'but I don't know if you've noticed, I am on my own on this side of the table and all our employees are about to arrive at work and wonder where the hell the three blokes who run this place have disappeared to.'

'So what do you want us to do?' said the first one.

I hadn't actually thought about the answer to this question. I just presumed the board would know what to do. I opened my mouth and hoped something half-sensible might come out.

'You need to reassure them that it's because of their efforts that we find ourselves in the position of having to do nothing.' So far so good. 'And then you need to tell them how good they are and ... er ... give them some more money.'

I have no idea where this last bit came from.

'You want us to give the management a bonus for walking out?'

I wasn't sure if I did or not but I wasn't about to stop now.

'Yes, more money, they're businessmen after all, that's what they're about. We need to get them back in the door and re-incentivise them at the same time. A cheque each is the only way.'

Now this, dear friends, is me being extremely bad at business but extremely good at selling. Let's face it, this was a terrible idea. People often say what a great businessman I am but there is nothing further from the truth. I am many things, but I am not, never have been and never will be a great businessman.

Although the management had an almost justifiable beef, there's no way they should have deserted me in the first place, let alone been rewarded for doing so.

Indeed, when I foolishly tried a similar stunt a couple of years down the line, the whole episode ended up costing me £13 million and I didn't work for the next three years.

But I must have been very convincing on the day because the board actually agreed to my suggestion, authorising me to dish out some new share options in the direction of my management team – if they deigned to return to work, that is.

I skipped off to the restaurant where they were waiting, happy to be the bearer of good news and confident they would see sense.

When I turned up they looked like three naughty school-boys hoping to high heaven they weren't going to get caned. If I'm totally honest, they looked like they thought they might be about to get fired. I suspect that they'd had time to reflect on their impetuousness and were perhaps beginning to think better of it. No need, though, for I only brought glad tidings of great joy.

'You are all bonused up and back in business', I declared to three visibly relieved and frankly somewhat surprised faces.

I only wish someone had been able to say the same to me later when, as I've said, I tried a similar stunt, but there I go, jumping the gun again.

Now, houses next and how to buy a really big one that you definitely can't afford.

TOP 10 MUST HAVES WHEN I BUILT MY DREAM HOUSE

10   Helipad

9   Trout lake

8   Hot tub (wooden – outdoor)

7   Village shop in the kitchen

6   Library

5   Waterfall in the library

4   Identical replica of my local pub

3   Steam room

2   Cinema

1   Space

WITH THE ROCK-STAR LIFESTYLE COMES THE ROCK-STAR MANSION and all that goes with it. It's all so unoriginal, I know, but nobody teaches you how to be rich and I fell for every cliché in the book.

I'd been looking for a place 'out of town', as they say, for a year or two and as the millennium was looming I still hadn't seen anything that remotely took my fancy. Not for want of trying, I might add, as I spent most weekends viewing properties from the east coast of Kent all the way down to the sand dunes of Dorset.

If there was a big house with land for sale, I wanted to see it. I looked at castles, farms, lighthouses, windmills – I even looked at one place that had its own airstrip where the chap who owned it said I could have his Fokker thrown in for free!

So far, though, for one reason or another, nowhere had quite clicked. In fact it was getting to the point where I had just about exhausted all combinations of commutable counties and different types of dwellings therein. I needed something to happen to help me change my mindset, and it did, on a skiing holiday to Whistler in Canada, of all places.

This holiday was a freebie and, like most freebies, was probably more trouble than it was worth. After all who would travel several thousand miles to another continent for a skiing holiday that lasted just four days? Me and my old pal Johnny Boy Revell, that's who. We were both from council estates and still hadn't quite got over the fact that people were willing to give us stuff for free.

We almost felt like we had to go, despite the immense jetlag and the fact that by now we were both well off enough to pay for ourselves to go first class practically anywhere in the world. But a bargain was a bargain and so off we trotted deep into the snowy peaks of the Canadian Rockies.

Barely able to keep our eyes open when we arrived, we just about managed to hire a Chevrolet Silverado 4x4 pickup truck, throw our gear in the back and get on our way. We were soon to discover there are some things that can blow the cobwebs of jetlag clean out of the water.

Almost the second we hit the mountain road we became overwhelmed by what lay before us. In less than half an hour we were in a wilderness of calm and serenity, a world away from the hubbub of the tempestuous media rat race. There really was nothing but a blanket of white for as far as our tired eyes could see. Truly spellbinding.

As we continued on our way, we passed countless expanses of icy blue water, one of which was so breathtakingly beautiful we just had to stop, get out and stare at it for a few minutes.

As the wonder of the Rockies continued to astound, a newfound sense of peace slowly began washing over the pair of us but, where I was concerned, I could also feel a slight trace of anger beginning to gnaw at its heels.

'Where is this anger coming from?' I thought. 'This isn't right, I was about to be really content. Please leave me alone.'

But it wasn't going anywhere. It wanted a word.

'Why on earth haven't you sorted out a house in the country back in the UK yet?' it snorted. 'You spend every weekend cooped up in your flat in London crawling from one ugly watering hole to the next when you could be out and about feeling the way you do now. You have the money, go get a life!'

I had to concede this anger had a point. I made a private deal with it to do two things when I returned back home.

1. I would buy a Chevrolet Silverado 4x4.
2. I would buy a house in the country within a month.

True to my word, I ordered the Chevy immediately upon my return, to be delivered on Christmas Day 1998. As for the house, I concluded that because I had looked at well over a hundred in the last year, at least one of which must have been suitable, it could only be reluctance on my part to commit to a big move out of the city that was the problem, rather than not having found a suitable property.

So here's what I decided to do:

I would simply instruct an estate agent to take me to look at the five best houses currently for sale in the south-east of England, regardless of cost. After seeing all five, I would then undertake to buy the one that I liked the most, even if I didn't really like it that much at all. This way I was forcing myself into a 'yes' situation.

I know this philosophy is a little extreme, especially for a boy who started life on a council estate with little more than his pocket money, his push bike and a paper round, but this is where I now found myself and I was determined to make the most of it.

There was more drastic action to come.

Because these houses were likely to be tens of miles apart, maybe even hundreds, it was going to be quite difficult to compare and contrast them. I therefore informed the agent to arrange all five viewings consecutively on one single day and to meet me that morning at Battersea heliport. I also kindly requested he seek permission from the vendors concerned for us to land in their gardens. We were about to have the viewing trip of a lifetime.

When we climbed up above Richmond Park on the Wednesday morning in question the rest of the world was at work. I don't know who had to try the hardest to play it cool, the agent or myself. We were both grinning from ear to ear.

Extravagant as this strategy may seem, there was more than a grain of sanity in what we were doing. After all, we were dealing with houses worth several million pounds each, and if it took a one-day lease of a Twin Squirrel to secure the right one, then it would be money well spent. The fact that it was a tonne of fun in the process was merely a bonus, albeit a pretty big one. Plus it meant I could also get to spy into the gardens of any potential new neighbours whilst we were at it.

The first property we looked at was in Windsor, right on the River Thames. It was huge, Georgian, white and stunning. After a quick scoot round, enough to gain a mental picture, we were back on board and up and away again. Next stop Chichester, to look at a renovated castle. This was also very nice. Protected by its own moat, with fabulous lawns, the present owners had spent a small fortune renovating their home by blending ultra-modern with genuinely ancient. As a result there was lots of new glass, mixed in with old stone – a real wow house, but just a bit too far away from London to make it practical.

Two landings completed, two houses down and Windsor was still winning. Time then for number three. The pilot tracked back over the South Downs, overflying Goodwood and Midhurst, before landing on the lawn of a fabulous house just off the A3, complete with its own lake, working water-mill and state-of-the-art recording studio.

'Who lives in a house like this?' I could hear the voice in my head say.

'Roger Taylor from Queen's place,' whispered the agent, as if he'd heard me.

The story goes that when Queen had their first hit album, Roger went straight out and bought this house. It didn't occur to him that they might not have another one; Roger told me this story himself. He also told me about the first time Freddie Mercury came over to visit. He said that Freddie couldn't believe how audacious the band's drummer had been with his recent purchase, so much so that he immediately felt compelled to return to London to buy a brand-new white Rolls-Royce from Jack Barclays. Having achieved this in no more than a couple of hours, Freddie was back at Roger's in his new wheels in time for tea.

Roger couldn't have been more welcoming that day and his house was to die for; so fabulous, in fact, that he ended up withdrawing it from the market and staying there himself, though not before adding a new library wing – all 7,000 square feet of it.

Time then for house number four.

Ladies and gentlemen, I present to you Hascombe Court, a turn-of-the-century manor house set in forty-seven acres of Gertrude Jekyll gardens, situated a few miles south of Guildford. This house was heaven on earth, sitting atop a hill overlooking the quaint little village from which it took its name.

No more than fifteen minutes after we landed there I made a call to my long-suffering accountant.

'Kirit, I would like to buy a house.'

'OK, that's fine, where is it and how much?'

'It's near Guildford and it's £4 million, which is a bargain because it *was* £5.5 million.' This was true; it had been on the market for over a year. I couldn't believe no one had snapped it up.

'Chris, you don't have £4 million.'

'I know that, but can we get it?'

Poor Kirit – who actually isn't poor at all but you know what I mean – he's had to cope with several telephone calls like this over the years, the most recent being when I bought a car I couldn't afford at an auction in Italy in 2007. That phone call followed exactly the same lines and both times I'm happy to say he came up with the funds required to indulge my desires.

I never ask how he does it – I think it's probably best I don't know – but following such episodes I try not to call him again about anything for as long as I possibly can.

On this occasion I would have to call Kirit back sooner rather than later as it transpired that Hascombe Court and its forty-seven acres turned out to be only the half of it – literally.

After the phone call I discovered that over the road was the second half of the estate which was made up of a farm, three cottages and another hundred and twenty-seven acres which was also up for sale.

'Kirit, I need a further £1.5million, there's more of the estate to be bought.'

'I see,' he sighed.

I was so sure about Hascombe Court that I didn't even bother going to look at house number five, asking the pilot to return us safely and swiftly to London.

Within four weeks I had completed the purchase of both lots for a total purchase price just shy of £6 million. I suddenly had an idea how Roger may have felt all those years before, wondering where his band's next hit might come from, but you know what? I really didn't care. Besides, I could always sell it again if I had to, which was a bloody good job because that's precisely what was destined to happen.

They say one of the best ways to go about making a small fortune is to start with a big one and lose most of it. That is exactly what the stars had lined up for me but I was yet to do the losing bit. So, let's find out how that happened first, shall we?

TOP 10
RESTAURANTS I'LL NEVER FORGET

10 The Italian when I was 20 where a date asked for Parmesan cheese to go with her pasta. I thought it was a greedy request for an additional course

9 My first Chinese. I got cramp from trying to eat with chopsticks

8 My first Indian, where a 'mate' told me to go for the phal. The phal was still going for me the next morning

7 The French restaurant where I had my first meal with Michael Grade (former head of Channel 4). I ordered steak tartare and had no idea it was just raw meat

6 Lunch in the Palm Grill in Los Angeles with Bernie Brillstein and Brad Gray when I was 29, just after they offered me $11 million to work on TV in the States

5 Lunch in Langan's with Ronnie and Peter O'Toole

4 Dinner with Billie in the Four Seasons the night before we were married in Las Vegas

3 The wedding lunch at Alambique in the Algarve, which is run by my best man Paulo, and where my wife Natasha and I started our new life together

2 Lunch in Little Italy with Jade and her mum after finally getting my shit together to do something about my relationship with my daughter

1 Lunch, again at Langan's, with my management team – read on

FOR A BRIEF WHILE THE MANAGEMENT TEAM were back in the building and back on side, but I could tell there was an ongoing and underlying frustration sapping their spirits. They were now under strict instructions that our fledgling golden brand was only to be polished, no longer pawned, in the quest for additional treasures.

It was at this point I realised I could do little more than I already had done to appease them, and that in reality I owned the company in name alone. I may have been signing the cheques but I was definitely not calling the shots.

Unrest soon began to set in for all of us and unrest, by its very nature, tends to grow as opposed to diminish. My guys were once again becoming more and more like caged tigers with the passing of each day. They were desperate to be cut loose and make the company more money, but instead they had to close their minds, eyes and ears to the countless business opportunities that were piling up in their in-trays.

I decided we needed a chat to clear the air.

'Lunch?' I suggested to DC.

'Oh yes,' came the resounding reply.

'Langan's?' I suggested.

'We'll meet you there', he confirmed.

Langan's Brasserie is by far the best place for lunch I have ever been to in my life and I have been fortunate enough to have been to quite a few. Located just off Piccadilly, opposite Green Park, Langan's doesn't do quiet in any way shape or form. If you want quiet, Langan's is not the place for you. For everything else, however, it's brilliant.

Its energy, atmosphere, opulence and patronage are unique. And it's always busy, even on the first Monday in January, notoriously the quietest day in every restaurant in the land. From lunch at midday right through to last orders at midnight, Langan's never stops buzzing.

I've yet to be invited down to the kitchen but can only presume it's a sight to behold, as the head chef and his loyal team churn out dish after dish of some of the most comforting food known to mankind: good old English fare, fearlessly fatty and dripping with calories.

There's the sausage and mash made with far too much butter, the beautiful cod in batter so brittle it explodes in your mouth, the liver and bacon so bountiful it obscures the evidence of any plate beneath, and the croustade d'oeufs de caille – a sort of quails' egg pasty – which is so good that quite frankly it should be illegal.

The waiters who run the whole show are dressed like boxing referees in black trousers, crisp white shirts with black dickybows and black silk waistcoats. They pride themselves on efficient service yet still appear to have plenty of time to chat to the customers whilst simultaneously being rushed off their feet. I've never quite figured out how it is they achieve such an illusion; maybe they're all secretly magicians.

The artwork is also a sight to behold, providing the most colourful of backdrops to this already vibrant theatre of food and fantasy and, like most things in Langan's, it also has a story to tell. Struggling artists yet to be discovered would offer up a completed canvas in return for a few months' free feeding. These very paintings still adorn the walls there and include works by such well-known names as David Hockney and Guy Gladwell. For what such paintings are worth today, a fellow could easily eat out anywhere in the world without having to worry about the bill for the rest of his life.

The real legend of Langan's however, is the original owner, Peter Langan himself. Sadly no longer with us, I'm sorry to say I never had the pleasure of meeting him, which is a real shame because from what I've heard he was quite a character, to say the least.

Langan stories are infamous in the catering trade. There are myriad tales of the Irish chef-cum-restaurateur who somehow persuaded Michael Caine to become his partner. No bad thing as it turned out, as Langan repaid Michael's belief in him with impressive profits year after year. In fact Caine is the only celeb I know who has ever made any money out of owning a restaurant – and I feel qualified to say that, having owned three myself!

Langan's eccentricities were born not only out of his love for his restaurant, the running of which entailed ludicrously long hours, but also from the countless bottles of bubbly he managed to consume on a daily basis. He was a big, big drinker: champagne and cider being his two favourite poisons of choice.

In the end it was the dreaded bottle that got the better of him, but not before he had formulated some interesting theories on life, love and justice.

On one occasion, for example, he was witnessed crawling under the tables during a lunchtime service, on his way to bite the ankle of a lady who'd thought it completely acceptable to bring in her beloved toy poodle. Having arrived at the ankle in question, Langan duly chomped into it with all his might. Neither the dog nor the lady was ever seen there again.

My other favourite Langan tale features him dressing up as a tramp and standing on the street outside the front door of his establishment, begging for money. This was a game he loved to play where, if any benevolent soul did happen to afford him a shilling or two, he would dramatically reveal his true identity before asking them inside to join him as his guest for the rest of the day and – no doubt – most of the night.

I'd love to have met Langan but despite his legendary status, ultimately there is nothing remotely funny about someone who drinks too much; it's always the drink and not the drinker who has the last laugh. And so it was with Peter. In a desperate attempt to win back his battle-weary wife he set fire to himself as a cry for help, but he ended up overdoing it and it took him six weeks to die of his injuries.

After Peter so tragically died, Michael, having been bitten by the restaurant bug, remained an active partner in the business and could often be witnessed dining with his friends and colleagues at table number one.

Table number one can be found in the left-hand corner just as you walk in. It's renowned as the best table in the house because from it you can see the rest of the dining room without having to look round – basically you can have a good old nosey without anyone noticing. Most top tables share this trait, though I doubt many of them have as much to be nosey about as Langan's does.

There is no other place in the world that shares its unique blend of dining enthusiasts, where MPs mix with football managers, ladies who do lunch mingle with gentlemen who would love to do them, and Essex girls flock to trade city boys. This heady cocktail of clientele and culture-clashes often leads to a marathon of musical chairs, with tables of four or five frequently merging to become larger gatherings that often have to be politely asked to vacate their tables as the next diners are waiting to be seated – for dinner.

I've been fortunate enough to sit at table one from time to time and it's always been a joy, as the waiters acknowledge one's ascent to the top spot with a respectful nod. Table one is presided over by Peter Langan himself, thanks to a fabulous Guy Gladwell painting that hangs on the wall next to it. The great host has been immortalised in one of his trademark pale grey linen suits, which is all he ever wore; he had six, all identical and usually spattered and stained with the remains of whatever it was he had been eating and drinking that day.

The genius of this painting lies in the fact that the subject has his back to us and yet it's so obviously him. He has his right hand in his pocket as he appears to walk away, but I have been assured, by people in the know, that he isn't actually walking anywhere, he is leaning against a door with one heel in the air as he struggles to balance whilst he takes a pee through the letterbox.

So lunch it was for me and the guys, not at table one as it happened, but not far off. We could see enough of what we wanted to and we were all set to get down to business as well as eat, drink and be merry in the process.

That day's lunch party was made up of the aforementioned David Campbell, a lovely man and good friend, Andy Mollet, the financial director, a solid and trusty numbers man, and the managing director, whose name escapes me for some reason, primarily because I want it to.

After loosening up with the usual round of excellent Bloody Marys followed by a cold beer each, it was time to embark upon the blissful task of perusing the mouthwatering Langan's menu.

Whenever I do lunch where there is business also to be done, I find it difficult to eat anything substantial. With passion being required for both, I can seldom split myself between the two, and as business was in the pound seats on this occasion, I plumped for the double Caesar salad option. This is something I used to do a lot; Caesar salad as a starter *and* as a main course – Hail Caesars all round and no hardship, as the Caesars at Langan's are to die for.

With our food orders now in, our pow-wow was ready to get under way although it stalled momentarily as we did that classic thing of 'everyone chatting about any subject other than the one they're there to talk about' – the human version of starlings swarming at twilight until one of them takes the plunge.

Finally we were off and started by mulling over our thwarted bid for the *Daily Star*, before moving on to where we felt we were at the moment, both as a company and as individuals, taking into consideration the constraints under which we currently found ourselves.

The question in a nutshell was, 'What could we possibly do next?'

It was patently obvious that we were in a Catch-22 situation; we'd become too successful, too quickly, and now had our hands tied. We were millions of pounds ahead of our projections in turnover and profit – three years ahead to be precise – and the board had no inclination whatsoever to risk a penny of it.

But there had to be something we could do. Even in a dark room with no windows you can still 'think' light.

'Alright,' I said, suddenly realising there was only one creative option open to us. 'If we're done, we're done. Our next big idea, gentlemen' – I paused briefly at this point partly for dramatic effect and also to make sure I had my colleagues' full and undivided attention – 'will be to sell the company three years ahead of schedule. This,' I declared, 'is definitely something we can do.'

These words were as much of a shock to me as they were to my three dining companions, but I knew it was a good idea because I suddenly acquired that sick feeling in my gut, the one you get when something is either very right or very wrong. Fortunately for all concerned this felt like the very right type to me.

There were of course issues with such a tumultuous decision; when are there not? For example, did we really want to give up this goldmine of a company before we had to? Would the company grow in value anyway without us doing anything drastic and could we reap more dividends? Why not just relax and take it easy for another year or two?

After discussing my eureka moment for a short while, the boys came up with a prophetic and convincing outline of where the business was now, considering advertising revenues, the listening figures and other important factors, including, most importantly, where the business was likely to be at our planned exit point thirty-six months hence.

As far as they could see, it was difficult to envisage the numbers getting any better than they were at present. In fact, they went on to add, it was conceivable the numbers had already reached a plateau and if anything might even begin to get worse.

As we continued to weigh up the scenario, it became increasingly hard for any of us to argue against the idea of an early sale. We therefore concluded that this was a suggestion we felt justified in putting to the board at the earliest available opportunity.

Having unanimously agreed on this course of action, a palpable air of optimism – something that had been conspicuous by its absence of late – suddenly returned.

Eighteen months after borrowing £85 million to snatch Virgin Radio from under the noses of the Capital Radio group, we were going to put the station back on the market at a guide price of between £175 million to £300 million.

Not a bad bit of business – if we could pull it off. Either way, one thing was for sure. The boys had the fire in their bellies once again.

It's amazing what a good restaurant can serve up.

TOP 10 UNFORGETTABLE SHOWBIZ MOMENTS

10 First show on the radio (Manchester Piccadilly Radio circa 1988)
9   First *Big Breakfast*
8   Last *Big Breakfast*
7   First Radio 1 *Breakfast Show*
6   Playing golf in front of 30,000 people with Catherine Zeta-Jones against Bobby Ewing and Cheech from Cheech and Chong, when Catherine was playing so badly she started to cry – and that was only on the second hole!
5   Leaving *TFI Friday* on a speedboat up the Thames with Paul McCartney
4   Watching Elton John present the last ever *TFI Friday* in my place as I had gone AWOL
3   Locking up the Giants Stadium for U2 in New York after they'd gone home. Of 60,000 people, I was the last to leave
2   First Radio 2 *Breakfast Show*
1   The mad wine night at Andrew Lloyd Webber's house in the South of France

THROUGHOUT THE WHOLE OF THIS PERIOD and for the last three years, I had been dating a saint of a woman by the name of Suzi Aplin.

Of all the amazing females I have had the ridiculous good fortune to be with in my life, there is no one who deserves a medal for services to this delusional, fruitcake of a man more than Suzi does. Suzi Aplin – televison producer, live wire, force of nature and all-round, solid-gold human being.

Suzi and I got it together after a night of drunken passion, there's no use trying to sugar-coat it and pretend otherwise. There was no romance, there was no plan, we simply started the evening in a comedy club in Greenwich and ended up back at her place later that night. The next morning we found ourselves food shopping in Suzi's local Waitrose like a couple who had been together for years.

Suzi was, and still very much is, tall, blonde and vivacious with marvellously long legs, even for a girl of five foot ten. She is also slim, maybe a little too slim, but willowy enough to get away with it, and even though she has a classically pretty face, she has not the first idea how beautiful she really is.

As well as all these wonderful physical attributes, the package gets better the deeper you dig. She is blessed with almost inexhaustible energy and is as positive as I believe it is possible to be about everyone and everything. She can be frank when she needs to be, honest and diplomatic when it's called for, and ditzy and dithering when she gets in a bit of a tiz – but of course this only adds to her charm. She also has the ability to listen and laugh in all the right places and lend a friend a kind shoulder when they need someone to lean on. Oh, and she's ever such a little bit posh – which I love ...

She is, I suppose, perfect – and if you're thinking to yourself why did I ever let her go, please let's not go there, at least not yet.

I first encountered this wonder-woman when I was working on *The Big Breakfast*. Suzi was the guest booker – one of the toughest jobs in the business, always fighting against other shows for first dibs on the latest people in town, then having to deal with all the egos and politics that follow such characters around.

Suzi was renowned as one of the best at her job, a fact confirmed by the constant headhunting she faced to go and work on other shows. She had formed excellent social and working relationships with all the necessary music, film and PR companies and, as a result, was able to deliver A-list guests where others only failed.

When I needed a guest booker for my new show *Don't Forget Your Toothbrush* I didn't have to look very far. Suzi was top of my list and as my new production company shared an office with Planet 24, the producers of *The Big Breakfast*, she was also only a few desks away.

Charlie and Waheed, my former bosses, were reluctant to let her go, but as my new show's need was greater than theirs plus they had a vested interest as they were my partners, they kindly if reluctantly allowed me to nab her.

Suzi had always been easy on the eye and had enjoyed the attentions of many a male admirer but I have to say thus far I had not included myself in that group and, although we were great mates, never in a million years did I think we would end up as an item.

Perhaps a deeper connection between us began to grow as a result of us working more closely together, and then subconsciously came to a head the night we hooked up.

'In wine the truth', as the saying goes, a phrase Suzi used a lot and there was certainly plenty of wine involved on that Friday night back in Greenwich. Having said that, it could easily have ended up as a quick fling until, that is, I opened the *Sun* newspaper a couple of days later.

Suzi had been in a cafe, on the Sunday after our serendipitous sneaky session back at hers and had been discussing the post-mattress aftermath of what had happened between her and her boss with a close friend. I think one could refer to what was taking place as a bona fide girly chat.

This would have been all well and good had not one Piers Morgan been sitting directly behind them. Piers, another recurring name in my story, who was still working as a gossip columnist at the time, was no more than three feet away, enabling him to hear every single word they were saying. He later told me he couldn't believe his luck.

What Piers did next is ... exactly what Piers was paid to do. He printed the highlights of Suzi and her pal's conversation almost word for word for the nation to read over their cornflakes in a two-page spread.

When I read his article I was almost speechless, not because I was angry or shocked – far from it – the press were part of my everyday existence, but because of all the lovely, complimentary things Suzi had allegedly been saying about me.

I called her straight away.

'Oh my God, I'm s-s-s-so sorry, and I'm so embarrassed,' she stuttered before I could squeeze in a hello.

'Please d-d-d-don't think I'm like that, I'm not one of those girls that does this. I don't know where they got the story from. It's almost as if he was there. I have to say, I did s-s-s-say those things but only to my friend. I don't know how they found out – I know for a fact Sam wouldn't have told them. I trust her with my life. I completely understand if you want me to leave and go and find another job somewhere else.'

She may well have talked for a full five minutes before coming up for air and letting me get a word in.

As she paused for breath I seized my moment and explained to Suzi that Piers had revealed in the piece that it was he himself who was behind her in the cafe, and that far from being annoyed or embarrassed about what he'd written, I was chuffed to bits by what she'd had to say about me.

Once Suzi had calmed down there was only one way to look at it, as far as I was concerned. Piers had done us both a huge favour as I now knew how she felt about me – along with the rest of the country for that matter – and his revealing column inches had vicariously awakened me to how I felt about her. The more I thought about her, the more I realised what a catch she was and what an amazing girlfriend she'd make. I concluded that I needed to do something about this, and fast; I would ask Suzi to move in with me.

This may seem a little drastic, but as you may have deduced by now, I'm an all-or-nothing guy. Admittedly this is not a trait that always led to the smoothest of rides, but that's just the way I am, I can't help it. Besides, neither Suzi nor I had time for a relaxed and measured courtship; we were both workaholics and unless we went home to the same bed every night, there was a good chance we might not see each other for weeks.

After a lot of fun and a couple of false starts in my flat in north London, my former guest booker and I made the transition to an official grown-up couple, moving into a rather grand town house in Notting Hill in the process. Suzi and I were now an item and the various boys and girls we had both been dating of late were duly told to back off for the fore-seeable future.

The more I came to know my new girlfriend the more I liked her.

Suzi loved food – although you would never know from the size of her. She also loved to smoke, not prolifically but poet-ically, drawing the maximum available pleasure from every individual drag. Most of all, though, she loved her red wine.

Her penchant for red wine came not so much from its alcoholic content and its effect but rather from its smell, colour and – of course – its taste. She sipped wine from her glass like no one I've ever seen before or since, her eyes closed, waiting for what was to come, her lips curling upwards at either end almost in a wry smile at the thought of the ecstasy of a full-on sensory assault.

Her passion for wine, food and fags often took us to France, where they seem to do these three things quite a lot and without worrying about them too much.

Holidays – nice ones – and especially in France, were new to me. Up until this point holidays had been an unwelcome cross I had to bear. I did go away from time to time but I had never really enjoyed myself and I could never wait to get back. I loved working and I hated airports, plus I burn at even the slightest mention of the word 'sun', so what was there to like?

Suzi was clever, though. She was having none of that. If I wanted to be with her, not only was I going to have to go on holiday, I was going to have to enjoy it.

She would not be patronised by the presence of a token companion, she wanted to see and feel me having as good a time as she was or there was no deal. How she managed to successfully extract this out of me where everyone else had failed I have no idea, but extract it she did and we always ended up having a blast.

All of our vacation destinations were pretty top notch, to be honest, but it was the Côte d'Azur that we loved to go to most of all. There is no place on earth like the South of France with its picture-perfect coastline all the way from Monaco to the Cap d'Antibes; glorious mountains crashing into the blindingly beautiful Mediterranean Sea below.

Whether you are having lunch at a waterside restaurant in the pretty village of Beaulieu-sur-Mer or looking down over a thousand feet from one of the exclusive restaurants perched on the side of Eze mountain, there is nothing not to like – except perhaps the bill. As well as topping the league in the beauty stakes, the Côte d'Azur is also the most expensive place I have ever been to.

That said, budget and availability permitting, Suzi and I would always try to stay at La Voile d'Or (the Golden Sail), a small but perfectly formed bijou hotel situated right on the rocks just above the sea in Saint-Jean-Cap-Ferrat, probably my favourite place on the planet.

Like several of the hotels in the region, La Voile d'Or didn't take credit cards until very recently. When Suzi and I were going there it was always cash only.

I think such hotels have been forced to change policy as with a single fried egg now costing as much as £10, the size of the bags full of money required to settle residents' accounts were becoming noticeably impractical.

I understand this was particularly evident at the most famous hotel in the region, where a basket of bread at your breakfast table will set you back £36 and that's before you even think about daring to order any tea, coffee or croque-monsieur. I have stayed at this place three times, most recently in 2009, and the sight of *l'addition* arriving never fails to bring me out in a cold sweat.

Not to worry though, eh? What's money for, if not to spend on the things you like with someone you love? What Suzi and I could afford we would enjoy, and what we could not we wouldn't worry about.

We always talked about what it must be like to have a house in Saint-Jean, the dream to end all dreams, but there is a knack to owning houses abroad. The secret is that unless you have infinite wealth, it's imperative that you are a founder-member of a future trend as opposed to someone who ends up paying through the nose, having turned up late to the party.

Take Noël Coward and Ian Fleming, for example, and their respective retreats in Jamaica when it was the last place on earth a European might think to live. They picked up their slices of paradise for virtually nothing. The same can be said of John Lennon and his various forays into Malta, and let's not forget Richard Branson and the legendary bargain that was Necker Island. The story goes that he paid ten per cent of the asking price – just £300,000. Not bad for your own island; he now charges double that if you want to rent it for just one week.

And so it was with Saint-Jean, we just didn't realise it at the time.

David Niven had lived there once upon a time and his house was for sale during one of our early trips. Set just off the main drag towards the shore on the path to Eze, it was a magnificent movie-star mansion, almost Gatsbyesque in its grandeur, and with its own private jetty and walled tropical garden thrown in.

I recall the price tag being £4.7 million.

'What?' I remember thinking back then. I couldn't believe anywhere in the world could be worth that much. I was of course entirely wrong about David Niven's house, which has since changed hands for ten times that amount. A good house is only expensive once, they say. After that you will never be able to afford it.

Suzi and I were destined to miss the French property boat big time, but this was not the case for Bono and his musical colleague the Edge. They had bagged themselves a relative bargain on the beach nearby just a few years before.

No sooner had the Dublin rockers made their first few quid banging out their irresistible brand of rock and roll than they heard of a beach-front villa up for grabs for a couple of hundred thousand pounds. A fortune to them then, but they knew something Suzi and I didn't and, without pausing for breath, they snapped it right up. They bought it between the two of them and proceeded to share the house straight down the middle whenever they could get away. Each of their families had half the villa, with both families coming together in a communal living room and kitchen.

It's testament to the two men's friendship that this arrange-
ment worked for over ten years before they succeeded in
getting planning permission for a second property on their
not unsubstantial plot. They now enjoy a villa each, as well as
a combined net value of tens of millions of pounds.

I know the above is fact because I've been there. Bono, who
had appeared on *TFI Friday* several times, heard Suzi and I
were in his 'Manoir dans Le Midi' and tracked us down to our
hotel, where he extended, via a rather creative fax, a generous invite for us to come over and enjoy a slab of pizza and a
glass or two of wine with him and his clan. The fax requested
an RSVP and informed us that he would pop by and pick us
up if we were interested.

Interested? What do you think?

When the night in question arrived, Suzi and I sat outside
on the terrace eagerly awaiting our 'lift' whilst desperately
trying to act cool and not drink too much, by playing Scrab-
ble of all things. However, by the time our man arrived, we
were both a bottle of champagne to the good and as giddy as
kites. So much for our strategy.

All the other guests in the bar, meanwhile, did a double-
take the moment Bono walked in. You see, in real life he sort
of does and yet at the same time doesn't quite look like Bono.
It can sometimes be difficult to be sure.

I would be lying if I denied the swelling sense of pride I felt
as he spotted Suzi and me beaming back at him across the
lawn. He strode over purposefully, shades on, arms wide
open, the perfect rock-star welcome.

As we hastily and somewhat nervously gathered up our
things, the normally surly French waiters began throwing

smiles in our direction. Smiles we thus far had been unaware they were capable of producing. Strange, that.

The drive back to Bono's house was right up there in my top ten celebrity journeys. There in front of the main door was parked his gleaming black BMW convertible, roof down, all set and good to go. A turn of the key, a growl of the exhaust and the screech of rubber and we were off into the balmy Mediterranean air with the lead singer of one of the greatest rock bands in the world as our chauffeur.

Did it get any better than this? Well yes, actually it did.

As we exited the village of Saint-Jean, Bono turned up the car stereo and started singing along at the top of his voice to The Carpenters' *Greatest Hits*. This was another one of *those* moments – of which there have been many because I have been very lucky. The surreal ones are the best and they don't get much more surreal than our night with Bono.

Once we arrived at the bargain villa on the beach, the food and wine began to flow along with the stories. Lots and lots of stories. Bono loves to tell a tale or two, most of them wonderfully outrageous. Like the time he and his mate Gav ran out of brandy one night so decided to take a small dinghy out to sea in search of the US Navy and more booze.

Beaulieu, next door to Eze and Saint-Jean, is a deep-sea port and as such can accommodate the biggest ships in the world including, on this occasion, a humongous US aircraft carrier.

'They love U2, the Americans,' Bono said to Gav as they made for open water, 'they're bound to have some brandy on board, sure they'll be up for giving us a bottle.'

Now, two things here. Firstly, it was the middle of the night and the sea can be a dangerous place at the best of times, and secondly, how on earth were the US Navy supposed to know this was Bono and his mate Gav requesting benevolence and not some murderous terrorists surreptitiously attempting to stick a limpet mine to the side of their warship?

The story goes that once safely located next to the carrier in their minute dinghy, our two thirsty adventurers looked up to register a vessel the size of a small city bearing down upon them.

'What did you do next?' asked Suzi, barely able to speak for laughing.

'I took out an oar from the boat,' replied Bono, 'and I started to hit the metal hull as hard as I could – clang, clang, clang ...'

'No way!' we both exclaimed like a pair of school kids. We were gripped.

'Way,' came the reply. 'And then ...' he continued, 'after about a minute, Gav now having joined in, we hear the whirring of chains being lowered and see what looked like some kind of mini destroyer descending down towards the water a few hundred feet away.'

'Shit,' shouts Gav, 'that boat's got a gun attached to it. Start the motor, Bono, they think we're attacking them. Fuck, they're going to blow us up!'

Suzi and I at this point were on the floor killing ourselves laughing and Bono, not immune to a fit of the giggles himself, was finding it increasingly difficult to carry on spinning his merry yarn.

When he finally did manage to finish, we all had tears streaming down our cheeks. It transpired that the night watch on board the US naval craft had indeed identified a security breach in the form of Bono and Gav in their dinghy, and launched a gunboat patrol to check what on earth was going on.

Suffice to say they caught up with our two barking-mad buccaneers within seconds, both of whom were on the brink of having a heart attack. Bono said it was still the most frightened he's ever been and Gav likewise. But did they ever get their brandy?

Well, he said no but I suspect otherwise.

But Bono wasn't the only well-known surprise Cap Ferrat had in store for us that week. When you go to extraordinary places, extraordinary things tend to happen and we weren't done yet.

TOP 10

THINGS THAT COME IN A BOTTLE

10 HP Sauce
9   Worcestershire sauce
8   Dandelion and burdock
7   Extra virgin olive oil
6   Vinegar
5   An ice cold beer
4   A pint of fresh, full fat milk
3   Heinz tomato ketchup
2   White wine
1   Red wine

THE FOLLOWING THURSDAY AFTERNOON, the sun was high in the sky, the sensible people were having a siesta whilst the sun worshippers were beachside busy baking themselves. As Suzi was happy to sizzle with the best of them and I was neither tired nor mad enough to expose my milk-white body and already sunburnt face to yet more heat, I decided to mosey on down to the town to enjoy a quiet read and a cold drink in the local patisserie.

After doing exactly that and whilst ambling back up the gentle hill towards the hotel, I noticed in the distance an equally pink-faced gentleman walking towards me. I smiled to myself, more out of a sense of camaraderie than anything else, but as he drew closer I couldn't help feeling he looked familiar.

'Blow me,' I thought to myself as we continued to converge, 'he looks for all the world like David Frost.'

Several more steps towards each other and ...

'Blow me again, it *is* David Frost.' And sure enough it was.

At almost exactly the same time I recognised him, he recognised me. We'd never met before, yet here we were now, red face to red face in an almost deserted French village. *Les deux rostbifs rouges, très extraordinaire!*

'My dear boy,' he announced, 'you're always much taller.'

What the heck did that mean? And before 'Hello', or 'How are you?' Hilarious.

'David, what a perfectly pink pleasure this is for both of us,' I replied.

'Indeed, indeed – hey, I'm staying at Andrew's, you must come round for a drink one night.'

I had no idea what on earth he was talking about.

'Oh, yes, er, right, of course, we must. I'm with my girl-friend you see.'

'Excellent, then you must bring her along as well. I'll get one of the girls on to it. Where are you?'

'We're at the Voile d'Or'.

'Righty-ho, we'll get you there, then.' And with that he was off.

I still had no idea what he was talking about. Who was this Andrew to whom David was referring, and who were these girls?

I half expected to hear no more about it, but I have since learnt to take members of the old school at their word. Later that evening there was a call to our room.

'Hello,' Suzi said.

'Ah, hello, this is Maddie Lloyd Webber here.' Ah, it was *that* Andrew and *those* girls to whom David had been referring. 'Frosty says you and young Mr Evans might like to come for dinner one evening. Would that be agreeable?'

Two evenings later, the 'boys', i.e. David and Andrew, were dispatched by the 'girls', i.e. Maddie and Carina (Frost), to fetch Suzi and me from our now familiar spot on the hotel terrace. Needless to say, after our second famous pick-up of the week, the waiters could not have been nicer to us for the remainder of our stay.

We sauntered down the road to Andrew's house, which was no more than a few minutes in the direction of the Cap itself. Andrew, the great composer and impresario, walked ahead with Suzi while I trailed a few metres behind with David. Andrew and Suzi talked wine whilst David and I talked telly.

Now, there's success and then there's Lloyd Webber success, as we were about to discover.

When we arrived at our dinner venue, Andrew and Maddie's house was nothing short of amazing. I won't go into detail – that wouldn't be fair – but let's just say it was off the scale.

There is a wee tale, however, that I do feel at liberty to share with you.

'Suzi and I had a delightful conversation walking up the hill,' proffered Andrew as we sat down to commence dinner. 'Suzi asked me what, in my opinion, was the greatest wine in the world, which, I believe, to be a 1947 Cheval Blanc.' At this point David and several other guests nodded their approval.

'So, if everyone is in agreement, I propose that after the Rothschild '55' (of which there were two magnums opened on the table to have with the starter), 'we move on to a couple of bottles of the best of the best for the main.'

Was I hearing this correctly? Had Mr Lloyd Webber just announced that we were to have not one but two bottles of the greatest wine the world had to offer? It certainly appeared so. Not only that, but how about the two babies currently taking pride of place in front of us; easily the best wine I'd ever had in my life thus far, but already about to be relegated to second place.

The night turned out to be fascinating on many counts; I have an idea most Lloyd Webber dinner parties do. The conversation was like a script from a film, with talk of presidents, prime ministers, gangsters and movie stars, all vying to be invited to this or get a part in that. There were also a few surprise visitors as the night went on, but those names are also for Lord Lloyd Webber's book. If he ever writes one, what a book that will be.

When the moment came for the '47 Cheval Blanc to be served I'll never forget Suzi's face when Andrew asked her to taste it, on behalf of all the guests. She was as nervous as I'd ever seen her. This was going to be the sip of her life.

Suzi raised her glass, closed her eyes and pursed her lips in her usual expectant manner, but this time as she tilted the glass towards her the deep-red ruby liquid inside seemed to light up with an extra special promise of the magic to come. We all waited, almost scared to breathe, for her verdict.

'Yum, that's lovely!' she declared, a brief response admittedly but an entirely acceptable one at that. Besides, what else is a girl supposed to say in front of a man who was not only our host and provider of the wine but also known to be one of the world's most prominent wine connoisseurs?

Moreover, Suzi was absolutely right. The Cheval Blanc 1947 was indeed lovely.

I only wish I could taste it again today now that I know just a little bit more about what a good wine should taste like.

Upon our return to England, Suzi and I couldn't resist following up our great wine adventure by paying a visit to our local vintners. The sommelier there was our very own grape guru and we couldn't wait to ask him which wine, as far as he was concerned, was the best wine in the world.

Without missing a beat he replied, 'Alors, mais bien sur, zere is no question, Monsieur, Madame, zat is zee famos 1947 Cheval Blanc – sans doute!' His eyes misted over as he pronounced the name and vintage of the famous château. 'Why you ask?'

'Because we had some last week,' I said, trying not to sound too pleased with our revelation ...

'Non Monsieur, ce n'est pas possible. Zee only person known to 'ave zat wine ees your music man, Andrew Webber Lloyd. You cannot get it anywhere else!'

'I know,' I said, this time having to try really hard to avoid the smug zone. 'We were at his house last week and he gave us some.'

Upon hearing this, our friendly wine merchant took a beat to see if we were joking, then for a brief moment looked as if he might cry, or faint, or both. Thankfully this was only a temporary glitch as he was soon back with us, insisting we tell him all about our experience, whilst offering us a glass each of something 'he just happened to have open' as a small bribe.

For the record, thank you Sir David for getting us the invite to the Lloyd Webbers in the first place. Thank you

Maddie Lloyd Webber for following up with the phone call. Thank you Suzi for striking up a wine conversation with Andrew whilst walking down the road with him. Thank you Andrew for being so generous as to share with us your liquid treasure. Thank you Monsieur Sommelier for providing a wonderful and enthusiastic epilogue to the piece. And finally, thank you God for inventing grapes in the first place.

TOP 10

PERKS I GAVE OUT AS A BOSS

10 Meals and booze – hundreds of thousands of pounds worth – fabulous fun all round
9   Holidays
8   Cars
7   Golf membership
6   A wheelchair!
5   Rolls-Royce and driver
4   Christmas bonuses – always (very important this one)
3   Share options adding up to millions
2   A year's salary to close colleagues
1   Ten per cent of annual salary to every employee in the company

ANOTHER GOOD THING ABOUT THE SOUTH OF FRANCE is that Nice airport is less than two hours away from London by plane, very handy if one has to return at short notice; something that was very much on the cards, as Suzi and I had embarked on this last trip shortly after our Langan's decision to sell the radio station. In the meantime, DC and I were keeping in touch via telephone.

'How's France?' he asked during one call.

'Oh, you know – quiet,' I replied.

'Yeah, right.'

'How are things there?' I enquired.

'Equally quiet,' he said, laughing.

'Ah, I see.' I realised there was a quid pro quo on offer here. 'Alright,' I sighed, 'will you tell me yours if I tell you mine?'

After a potted version of what Suzi and I had been up to in the last few days, DC wasted no time in getting down to the business of our business.

Having made the decision to sell the Ginger Media Group, the next step was to figure out exactly how we might go about it. This was the main thrust of David's industry over the last few days. Whilst I'd been off gallivanting with various members of the entertainment industry, DC had been hard at it.

'We've met with the major players from the banks who handle this kind of thing,' he began, 'and I'm delighted to say that Goldman Sachs look like they might be willing to take our sale on.'

I had no idea of the significance of this but it sounded like I ought to. I asked David to enlighten me further.

'Goldman Sachs,' he explained, 'like all the big banks, offer many corporate financial services, as long as there's plenty of fat on the bone left over for them. The thing is, though, at a projected sale price of *only* £175 million to £300 million, we as a company would not normally be worth their while, let alone the wholehearted attention and focus of one of their hot-shot city-slicker sales teams.'

'Ah, I see,' I said, trying not to sound too underwhelmed.

Eventually, after more detailed explanation I got it – sort of – and began to understand why DC did what he did for a living and I talked on the radio.

As the week progressed, my crash course in how to sell a company continued and I couldn't help feeling that all the stars were once again lining up in our favour. Every phone call seemed to be a step forward, every conversation taking us closer to our goal.

The man from Goldman Sachs was convinced he could pull off the kind of deal we were after, and much sooner rather than later by the sounds of it. In fact, when I arrived back in Britain he already had several very interested parties banging on our door. Three stood out in particular; they were the French company NRG, the American company Clear Channel, and from Scotland, the Scottish Media Group.

It was soon time for me, along with the rest of the board, to attend another series of secret meetings around more of those ghastly, bad-taste mahogany tables.

I was never quite sure during these meetings whether we were courting the buyers or the buyers were courting us. I suppose there was no question they all wanted to sleep with us, but who was going to take their clothes off first?

As the discussions developed, just as when we were buying the radio station ourselves, it appeared that I was the main concern. Although this time it was not because I was seen as a risk – on the contrary, I had almost doubled the radio audience since taking over *The Breakfast Show*, adding millions of pounds to the bottom line – but rather because, along with my hosting *TFI Friday* every week, a lot of the value of the company now rested on my shoulders. The big question on everyone's lips was, if we did sell, would I stick around and carry on and if so, for how long, and how much would I want paying?

Furthermore, when it came to my future salary they wanted to know if I would be prepared to take some of my fee in shares as opposed to having it all in cash, thus providing me with an incentive to carry on performing at the highest level.

The answers to these questions were key to any potential new owner.

I assured anyone who would listen that I had no intention of going anywhere. After all, this was what I loved doing and especially so when it was on my own terms. When it came to the issue of my salary, I had already taken a massive wage cut to increase our profits and therefore our value, and as long as I still had shares in the new company, I said I would be more than willing to continue on the same terms.

This is exactly what the parties concerned wanted to hear and helped bring the best out when it came to bidding. Several firm offers were made for our little outfit, the most attractive of which was £225 million from the Scots.

Were they really going to make us over a £100-million profit on a company that had only existed for just over two years? Yes they bloomin' well were, and what's more they did.

In March 2000 the biggest deal of my life was completed and the instant the papers were signed, I was out of debt and my bank manager's new best friend.

A few weeks later I was handed a ridiculously fat cheque. So fat, in fact, that I was officially, according to the *Sunday Times* Rich List, the highest paid entertainer in the UK.

There it was for real, an actual cheque with my name on the top line and a figure of twenty odd million pounds underneath it. I remember taking the cheque to the pub with me for the next week. My accountant went spare, not in case I lost it, but because of the amount of interest I was losing out on every day.

Everyone was happy, how could they not be? SMG had got their hands on the media company everyone was talking about, my team and I had all become significantly wealthier – five of them became millionaires overnight – and not only that, we all still had our jobs and were being paid a small fortune to do them.

This, however, was also when I came across my first example of the difference between proper businessmen and a DJ who just got lucky.

'We must give everyone a slice of the action,' I announced gleefully.

'What do you mean?' asked one of my now former backers.

'Well, how about every member of staff receives a bonus for, let's say, ten per cent of their annual salary, except for my immediate on-air team, whom I propose should receive a whole twelve months extra pay,' I suggested.

'Good for you,' said the same guy, 'but we'll be returning all of our profit back to our shareholders, every penny I'm afraid. Good luck, though, it sounds like you're going to need it with ideas like that.'

'But why?' I remember thinking at the time. 'Why would we not want to reward everyone involved in our success?'

Of course his view was that only a handful of us had taken any risk, whereas our staff had taken no risk whatsoever, remaining secure and decently paid throughout.

Even though I had to concede he was perfectly astute in his summing up of the situation, in the end I gave everyone a bonus anyway. It all came out of my share of the pot and I was more than happy to do so. The bill came close to

£800,000 but out of what I had made it was more like a graze than an open wound. In fact, it felt great. For me at the time, new money was like fresh butter; I thought it should be spread around whilst there was still plenty left and it tasted nice. Idiot.

Nice idiot, but still an idiot.

Having done my own bit of spreading, a party was declared. A party which I think may also have gone on for several days, I'm not quite sure. But then again, I was about to become unsure about a lot of things.

TOP
10 DODGY DECISIONS I HAVE MADE

10 Buying 220 acres of land in Portugal for about £7 million
    with barely any planning permission for anything
9   Forming a new production company to make shows in
    which I had little or no interest
8   Producing other people generally
7   Agreeing to turn up to the Comedy Awards very much
    the worse for wear after being 'found' in a pub
    nearby
6   Donating £100,000 to Ken Livingstone's mayoral
    campaign
5   Doubling it to £200,000 after Frank Dobson (Ken's rival
    Labour candidate) criticised people for being ginger
4   Buying a Chelsea mansion because I was bored waiting
    for the pub to open
3   Withdrawing £300,000 in cash from the bank so I could
    pretend I had won on the horses, thus getting people to
    stay and have a drink with me
2   Taking the Scottish Media Group to court and losing
    comprehensively
1   Refusing to let a nice man from a big bank give me a
    cheque for £56 million

AS MY PART OF THE DEAL I had accepted forty per cent of the
value of my old shares in cash, with the other sixty per cent
being held as shares in the new company. These shares were
to be released to me in three tranches of equal amounts over
the next three years. After that it was up to me whether I sold
them, kept them or lit fires with them.

Everyone at the time said I was mad to accept so much paper as opposed to real money, with the other main players in the deal negotiating a much higher percentage of cash payment for their equity.

'Not so smart now, though,' I thought a few days later, sitting in DC's office watching the share price of the new company rocket from our sale price of £2.00 to a high of £3.76.

This meant that where I had been sitting on £30 million pounds' worth of new equity at the point of sale I was now, just over a month later, sitting on a value of £56 million.

It was time for another conversation with Goldman Sachs, except now it was they who called me, shortly before dispatching a very nice man to come and visit me. He represented one of their investment funds.

'Chris, we would like to offer you £3.76 per share for all your shares today,' he said, sitting opposite me in an office I'd borrowed. 'That, as I'm sure you know is £56 million,' he went on. 'What do you say?'

Well, to be honest I didn't know what to say. I was already richer than I ever imagined I would be and these latest figures being tossed around were plain silly, but before I could even consider a decision, I had something to discuss with the nice gentleman on a point of clarification.

'Er, I don't actually have all the shares yet. I only receive them a third at a time over three years.' Of course this was not news to him.

'We are aware of that, Chris. What we are suggesting is that we buy them forward – that is to say we buy all your shares off you at an agreed price today, no matter when you get them. The price is firm.'

Now I have done many stupid things in my life but what I was about to do next is right up there at the top of the list. I suddenly convinced myself that there were dastardly goings on here, after all this was Goldman Sachs. Why were they so keen to totally buy me out and at such a premium?

'Surely they must be up to something,' I concluded to myself. 'Why the hard sell?'

I tried to look intelligent for a second, tapping my fingers under my chin in a contemplative manner before declaring with gusto, 'No thanks very much, I'm fine as I am. My shares are not for sale to you or anyone else.' Upon hearing this, the nice gentleman from the big bank turned ashen. It was obvious to him I'd just lost my mind.

He tried to help me.

'But Chris, do you realise how good a deal this is for you? It's a guaranteed profit of almost one hundred per cent on the huge profit you've already made selling your company.'

But I was not to be moved. I was determined to turn down this second 'offer of a lifetime', no matter what. In fact the more he tried to reason with me, the more I became suspicious and convinced myself I was right.

By the time the nice man eventually gave up trying to give me £56 million for nothing more than a signature, he was incredulous.

In that one encounter I had become delusional. A fathead of seismic and cataclysmic proportions.

Whereas before I had understood my limitations when it came to business and accepted that thus far I had enjoyed no more than perhaps a highly fortuitous roll of the dice, I had now unwisely entered a state of mind where I presumed to actually know what I might be doing.

Mistakes don't get much bigger than this.

The nice man from Goldman Sachs left the meeting shaking his head in disbelief. Over ten years later I'm still shaking mine. Excuse me for a moment whilst I just go outside to scream.

TOP 10 WAYS DRINKING TOO MUCH LEADS TO FOOLING YOURSELF

10 You pass off being scruffy for being eccentric

9   You pass off being drunk for being creative

8   You pass off being an angry pain in the ass for being misunderstood

7   You pass off not eating for being fit and lithe

6   You claim contentment is for the unambitious

5   You see responsibility as the badge of the dull

4   You mistake standing in a bar for hours on end talking shite for having a good time

3   You only have relationships with people based around alcohol

2   You are genuinely surprised when people disappear to go home

1   You think that anyone who goes to the pub all day, every day, may actually have something to offer the world

I MIGHT NOW HAVE UNWITTINGLY EMBARKED upon the most rudderless stage of my still relatively young life but at least I no longer owned the radio station, which suddenly felt more like a plus than a minus. After just over two years at the helm of a major business, a weight of which I had hitherto been unaware seemed to lift off my shoulders, leaving me instantly feeling lighter.

Gone for ever were the days when I needed to worry that we were spending too much money on new equipment or vastly expensive poster campaigns that seemed to have little or no effect. I could also forget about the fact that we were paying immense amounts of money to several very average broadcasters to do little more than tell the time and announce a competiton every now and again.

In many ways I was freer than I had ever been before. I had all day every day after *The Breakfast Show* untouched, *TFI* was still flying and I was now perceived as a whizz in business (except of course by the people who really knew what business was about). And all this before I turned thirty-four.

So where does such a heady cocktail of success and opportunity leave a guy? Well, in my case it left me as high as a kite after coming off air every morning, in the middle of one of the most exciting cities in the world, with no more work to do and a truckload of disposable income burning a hole in my bank account.

It's obvious now, when I look back at those days, that I was destined to go off the rails.

How about this for a clue?

Meticulous planning would go into my 'recreational' activities after the show each day and I convinced myself that in spite of these 'plans' I still had a hold on reality. But it was the almost frightening level of attention to detail that should have alerted me to the fact that there might be the beginnings of a larger problem here.

It was almost as if the producer in me had been enrolled by the devil to ruin my life as efficiently and comprehensively as possible.

I would begin my post-show programme of preparation for the day with a trip to the gym. Ironic, given what was to follow, but in my mind the fitter I was, the more unhealthy a lifestyle I could get away with. I would work out for all I was worth for an hour every day, followed by a forty-minute in-and-out sauna session, rounded off with a sleep in the relaxation room – it was a very posh gym.

The relaxation room was a big circular space lined with white leather recliners, all of which were arranged in semi-circular rows facing a huge fish tank. There was suitably soft lighting and subtle, ambient music that seemed to come from nowhere and the room was dominated by a huge planetarium-style curved ceiling that came fully into view the instant you pushed back on your chair.

It wasn't difficult to drift off in such a soporific atmosphere unless one of the larger club members had drifted off before you and had settled into a period of full-on, fat-neck snoring. This could be very debilitating when it came to trying to sleep, although it did raise a smile on the odd occasion when one of these chaps snored so loudly they woke themselves up with a jolt.

Snorers permitting, I used to have around an hour's sleep in the relaxation room; very deep, very rejuvenating sleep, or at least that's what I convinced myself it was – enough to last me for the rest of the day.

After the magic kip, I would jump under a cold shower, get dressed and I was all set. This routine made me feel brand new, come lunchtime and, regardless of what I may have been up to the night before, I was more than ready to go again.

See what I mean? While the rest of the world was at work every day, I was preparing myself to get perfectly wasted and slowly but surely dealing myself out of the game.

After leaving the gym, lunch would begin. I'd usually rope in a few pals for company and we would start with a cold beer before moving quickly on to the wine, white or red, it really didn't matter.

A couple of glasses in and that protective alcohol-induced soft haze would descend slowly before my eyes like an invisible film, insulating me from the real world. As it took effect, smiles became bigger, conversation flowed more freely and the concept of time became almost non-existent.

This weird time factor was the most fascinating aspect of what alcohol used to do for me, or to me, if you like. The hands on the clock lost all meaning. It was this disconnection from reality that I enjoyed the most. I saw booze as my key to the ever-elusive philosophy of living in the moment. Living in the 'now', as they say in all those books and not having to worry about the before or the after. Simply focusing on being in the present, except of course – it's not that simple.

I'm not excusing my drinking or trying to justify it, I'm merely trying to explain what it felt like. I remember taking various drinks on board, and waiting for these periods of cerebral protection to kick in. With the thought of this safety blanket wrapped around me I could look forward to forgetting about the growing muddle of things in life I didn't understand – or perhaps more accurately, didn't want to face. Within a couple of hours I knew I would be free.

This pattern of behaviour became almost pathological, no matter what was going on in the rest of my life, whether it was the afternoon or evening, raining or sunny. In fact I dread to think of the number of beautiful, God-given days I lost to the allure of booze.

I invented all kinds of rules to convince myself I was still in charge. If I could put off the start to my drinking until at least twelve hours after I had last stopped, then I would deem that a good day, a great day in fact, fooling myself into thinking I had attained some kind of control. Ridiculous, I know, but this was typical of the kind of justification I would cling to.

I also made another 'rule' that once I'd had a drink I would not talk about anything to do with business. Everyone knew that when I was out, I was out. They were more than welcome to come and join in, but all talk of work and anything to do with it was strictly off-limits.

With lunch over, the company would often dwindle as most people had jobs to get back to. This is when I would find myself hanging around with strangers while I waited to see who was coming out to play next. I'd put in a few calls to friends who might be up for a drink or two later, before heading off to the fifth-floor bar at Harvey Nicks in Knightsbridge – the perfect venue for an afternoon pick-me-up.

Harvey Nicks bar was always guaranteed to be in full swing by mid-afternoon with ladies taking what they believed to be a well-deserved half-time glass of fizz in a break from another credit-card-melting shopping spree. 'God help their husbands,' I used to think, as it was obvious that the vast majority of these wives, mistresses and whatever the others were, probably did little else with their days other than perhaps associated visits to the hairdresser, manicurist and other diversions that cost as much money as possible.

From Harvey Nicks I might move on to Motcombs, a local wine bar and a complete throwback to the eighties, with a cast to match – a more experienced and, dare I say it, more sagacious group of professional drinkers you would be hard pushed to meet. If Ernest Hemingway had drunk his whisky in London, it might well have been in Motcombs.

The guys that patronise this place are a breed unto themselves – an irresistible mixture of saints and sinners, all of them capable of belonging to either group, depending on which way the wind is blowing. From silver-haired songwriters to sport stars of yesteryear, you can never be quite sure who you're going to bump into when you drop in to Motcombs …

My early evening port of call would be for a couple of cleansing pints of beer at one of Belgravia's excellent cluster of pubs. I used to convince myself that after what I had been drinking, these pints were the equivalent of water and would help to sober me up, ready for the evening session back in Soho. When I felt enough 'sobriety' had been achieved, I would grab a cab and prepare myself for the home straight, where the really serious action would begin.

Just writing all this down makes me wonder how on earth I kept going and, more importantly, why on earth I kept going with such pointless marathons of self-destruction. At any point I could have gone home to bed but I never considered that option. Home to me was where everything stopped, and all there was to do was wait for tomorrow.

And so it continued. After the bars in the late evening, I would take another cab to the clubs, where I would stay until the lights came on and it was chucking-out time. This was invariably somewhere around three o'clock in the morning and yes, I know, I had a breakfast show to do less than three hours later, but I considered myself invincible and somehow I managed to pull it off.

My ability to get blitzed on such a regular basis and yet still be able to host a radio broadcast come 6 am the following morning inevitably gave rise to the suspicion that some additional stimulus might have been part of my daily diet. This not unreasonable conclusion – that I was hoovering up the white stuff in between downing the hard stuff – was, however, entirely misguided.

I think if I had strayed into the world of cocaine and whatever else was around at the time, then I really would have been in serious trouble. The thing is, drugs scare the life out of me, they always have and always will. I have an inbuilt off-switch where they are concerned and I've never even dabbled.

The joke is that I was unofficially blacklisted on several occasions because I didn't 'subscribe' to being one of the coke in-crowd. Those who did indulge in this particular vice became suspicious of those who did not and once it became common knowledge I was in the 'did not' camp, I was frequently persona non grata in certain circumstances. What they didn't realise is that I was usually so out of my mind on booze anyway, it would probably have taken half of Bolivia's national product to register even a mild high where I was concerned.

The bizarre thing is that I was hardly ever offered drugs anyway which, when you think of the circles I've moved in, is bordering on weird. Maybe I give off a natural anti-drug signal to any ne'er-do-well who might otherwise think to darken my door, or maybe God thought I was doing just fine ruining myself as it was, without the need for any additional help.

There was one exceptionally polite offer of drugs that I did encounter, however.

A very good and immensely talented friend of mine who liked the odd 'toot' was celebrating his birthday, to which he had invited me. Halfway through the night, he beckoned me to the loos where he informed me that another pal had bought him the present of a small 'wrap'. He assured me that contained within the wrap was the *crème de la crème* of cocaine and, although he was aware that I did not partake in such practices, he wanted me to know that if ever I was going to have a go, then this was the stuff to have a go with ...

For a moment I must confess I was tempted, but again, thank God, I declined.

Alcohol may well have got the better of me at various stages of my life; this is something I completely accept but I'm almost sure, had I ever wandered down the drugs route, I would have been in my box and six feet under a good few years ago.

TOP 10

QUOTES TO GET YOU THROUGH MOMENTS OF DOUBT

10 Don't mistake knowledge for usefulness
 9 The present is short, the future doubtful and only the past certain
 8 Passions must be attacked by brute force and not logic
 7 Strive not for a fine life but for a fine day, every day
 6 Beware those who long for the future and claim to be weary of the present
 5 Neither a second nor a year is replaceable
 4 There is nothing above the man who is above fortune
 3 Prosperity is nothing without inner peace
 2 Don't spend too long getting ready for the best days otherwise they will be over before you get started on them
 1 Life is long if you know how to use it

INCREDIBLY, SUZI AND I were still together during my early days of post-sale paradise seeking. For a while she arranged to meet up with me in the evenings after she finished work, in an attempt to remain a part of my life, but as there was less and less of me to meet, this was only destined to end one way.

Eventually she would give up on me after our lives became too much of a party she no longer wanted to be at.

It was never a party that was organised, it just sort of happened. And like most parties, when I first arrived, and for some time after that, it was most enjoyable. We all just forgot to go home.

I think it would be fair to say that very few people involved around my company and my shows during this period did not have a riot. There were simply too many fabulous things happening day-in, day-out, and we felt this was our time. We were old enough not to be considered kids any more, but not too old not to behave like them. Either side of 30 is the age I recommend to sow whatever wild seeds you possess. At least, it was for me and my lot.

Let's have a look at what was going on. Oasis and Blur were friends, rivals and then enemies. Oasis died; Blur (it seems) live on but now the mad, bad, often sad lads of Britpop are approaching middle age and their muse threatens to move out on a daily basis. When I presented *Top of the Pops* – the only time I did so – the two bands went head-to-head in the battle for number one. I can't even remember being there.

Everyone was banging down the door to come on *TFI Friday*: McCartney, Bowie, Iggy Pop, Aerosmith, even Van Morrison. And how about the Stones, who thought it might be an even better idea if we went and made a whole documentary on them? Me and a production team of five, all flown first class to Chicago, to make a one-hour movie of them on tour. Fine by me.

'Chris, Jon Bon Jovi's making a movie. Do you wanna go out for dinner with him and his wife to talk about getting involved?' I declined, but we went and filmed him on location for *TFI* anyway. Michael Caine invited us to film a skit in his Chelsea penthouse. Helen Mirren took me on as her new DI. One week, in our opening titles, James Belushi served behind the bar and stayed – all night and most of the next morning. Sean Bean went to the pub in a car we'd provided for him to go home in and kept the driver waiting ten hours – no problem. We acquired special gold-leaf tequila for

Jimmy Page – well, you have to when he and Robert Plant agree to turn up and play.

After every show, without fail, there was a party. Close to two hundred of them, drinks all round at the studio, at the pub over the road and at the house we'd seconded next door for the five years we were in residence.

Famous faces, energy and access. We were festooned with an endless army of gorgeous girls and boys, each one of them desperate to be part of the action. And all this fuelled by PR reps appearing from every side, flashing their company credit cards to pay for whatever we wanted.

For the first two years, such levels of excitement seemed entirely sustainable and, throughout everything, Suzi was by my side. We may have parted for some or all of the night when we were partying, but one way or another we would always end up bundled in the back of a car together come home time.

As well as being one of the main players behind *TFI* making it successfully to air every week – and at a profit – Suzi ran our lives completely. Having said that, I was basically allowed to do whatever I liked. I had not yet become unreasonable but was nevertheless still very much full-on. Not that Suzi was a shrinking violet, by any means, and not that she minded the party coming home from time to time, which it did a lot.

Our house in Notting Hill was generously sized and quite posh for two 30-somethings working in the media, and it often found itself home to the waifs and strays of another night of enthusiastic debauchery. Pals like Shaun Ryder and Ronnie Fraser came back to party with us, along with a whole string of other friends, acquaintances and hangers-on.

* * *

And then there was Gazza. Paul Gascoigne – England's finest-ever No. 8, who was a hero first, a friend second and now, frankly, I don't know where he's gone.

The first time Suzi and I met this much misunderstood phenomenon was at his wedding. I should have known when he sent an abnormally large white limo for us that this was not going to be a normal relationship. The second time I met him, I was invited to dinner for his wife's 30th birthday party. Would I ever meet him under normal circumstances? Not really, no.

Here's just a taster of the kinds of thing that could happen when Gazza was around.

On one occasion he had an injury that was keeping him out of the England team. He was still due to go to the game, which was being held at Wembley, and he asked me to accompany him. We were supposed to be sitting next to Sir Bobby Charlton in the royal box.

Both of us were reluctant to go, so we stopped off on the way for a pint and ended up giving away his tickets to two 'bubbly' ladies. We then watched the game in the pub and duly witnessed Sir Bobby on the telly at half-time, wondering who the heck his fellow spectators were.

Another time, Paul asked me to acquire a tour bus – 'Ya kna, like them bands have' – to meet him outside the ground at Wembley after the game. He assured me he could get the gaffer to take him off with ten minutes to go, so we could beat a hasty retreat. 'Get some pals and some beers and wait for us in the lay-by outside the conference centre, why aye.'

I did as he requested but whilst waiting in the lay-by it suddenly dawned on me how unlikely it was that Gazza would be taken off just so he could meet up with us ahead of the crowds. Of course, I was wrong. With seven minutes to go, Paul was substituted. He ran straight off the pitch, straight out of the ground, took his boots off and ran full-pelt towards the bus, still in his kit. We could not believe it. Within seconds he had swapped clothes with one of the lads who was now smiling ear to ear, proud as punch to be wearing Gazza's sweaty, muddy kit whilst the game was still going on.

My favourite Gazza story, though, has to be the four days I spent in Glasgow with him when he played for Rangers. Too long to tell in full, so how about this potted history?

Land Glasgow airport with Will from *TFI Friday*, meet Gazza at Ibrox, go training with the team, meet Walter Smith, the manager. Go back out to pitch, to play one-touch whilst Gazza gets them to put *The Simpsons* on the big screen. Gazza disappears, drives onto the pitch in his new Merc SLK, tells me to get in. We are meeting some of the team at the Cameron House hotel. We drive there but decide to give his car away. We flag down a family in a red Astra and ask if they want to swap. They say they can't because they need more than two seats. We give them the car anyway and hitch a lift to the nearest garage to buy another.

'Can we have the worst car on your forecourt, please?' we ask.

'We have a death trap round the back for 300 quid,' says the guy.

We buy it and ask for a pot of black paint to black out the windows with. We then drive directly to the Cameron House Hotel, straight past everyone who is now wondering where we have got to, and into the waters of Loch Lomond.

Why? I have no idea. Because we could, I suppose, and to make ourselves and everyone else laugh.

The following day, Gazza hired a cruiser to take us camping on an island in the middle of the loch. Five brand-new tents, ten sleeping bags – all the gear and absolutely no idea.

Heinz, the German captain of the boat, and his wife could not have been happier to have us on board but when it came to docking at the island Heinz suddenly lost any ability to steer the boat. We smacked into the jetty at a considerable speed. We said nothing as he tried again but before he got near he struck several buoys.

'Heinz, man! What the hell are yee dan?' said Gazza, no longer able to hold his silence.

Instead of showing any repentance, Heinz became angry.

'Vass are you doink' on my boat anyvay. I haff never dreeven eet before, today ees zee first day my wife and I haff effer been on eet.'

It turned out that this was not our charter and Heinz was not our captain. We had climbed on to the wrong boat in the marina and Heinz had been so excited at seeing Gazza, he had just gone with it. Our skipper had since headed home as he thought we were a no-show.

Gazza was a frequent house guest of Suzi's and mine in Notting Hill and again there was never a dull moment, like the day he met the Pet Shop Boys after they had been on *This Morning* and brought them back for a plate of pasta and a sing-song round the piano – what a combination of person-alities that was. There was also a particularly memorable afternoon when Peter O'Toole was passing and clumped down the stairs to our basement kitchen unannounced after noticing our door was ajar.

He was due to appear on *TFI* that week and decided a spontaneous ideas meeting might be in order.

Every inch the actor, he was wearing an impressively large hat, which I can only presume was intended to aid disguise but instead served only to draw attention. His dramatic sartorial theme continued with a navy blue, double-lapelled overcoat that had a belt wrapped around the waist, not buckled as the designer intended but tied rebelliously in a clumsy knot. Beneath this he wore a pair of grey trousers hitched up high enough to reveal a pair of those questionable see-through socks favoured by the older gentleman. An impressive pair of big black Chelsea boots completed the outfit.

It was one of these boots he plonked upon our battered old pine kitchen table as he lifted up his leg before commencing to strum on my ancient classical guitar almost as if his life depended on it. After a few bars of painful twanging he proceeded to sing a country and western song, the like of which I'd never heard before and hoped never to hear again.

'Here, how about we do this?' he said, an obedient cigarette now hanging precariously from the side of his mouth. 'Better than a bloody boring interview!' he laughed. How could anyone have disagreed?

Of all the people I have met, O'Toole is probably the most impressive. He's certainly the most magical and unpredictable. The stories about what his lot got up to in their day leave most rock bands – and the likes of me back then – looking like little boys wandering around the playground wondering what their willies are for.

O'Toole, Harris, Ollie Reed and Richard Burton – there's no doubt about it, they were the original hell-raisers, with the diseased livers and death certificates (three of them to date) to prove it. We had some serious work to do if we were ever going to catch up with these guys.

Having said that, we were in the middle of giving it a bloody good go.

TOP
10 THINGS DRINKING CAN DESTROY

10 Your bank account
9   Your body
8   Your work
7   Your friendships
6   Your marriage
5   Your outlook
4   Your kids
3   Your brain
2   Your love of life
1   Everything that means anything to you

LOOKING BACK AT THE LESSONS I HAVE LEARNT in my professional life, the one thing I will never allow myself to do again is to waste opportunities. When I was in my mid-thirties, I was in such a fantastic position to get things done and yet all I actually did was request another beer or bottle of wine.

The thing is, I honestly didn't think I was doing anything wrong. I was still turning up for work every day to host my radio show as well hosting *TFI Friday* on Channel 4 every week. The audience figures for both were good and, as far as I could tell, everyone seemed happy.

When you drink heavily and for long periods over several years, in my case a good five years at least, sure, you know it's bad for you, physically, mentally and spiritually, but there is no denying the bizarre sense of freedom that also comes with it. Whether or not this freedom is actually real is entirely another matter but that's how it feels.

Of course, this only tends to be the case when one's drinking is going well. Inevitably the more one continues to drink, the more likely it is that the darker and more sinister aspects of drinking will eventually take over and consume you.

The problem is, at what point does the good drinking turn bad and how can you tell? Well, the answer is of course you can't. The only way you can avoid the onset of bad drinking after good is to quit whilst you're ahead. Unfortunately though, the more alcohol you imbibe, the less you are able to ascertain when this might be.

If you think you're having a whale of a time at a party and someone suggests you go home before you have to, why would you say yes? But there is an undeniable tipping point, that crucial moment when you know that one more probably means four or five more, and a significantly bigger headache in the morning – but by then it's too late. 'No' and 'home' are two words that no longer come easily.

When you allow drink to take over, your mind and body become increasingly unable to resist and will eventually give up and take cover, leaving you to fend for yourself. This is the moment the alcohol has won; the drinker and the drink have exchanged places, and the drink is now calling the shots.

This is why alcoholics can't stop once they have started. This is why, once they get sober, they can never have a drink again. To them, having just one sip of alcohol is like turning on a tap that cannot then be turned off again. It opens the floodgates and says, 'OK, the rules have now changed. Let's get shitfaced again.'

'Just a couple and I'll be fine,' they try to convince themselves.

But 'just a couple' is not a possibility. Alcoholics are not fitted with the right brakes.

One is too many and a thousand is never enough.

What a night of drinking does to our brains, one sip of a drink does to theirs.

I worried I was becoming an alcoholic for years. I still think about it now, if only for the reason that I couldn't bear the prospect of never again being able to have an ice-cold beer on a hot day, taste a magnificent glass of red wine with a juicy steak or enjoy a warm brandy with a cigar on Christmas Eve.

Some say being an alcoholic is not a choice a person can make and that you are either born one or you're not, others say different. I don't know for sure, but I confess there have been times when I felt I was definitely on some sort of slippery slope from which there might be no return. At such moments all I remember thinking was, 'It's just not worth it. I love my beer and wine far too much never to be able to have them again.'

Have I drunk too much in the past? Absolutely. Do I wish I hadn't? Absolutely again.

But I did and I'm still here. I got away with it and I thank my lucky stars. In the meantime I shall continue to enjoy the odd pint of pre-dinner real ale down the local, as well as the odd bottle of beautiful Bordeaux my agent recommends occasionally.

I am entirely aware, however, of the need for me to keep a watchful eye on my drinking habits in order to do so and will do my utmost to make sure I never find myself on the wrong side of the tracks again.

I do also think about giving up drinking completely to see what life might be like in an exclusively sober world, and I am not ruling it out. I talk about it quite a lot with a friend of mine who on two occasions nearly died through his drinking.

He ended up in the same hospital as George Best and was given the last rites before miraculously coming back to us. He is now in the 'can never drink again' category and has the pellets in his stomach to prove it. If he swallows so much as a drop of alcohol, he will become violently ill.

A high price to pay?

'Not for one second,' he would be the first to reply.

'The difference between you and me,' he said, 'is that my whole life was based around drinking. Having another drink was the first thing I thought about when I came to from whenever it was that I'd passed out last. I didn't "go" to sleep for fifteen years, I didn't "go" to bed once, in that whole time. I just fell unconscious whenever I couldn't drink anymore.'

He said that even when he had managed to stay sober for a while, all he ever thought about was alcohol. This is what's called being a 'dry drunk', a sure-fire sign you still have a long way to go in overcoming your addiction.

Scary stuff.

A fellow reformed alcoholic told him before he stopped, that if he carried on he would lose everything he loved and held dear, and this is exactly what was about to happen. I remember helping him get sober on one of the many occasions he'd gone over the edge. Those were three of the most traumatic days I have ever experienced.

He was in a real mess one day and turned up at my house unable to do anything other than stare at me. I rang his wife who told me there was no point in bringing him home until he had dried out. If I tell you she was in another country in their house at the time and she had no idea he was in England, it might help you understand the gravity of the problem.

I was shocked by the extent to which he had lost all self-control and ultimately all self-respect. We were in a coffee shop in Chelsea, where he thought nothing of vomiting into his cup in front of everyone, regardless of the fact that most of what came out of his mouth missed, ending up all over him and the table. He also soiled himself on countless occasions and became aggressive with me when I refused that famous request, 'Come on, let's go to the pub – one isn't gonna do any harm.'

Eventually I put him to bed and slept outside his door for the next two nights. When I delivered him back to his house after one of the more interesting flights I have taken, I guaranteed to his wife that he had not had a drink for seventy-two hours.

I know she loved him dearly but how she stayed with him through all those years I will never know. He has always been a good man at heart but a bloody nightmare when he was on the sauce.

I think it was my witnessing such a close friend going through such a needlessly tragic and mindless battle alerted me to the fact that I was playing with fire. If there were any chance I might end up like him I would have to change – although at this point I was still a while away from any real epiphany.

TOP 10 FACTS ABOUT SLEEP

10 Never try to sleep whilst wanting to pee, it's only going to get worse

9 Falling asleep on the sofa is a subconscious but very real manifestation of your fear of your own bedroom

8 Girls really don't like it when boys don't come to bed. They see it as some form of rejection – which it probably is

7 Girls sleep better than boys

6 Girls sleep quieter than boys

5 Girls sleep less smelly than boys

4 Good sleep is dished out by God to those who deserve it most

3 Lack of sleep is the most dangerous thing other than drink and drugs a person can do to themselves

2 A peaceful sleep is only second in importance to a peaceful death

1 Insomnia is God's way of telling you to shape up

GOING TO BED WHEN YOU WANT TO AND NEED TO is a sign of contentment and a soul at peace with itself. Of someone who is wise enough to take the hours necessary to fuel up for the next day in order to live life to the full.

Sleep is not, however, for the malcontent, who, far from embracing the wonderful gift that is sleep, ends up fearing it instead, running a mile at the mere mention of its name.

For years I was this man.

I've asked myself, many times, why this was. Maybe I feared going to bed because I knew my sleep would be anything but restful and calm. I have always suffered from the most horrendous nightmares and often wake up more tired than when I went to bed. I am convinced that my hair has turned from ginger to white because I spent a large chunk of the nineties supposedly asleep when it was actually just my body that was unconscious whilst my mind was taking part in a horror movie.

I have come to the conclusion that this unwelcome nocturnal cranial activity was the result of lots of unfinished business that littered my life. You have to tend the garden now and again otherwise nothing new can grow. My garden was well overdue for a good weeding.

For a long time I had tried to ignore the fact that I had a daughter whom I had not seen since she was a few months old.

Back when I was a wet-behind-the-ears 21-year-old in Warrington I got together with a lovely girl called Alison, and not long afterwards she became pregnant. We had a beautiful baby girl called Jade, but in those days I was just not ready to commit to bringing up a child. Immature and selfish, I know, but the truth.

Alison went back to live with her mum, taking Jade with her whilst I ran away to pursue my dreams of fame and fortune. At the time, I'm ashamed to say, I felt relieved. I didn't think for a moment how Alison must be feeling, or how it would be for Jade, I just wanted my 'freedom'. Besides, I convinced myself that Alison would meet someone else who would be a much better dad to Jade. Surely they were best shot of me.

But this pathetic excuse for the abandonment of my child had eaten deeper into my soul than I ever imagined it could and it would continue to do so until I stopped ignoring it. During the latter period, when I was drinking myself into the ground, the impact of not seeing my daughter for all that time began to creep slowly back into my mind like the first ripples of an autumn tide.

Having said that, I still didn't have the courage to try to right the wrongs. Far from it – I had become a leading expert in looking the other way the second anything or anyone worthwhile threatened to come into my life to make it better. All I had to do was look at the evidence.

Over the years I had acquired some of the best jobs in my industry and yet dropped them like a stone. I had also experienced the love, laughter and tenderness of some amazing women but they too were now part of the wreckage. And yet my answer? To carry on regardless and stay out drinking until I dropped.

There are several problems with this approach, of course – the numerous health issues, for example, as well as the possibility of being attacked late at night. The most pressing problem to me and my booze-soaked mind, however, was neither of these. All I cared about was the fact that when I eventually *had* to go home, I could no longer speak and so was unable to get anyone to take me. When I contemplate what a state this must have meant I was in, it makes my blood run cold.

This recurring dilemma, which I began to face more and more as my life continued to fall off the edge of a cliff, led me to make one of my most illogical decisions to date. I took the insane step of announcing to my beautiful girl-friend Suzi that I could no longer live in the house we shared.

My warped reasoning was that I had to move somewhere else that was easier to pronounce when I was drunk, thus enabling me to get home.

'This,' I claimed hopelessly, 'is why I have been coming home less and less recently.'

Suzi, I suspect, had by now all but given up on our relationship and was probably glad to see the back of someone who bore no resemblance to the happy-go-lucky, hard-working kid that she had fallen in love with five years before. If she had stayed with me any longer she would have been on the verge of becoming a victim and, as sensitive and caring as Suzi is, one thing she is not is an emotional punch bag for a bloke gone wrong.

Kensington Park Road was the address I was having drunken issues with.

When you're drunk, really drunk that is, words become like twelve-foot-high walls almost impossible to scale. The more you think about them, the more they become a lost cause – even before you've attempted to say them out loud. When you do finally have a go, the emphasis in your mind is so much on getting the first word right that the rest of what you want to say fades into oblivion. Your brain and mouth have fallen out with each other, and you have nothing left with which to pick up the pieces.

At such desperate times as these, my paranoia at the potential of slurring the word K-E-N-S-I-N-G-T-O-N would fill me with such pathetic dread that I would start thinking about it for up to an hour before I even had to contemplate saying the street name out loud.

When it came to the big moment I would often make several attempts to convince the cab driver that I wanted to go to Keshisham Park Road or somewhere similar. Various cabbies would wait patiently for an improvement in transmission, whilst others would quite rightly sling me out to sober up and see if I could do better next time.

So the long and the short of it was, I really did up sticks and move – first into a hotel for six weeks and then into an apartment opposite the hotel, both of which were situated at the infinitely less slurrable address of WILTON Crescent.

There you go, I assured myself, clean and crisp and easy. WIL-TON. Lovely. What an infinitely less scary name to be confronted with at the end of yet another mindless night of liver-bashing. Yes, yes, yes – WILTON CRESCENT, that will do very nicely, thank you.

Ah the joy, I remember thinking. No more having to practise KENSHNINGSHTON PRAK TOAD when I could feel the night and/or me coming to another sad and sorry end. Not only was Wilton easier to pronounce, but the geographical location of my new home meant that if I played my cards right, I could make it home without having to speak to anyone at all. This was because my new address fell within the recently designated £1 public-transport zone of central London. I was pretty sure that so long as I handed over my pound confidently and smiled at the bus driver he would presume that I was a £1-zone man – with no conversation required.

I was keen to test out my new plan and did so the very next night. I was thrilled to discover it worked like a dream. In fact, it worked so well that cabs very quickly became a thing of the past, with buses my preferred choice of transport. This was a position further compounded when I realised that the London omnibus was also the only vehicle legally allowed to travel west up Piccadilly towards Hyde Park, halving the time it took a cab to navigate the various one-way systems to arrive at the same place.

So, all very well and good for the drunken nutcase; he had successfully figured out the quickest and most efficient way to get home. But of course when he eventually did get home, there was no one actually waiting there for him.

Not surprisingly, Suzi had opted right out of this madness.

She remained for a further year or so in the lovely Notting Hill townhouse we had shared before calling time on it herself and picking up an apartment just around the corner. I heard afterwards that although the old place still held many affectionate memories for her, ultimately it made her sad.

Where there was once so much joy, love and laughter there was now only emptiness.

I thought I'd done enough by inviting her to 'relocate' with me. Not for a moment did it strike me that my grounds for moving were so far removed from the real world that no one in their right mind would have sanctioned such a ludicrous course of action by being party to it.

All I thought was that she didn't understand. No one understood. It was time for another drink.

TOP 10 BAD THINGS THAT CAN HAPPEN WHEN YOU'RE DRUNK

10 You start to over-tip
9   You don't go home
8   You think you can sing
7   You share good things with bad people
6   You covet strange women
5   Your morals take the night off
4   Your mind waves bye-bye
3   You give your phone number and email address to anyone
2   You black out
1   You can quite easily kill yourself

MY WILTON CRESCENT DAYS were the times when I was least myself.

It was a period in my life when I clearly wasn't thinking straight. Wilton was an address I moved into on the basis that it would help me sustain abnormal levels of self-abuse. This is not good karma and karma is something I very much believe in. Not in a hippy-shit kind of way but because anything you do, by its very nature, has to have consequences. Every action has an opposite and equal reaction, as the physicists say.

Wilton Crescent was always going to be a mistake because I'd gone there for all the wrong reasons – and caused hurt in the process – but I wasn't ready to see that yet. In fact having originally secured a lease on the ground floor/basement flat, I went on to acquire the other two flats that made up the rest of the property, thus taking over the entire house.

I have vague memories of considering turning the whole building back into one single dwelling, but of course that would have taken some effort and endeavour; two qualities that were no longer available to me.

The actual reason I took over the other flats was because I had a noisy neighbour upstairs, and another neighbour, on the top two floors, who didn't like my motorised scooter parked in the hallway. Effectively I paid for these two problems to disappear by buying them out. I ended up owning the building more by accident than design.

Other than the fact this situation gave me control, I had no use whatsoever for the two additional apartments and so ended up letting them to pals for next to no rent. I assumed the apartments were appreciating in value anyway so the money was not an issue, and I preferred them to be occupied for security reasons. The presence of people that I knew also meant that, technically, I was no longer alone.

I am not very good on my own, not for long periods. I enjoy my own company for a couple of days, and definitely when I'm working, but generally I do like to be around other human beings. I think they're more fun and more engaging than anything else that's been invented since.

It was choosing the right ones to be around I was beginning to have trouble with.

Many extraordinary things happened to me during the couple of years that I was resident in London's leafy Belgravia, an area that is officially designated as a village and a very posh village at that.

Other than Buckingham Palace, Belgravia has the lowest crime rate of anywhere in the country, largely due to its massive police presence, because of all the embassies that are located there.

I remember reading in the local magazine – an overtly lavish publication printed on several brief but very shiny and expensive-looking thick pages – that crime was down year on year from a colossal three crimes to now just two! A figure that the police were still not happy with and confident they could reduce even further. Two fewer crimes a year and their work would be done.

Ironically, however, it was whilst living in this ridiculously low-crime area of the capital that I came the closest to being arrested. Imagine if I had been – I would have sent the local force's statistics spiralling out of control, devastating their plans for policing perfection.

It all happened one night after another of my meticulously planned drunken evenings and speechless bus journeys home.

I arrived at my front door in the early hours of the morning, only to discover I had misplaced my door keys. As I had to be up in almost no time to host *The Breakfast Show*, gaining entry and grabbing what little time I had left for sleep became paramount.

With this in mind, I immediately set about searching for a missile. I had decided to smash a window, climb in, go to bed and worry about the consequences in the morning. After all, it was my house, my window.

After rummaging around in a skip parked nearby (people in posh areas are always having alterations done) I found what I needed in the form of half a breeze block. I marched back towards my house ready and willing to do what was necessary and, once in position, closed one eye to take aim. I followed this with a couple of unconvincing practice swings, before clumsily hurling the brick in the general direction of one of my beautiful Georgian plate-glass windows.

With an almighty crash the glass shattered. All I had to do next was jump the four-foot void from the pavement to my downstairs basement, land on the windowsill, balance and then sidle in through the newly smashed hole, trying not to pierce any of the arteries in my legs in the process.

There were several ways I could have met my maker during this mission impossible but hey, I was Superdrunk, and surely everyone knows that Superdrunk is invincible. Until that is, he ends up in the A&E department of his local general hospital, an unworthy drain on one of our most vital services.

Miraculously, I made the jump, although God only knows how. I've looked at that space many times since and I would never attempt to do the same thing sober.

Having achieved stage one, I was ready to move on – but surprise, surprise, guess what? I was stranded. I had landed on the windowsill and it was now all I could do just to hold on to the underside of the sash frame without falling off. I was so close to the window that I simply didn't have the centre of gravity to move in any direction. Even in my inebriated state, it wasn't difficult for me to realise that if I attempted anything, serious injury was a distinct possibility. Whichever way you looked at it, I was well and truly stuck.

As my fingers started to seize up and cramp began to set in, the nausea of blind panic started to envelope me. If I let go, I was heading for a twelve-foot drop into the basement area and the wrought-iron banister of the staircase that led down from the street.

I began preparing myself for the worst, when I was interrupted by one of the most redundant statements I have ever heard.

'Don't move,' a man's voice called out through a loud hailer.

What was he talking about? I hadn't moved for over a minute. I didn't need telling.

I just about managed to rotate my head enough to see the three red police cars that had screeched to a halt behind me, tyres smoking, sirens flashing. The red livery told me these were vehicles belonging to the special diplomatic police force that constantly patrolled the area. The same guys who cracked crime like no others before them.

'I *can't* move,' I said, almost apologetically, as armed officers now piled out from their respective vehicles.

'I wish I could,' I said, now almost whimpering, 'but I'm stuck and I have to warn you I think I may well be falling soon.'

'Bloody hell Chris, is that you?' the officer with the loud hailer remarked, having now put it down, realising that the moment for amplified conversation had probably passed.

'Yes it is. I'm sorry,' I said, feeling every inch the complete idiot.

'What the hell are you doing?' he asked, the incredulity in his voice almost comical.

'My place – locked out – need to get in,' I replied, resorting to basic caveman.

'You know people get shot around here for less than what you're doing,' he exclaimed in disbelief. 'What *were* you thinking?'

I should have been arrested on the spot. It would have been good for me, perhaps with even a brief stretch in prison thrown in, but instead I was mercifully rescued. The boys in blue forced my front door, opened my window and dragged me in the best way they could.

'For Christ's sake don't do that again will you?' requested the loud-hailer man, whom I could now see was a sergeant, 'or next time we'll shoot you just for being an idiot.'

As he and his colleagues laughed, I attempted an unconvincing smile.

'Would you like me to give you a mention on the radio this morning?' I offered feebly, the dawn chorus now alerting me to the fact that my work was no longer any length of sleep away.

'No, we flippin' well wouldn't,' came the emphatic response. 'As far as we're concerned, this never happened. Now sort yourself out and get that bloody window fixed – today!'

And with that, several good men who do a real job for a living, left one very embarrassed man who really had no idea what he was doing at all.

TOP 10 THINGS PEOPLE OFTEN THINK I AM BUT I'M NOT

10   Short (I am 6 foot 2)

9   A Manchester United supporter (I have always supported Liverpool)

8   A petrolhead (I love cars but I know next to nothing about what goes on under the bonnet)

7   Always hyperactive (I am very quiet and relaxed at home)

6   A low-handicap golfer (I have been off 15 for years)

5   Good mates with every famous person in the world (I barely know any of them)

4   A pint lover (what I really love is good red wine)

3   A huge Beatles fan (I love their music but know very little about them)

2   Cash rich (I am permanently cash skint)

1   A gadget person (I am in fact almost anti-gadgets)

I READ SIR MICHAEL CAINE'S BOOK *What's It All About?* soon after it first came out in the early 1990s and a damn fine read it was too. For a start, he very nearly died after he and some of his army pals contracted an often-fatal tropical disease whilst stationed in Korea.

After they were admitted to hospital and told they were going to die they were offered the chance of being guinea pigs for a new form of treatment which involved them having to be strapped to their beds for a few days which, if successful, could save their lives. They all went to the pub one afternoon in order to discuss what they should do. They were unanimous in agreeing to become part of the experiment.

After all they had nothing to lose. The experiment was an unexpected success and they all survived.

Another surprise for me was discovering that Michael didn't make it big in the business until he was in his thirties, and lived until that point in the shadow of his flatmate Terence Stamp. Stamp was a superstar whilst Caine was still flogging himself around any audition that would have him.

Michael cites one of his more successful roles during this period was that of air traffic controller for Terence when it came to ushering one beautiful woman out the back door before the next one arrived at the front.

Described as 'one of the most beautiful men of his generation', Terence was making the most of his fame, fortune and handsome jaw line, and it was Michael's job to make sure he didn't get caught with his pants down.

'Wow,' I remember thinking when I read that, 'just imagine ...'

I have often wondered to what extent I am influenced by the books and movies I have read and watched, and whether I subconsciously remember all the bits I like and then weave them into my own life. Of course I'm not saying for one second I was my generation's Terence Stamp, but it's amazing how busy your runway can get if you put your mind to it. Of all the places I've lived, Wilton Crescent was closest to becoming my Heathrow than any other.

Whether or not the women whom I have had the good fortune to get to know more intimately acquiesced to my advances because I was rich and famous I cannot know for sure, but of course I know this may have been a factor.

But does it really matter?

I realise some people may regard this statement as shallow, in fact I know they will, but bear with me.

Yes, rich and powerful men often end up with women who, on the face of it, are too beautiful for them. And ageing rock stars and film stars (again, mostly men) don't think twice about marrying someone half their age.

But do you really suppose they care what the rest of us think if she makes him feel ten, twenty or even thirty years younger, whilst she gets the life of her dreams? If a couple is happy in the shallow end, then so be it – leave them to it, I say. Sure, it may be more of a 'deal' than a genuine relationship, but most of our lives are riddled with clichés – it's just that we choose not to admit them.

The other much-maligned couples who get it in the neck for so-called questionable motives are famous people who choose to pair up with one another. God forbid two people in a similar job get it on, eh?

Before the advent of online dating, eighty per cent of couples in the western world met their partners at or through work. Take my romance with Ms Geri Halliwell, formerly of the Spice Girls. That was an interesting episode, to say the least. Geri was – and still is – a dear sweet girl and one with whom I shared a sincere, albeit very brief, relationship. Not what the press wanted you to think, of course.

I had never, in all my exploits, not even with Gazza in our 'let's surf on the roof of a white limo' days, experienced anything with the press that came close to the fuss that kicked off when I started dating Geri.

Not that I minded. As I've said before, famous people who complain about getting attention are in the wrong business.

But I will say that when Geri and I were an item, it did become somewhat intense.

On the nights Geri stayed over at Wilton, I would set off for the studios in what should have been darkness but there were so many paparazzi waiting outside it was like stepping out into the bright light of midday. I have no idea exactly how many paps were waiting to pounce during those mad mornings but it must have been at least twenty, their camera flashes so blinding that it was a good few minutes after I had managed to scramble into my car before I could see properly again.

I had to chuckle to myself. Here was I, a ginger kid from Warrington, being pursued as if it were the sixties and I were one of the Beatles.

For the record, Geri and I *were* a genuine couple, but of course it was a much better story that we were going out with each other purely for publicity, a charge I found laughably predictable and lazy. The last thing either of us ever needed was publicity.

The truth is that Geri and I got it together because we had a lot in common. We were both working-class kids done well, and we both fancied each other. I can one hundred per cent tell you that I was totally focused on that lovely little toosh of Geri's, rather than trying to lure the red-tops into giving us more meaningless column inches.

Indeed, my sole mission was to get as close a look as I could inside those famous spangled red hot pants, not to mention that sparkly Union Jack dress that seemed to fit her so well. Make no mistake, when Geri gave me the go-ahead I was in there like a shot.

Alas though, our flame-haired alliance was not meant to be. While Geri was one of the sexiest girls I'd ever known, it quickly became evident that we were two mad March hares destined for anyone but each other. I had checked out of reality one way (by being totally barking), whereas Geri was having her own issues for entirely different reasons.

She was a 24-hour-a-day perfectionist and now that she had the means to take her philosophy to a whole new level, her fastidiousness knew no bounds. This resulted in what appeared to me to be a frightening degree of organisation.

Geri was also single-minded. Nothing wrong with that – and no doubt one of the reasons she became so successful – but she made it very clear that if I wanted to be with her it was her way or the highway.

In retrospect, a bit of Geri-domination is something I could probably have done with, but in those days my eyes and ears were closed to anything that might be good for me. I had duped myself into thinking I liked being out of control and half out of my mind, so when Geri came along and I realised she preferred quiet nights in, as opposed to very loud nights out, I suspected this union was probably not the one for me.

Not that baling out of the relationship was by any means easy. Geri was gorgeous, interesting and fun enough for me to be easily tempted to hang on in there and see if we could bridge the gap between our differences. But Geri was looking for a truckload of love and I had shed mine a long time ago.

There were other girls too – some you may have heard of, others you won't have. There was a door-less door frame that led from my bedroom through to the hallway and as each lady departed, I saw her momentarily freeze-framed and wondered if she would ever come back. She rarely did.

It wasn't all about the bedroom at Wilton Crescent. For this was the height of my *TFI Friday* era and many of the guests who appeared on the show used to end up back at mine as we attempted to discover how far we could stretch another crazy night.

There was the famous Ant and Dec incident, which I only remembered when they wrote about it in their own book and it was picked up by the tabloids. They'd come back to my place after appearing on *Rock and Roll Football* and later that evening we were very merry, to put it mildly.

I was still with Geri at the time and we'd slipped off to bed, leaving the boys downstairs in the kitchen. Apparently it was Ant who came to look for us whilst Dec was having a serious word with himself in the loo. The story goes that Ant stumbled into our bedroom to witness some Ginger on Ginger action. I don't recall any of this but that doesn't mean it didn't happen.

Other famous pals who were always welcome included one of the most beautiful creatures on earth, the enchanting and hugely talented Anna Friel, the rebel-rousing tour de force that is Ray Winstone and even the surprisingly open-minded Ms Dannii Minogue.

Then there were the odd curve balls; for instance the six weeks during which the criminally handsome American actor Aaron Eckhart came to stay after turning up unannounced on the doorstep one evening. He claimed his agent had given him my address as his place of residence whilst he was filming his latest motion picture on location in London.

To this day I have no idea what he or his agent were talking about but no matter, I was more than happy to have another interesting, energetic and colourful character around, so I let him stay on the top floor. By the way, if you really want to know how American film stars stay so thin I can tell you; they simply don't eat – anything – ever. Aaron just smoked Marlboro Lights cigarettes – that's all he ever did; I never once saw a single morsel of food in his fridge. It was as clean and empty the day he left as it was the day it came out of the factory. How he had the energy just to stand up every day, let alone go and look beefy and gorgeous in front of a film camera, I have no idea.

My best guest story from the Wilton years is, however, reserved for Tara Reid, American film star and all-round Hollywood babe. Tara was over in Britain to publicise the first of the *American Pie* movie trilogy, her first port of call, luckily for us, being an appearance on *TFI Friday*. Just how lucky I would get, though, I couldn't possibly have imagined.

Tara was part of a three-pronged publicity assault on the UK's media, along with her two co-stars, Jason Biggs and the really good-looking tall guy – you remember, the one who was a bit too nice for his own good and a bit wet generally.

I'd already seen *American Pie* at a pre-screening, along with some of the production team before the stars were due to come on our show. We were all very much in agreement that the film was going to be a smash as it encapsulated the spirit of our times, very zeitgeisty. *The Graduate* of its day. In fact we were so convinced of its success that we declared that week's *TFI* the *American Pie* Special.

Now, here's the thing. Americans are really good when it comes to appearing on chat shows; they consider it a part of their job. Sell, sell, sell is the order of the day and absolutely right, too. Their attitude is, 'We've worked bloody hard to make the product, we might as well finish the job off and get as many people to go and see the damn thing as possible.' They also know it doesn't hurt to put in a few sharp performances in the interview chair in case any movie directors may be tuning in with thoughts about whom to cast as their next star.

This, I'm sorry to say, is the opposite of a lot of UK artists, who consider the interview circuit a bind that is beneath them and will do anything they can to get out of any such commitment – or at least get it over with as soon as possible, while looking awkward and uncomfortable throughout. Sell, sell, sell you fools and don't worry so much about what we might think of the real you. Alright, you'll never be as articulate as you are when reading from those wonderful scripts you're given, but we know that and it's OK, so lighten up.

It was no surprise, then, that the three young stars of what was to become a worldwide hit, not to mention a three-picture multi-million-dollar franchise, turned out to be a chat-show host's dream. They were charming, funny, sweet, cheeky and oh so positive, another American trait which we need to adopt. In short I couldn't have asked for more, but here's another thing, I wasn't going to have to – more was going to ask for me.

Along with Shannon Elizabeth, the actress who played the ridiculously hot Russian exchange student (surely no girl on earth has been that hot in real life – have they?), Tara Reid was the chief totty in the hippest flick of the summer.

After *TFI* was over, I almost always followed the same routine. I ran downstairs to my dressing room where I would get changed as quickly as I could and remove my slap with a couple of wet wipes whilst having a quick debrief with the producers and our writer, Danny Baker. Following this, we would go en masse back upstairs to the bar, or across the road to the pub.

This week had been declared a pub week. So there I was, walking down the corridor leading to the stage door, the corridor where all the dressing rooms were. As I neared the stage door, I heard what sounded like an American female calling my name. I stopped and turned around.

'Hello, did somebody call me?' I shouted back down the busy thoroughfare.

A moment later, the blonde bob of Ms Reid swung round her dressing-room door.

'Hey, Chris. It was me, Tara.'

'Hi Tara,' I replied. 'What can I do for you?'

Note to reader: Alright now, calm down and listen up because this next bit really did happen – you have to believe me. I promise I wouldn't bother wasting your time, and mine, writing about it, if it did not. This is exactly what Tara said next.

'Do you know any good pubs that might be fun to go to?'

As you can probably imagine, upon hearing this, I had to check to make sure I wasn't hallucinating and hadn't died and gone to heaven.

'Excuse me?' I said, just to make sure.

Clockwise from top left: Mr Dicky B, checking if my heart's still beating after I'd just paid him £87million for his radio station; Me with Gazza and Danny Baker at Virgin; What could possibly go wrong?; Guinness for breakfast anyone?

Drinking partners: Chris Evans, centre, Danny Baker, left, and Paul Gascoigne spent the afternoon at a clu

Evans spurns award to go drinking

By Alison Boshoff, Media Correspondent

HRIS Evans skipped an
yards ceremony yesterday
favour of going drinking
th Danny Baker, the radio
esenter recently sacked by

show in January, made a
brief appearance at the 1997
Television and Radio Indus-

sonality of the Year. He said:
"We were all going to accept
the award for a laugh, but

Groucho Club. His an
came as Channel 4 annou
that it did not want to
his chat show, *TFI Frid*
third weekly slot.

Clockwise from top left: Saying hi to Stephen Fry;
With the oh-so-cool Peter O'Toole; Lots of hair,
both me and Cher; St Suzi slogging it out with Mr
Nightmare; Dennis the Menace I have your jumper.

This page: 'Mmmm, I bet most of this hair is gone
ten years from now'; Anyone have any idea why we're
here?; There's no better chin-rest than an ex-Spice
Girl; Gazza you can stop sucking my cheek now.

WHEN BILLIE MET CHRIS

Simply Irresistible

Clockwise from top: The sales brochure for Lionel Richie's house that we bought in LA; A Grappa with a Granny at 8 o'clock in the morning in Venice; I've just lost a £15million court case, me!; Hats off, lips on; Boxing Day on a speedboat in Venice.

Clockwise from above: Billie marries Steve Davis; Who do I make this out to?; Private jets always make me this red; WANTED: Four blokes for looking far too British; Ugly bloke wins 'Can I touch beautiful girl competition' – again.

Clockwise from above: Pond Life, I dig myself another hole; Billie on the edge; Enzo my German Shepherd, 'Do I push the mad ginger bloke in or not?'; Billie goes topless; Billie – that's the girl I fell in love with; Billie put the knife down – please!

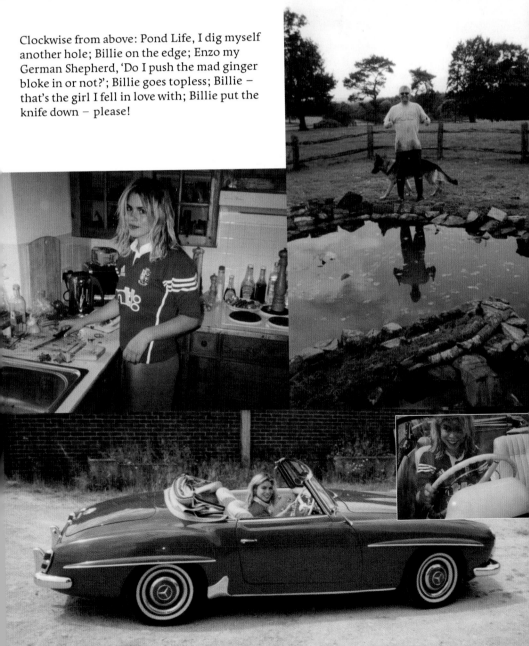

'Do you know where there are any good, fun pubs?' No, this was definitely real. Tara Reid was really saying these words out loud and to me.

And there was more.

'The boys want to go to a restaurant but I'm not into that. Perhaps you could show me a few – if you're not busy that is.'

Here's what the voice in my head said next.

'WHHHAAAAAAAAAAAAAAAAAAAAAAAAAAAAT?'

The thing is, as I have already mentioned at some length, pubs were my thing. I knew some of the best in the land and, as a result of several years of enthusiastic hanging out in such establishments, was a welcome patron in all of them.

Here's what I actually said whilst attempting to stifle my excitement.

'Tara, if you want pubs, you've come to the right man. I am Mr Pub. I'm not proud of it, but it's true. I'll give you all the pubs, drinks, stories and characters that go with them.'

'Really?' she said.

'Really really,' I nodded.

'Oh my goodness, that's so exciting, that's so sweet of you. Can you wait five minutes?'

'Tara, to take you to the pub I would happily wait several years.' I didn't actually say this, I'm nowhere near cool enough but it was what I was thinking. As it happened, I think I just smiled as if I had lost the ability to speak – which I had.

The result of this situation was not one night with this minx of the movie world but the next three!

Yes, three nights and three days with Tara bloomin' blinkin' Reid.

Tara saw more of London's pubs in the next seventy-two hours than I believe any US citizen has done before. We didn't leave each other's side until her car turned up to take her back to Heathrow airport on the Monday morning.

I swear the only piece of promotion Tara Reid ever did in Britain for the original *American Pie* movie was *TFI Friday* because having only arrived in the country a few hours before, she then went on the missing list for the rest of her engagements. I know because I was with her the whole time.

None of her publicists knew where she was and neither did her two co-stars, who continued the press junket in her absence.

And do you know? I've never heard from her since. Not a word, but that's kind of perfect.

I do wonder, however, if she ever recalls the crazy pub crawl she embarked upon with the ginger-haired talk-show host over in London that time.

What do you reckon – probably not, eh?

Ha ha.

And no, we didn't sleep together.

PART TWO

WHEN BILLIE MET CHRIS

TOP
10
WAYS TO KNOW YOU'RE
IN LOVE

10 When you feel like you could kiss her for ever
9   When love-making takes precedence over orgasms
8   When holding hands feels electric
7   When her breath feels like it might burn you
6   When you find other girls invisible, even on hot sunny days, when most of the female population is naked
5   When you see her as the little girl she once was
4   When you see how kind and considerate she is towards other people
3   When you see her laugh
2   When you see her cry and it kills you inside
1   When you see her give birth to your child

TFI FRIDAY **WAS ALSO THE VENUE** for my first meeting with Billie Piper – the pop-starlet slice of perfection who was to become my second wife.

The moment Billie was confirmed as a guest, we were all very keen to meet her and see what the young firecracker from Swindon had to say for herself. It was generally accepted that there was a lot more to this girl than just another saccharine-sweet chart sensation who found herself splashed on the front of the teeny magazines week in, week out. The word on the street was that, despite her tender years, Billie was a girl who knew how to party in the fast lane and had the stories to back it up.

I couldn't wait to talk to her. There are some people you just get a feeling about and Billie was one of those. Whenever

I'd seen her being interviewed, I felt maybe there was something she wasn't telling us.

Billie's appearance on *TFI* involved the usual walk along the gantry through the crowd to rapturous applause and excited whoops and hollers, followed by a pacey chat, fleshed out with a few clips and photos. In Billie's case it also included a spontaneous exchange of clothing behind a pair of curtains, and it was this exchange that piqued my interest even further.

The curtains in question framed a window that looked out across the Thames, and formed the backdrop to all the interviews that took place at the desk. At some point during our conversation, though for the life of me I can't remember how or why, Bills and I suddenly found ourselves giggling behind the cover of those famous but dusty old drapes whilst swapping my shirt for her vest. No doubt the TV audience wondered what the heck was going on.

When we reappeared I could be seen busting out of Billie's slinky black skin-tight top, whilst she looked slightly dishevelled but sexy as hell in one of those garish Liberty-patterned shirts I seemed to wear all the time back then.

Whatever the reason for this sartorial tomfoolery, it definitely broke the ice between us. It reminded me of the secret tent moment I had enjoyed with Kim Wilde back on *The Big Breakfast* almost a decade before, when I'd managed to kiss her just before we went live on air – a situation that resulted in us becoming an item for a while.

Clandestine moments like these, when the audience is watching but can't actually see what's going on, really do seem to hold plenty of truck when it comes to persuading various gorgeous members of the female race to become more interested in the television host trying to woo them. I think it's the element of danger that's exciting, but without the risk of anything really bad happening.

Billie, having to my knowledge never exchanged clothes with any other interviewer before me, had made a statement. At least that's how I saw it. Girls don't swap clothes with blokes they don't like; everyone knows that, not even for the sake of a good bit of PR. I concluded therefore that Billie must like me and I knew for certain that I liked her.

'There's something in this,' I thought to myself. 'This could go further.'

She was only eighteen, but she was a feisty young woman who had seen much more than such tender years would normally allow. And yes, at thirty-four I was almost twice her age but I was still far young enough not to have to worry about being perceived as a dirty old man just quite yet. Consequently if the chance ever presented itself, I would have no hesitation in pursuing Ms Piper further.

My chance came a fortnight later, when Billie, who was still promoting her latest single, appeared on my radio show. Once again we got on like a house on fire, and this time I managed to hand her my phone number and suggest she give me a call.

When I say 'my' phone number, what I actually gave Bill was my close pal Webbo's number, because I didn't own a mobile. I thought they were the devil back then and in many ways still do, though there's no denying their usefulness at times such as this.

A quick word about Webbo. I met him in a bar in Tokyo when I was being filmed for my disastrous golf programme,

Tee Time (that's another story). Webbo was one of the film crew, we got on famously from the off and he has since become a valued friend and colleague. In fact, he's been solid as a rock during the most recent quarter of my life.

With Webbo's help I was now contactable 24 hours a day – if he was able to stick with me, that was. This could have been pushing it, as Webbo's lovely but long-suffering wife Lisa had put up with a lot from both of us recently. This included one week when her husband went to work on a Monday morning and didn't get back home again until eight days later. This kind of behaviour had now tailed off, though a few selectively requested late passes were still sometimes available, depending on which way the wind was blowing.

'Tell Lisa,' I instructed Webbo, 'that of all the things I've ever asked you to do, this is by far the most important. Inform her that if you stay with me till Billie calls I promise never to keep you out again.'

'This is not gonna be easy,' said Webbo, whilst simultaneously biting his lip and stroking his chin like a dodgy builder pricing up a job. We both knew we were skating on very thin ice where Lisa was concerned but I begged him to give it a shot.

'Let me have a cigarette first, then I'll give her a ring.' He was gonna have a go. What a hero. Webbo went outside, and five minutes later he was back.

'She's not having it, not this time. She says I can stay out until this afternoon but then I have to go home.'

This would almost certainly result in disaster. Billie was filming *Top of the Pops* all day and was more likely to ring in the evening, if at all. I had to think and I had to think fast.

'Webbo, what does Lisa want?'

'What do you mean, what does she want?'

'In life – what does she desire?'

'Well she'd love a car; she's always talking about those Suzuki jeeps.'

'Right, perfect – phone her back and tell her I'll buy her one. All she has to do in return is allow you to stay with me until Billie Piper rings on that phone. We'll also put a time limit on it; forty-eight hours maximum. Any way up, Lisa gets her car.'

'You can't do that,' said Webbo, laughing his head off.

But I was deadly serious.

A second phone call was made to Lisa.

'Deal,' said Webbo, upon his return.

Webbo has since informed me that over the next few hours I was so busy praying for Billie to call that the rest of our schedule went out of the window – much to the chagrin of my other colleagues. It also happened to be the day of our team's Christmas lunch. To which I paid no more than a fleeting visit.

I really was smitten by Billie. I convinced myself – like a child wishing for a Christmas present – that the more I thought about her, the more likely she would be to appear. Although I didn't have a lot to go on at that stage, I couldn't help feeling that we were very similar and perhaps some of the same things were missing in both of our lives. Maybe we were destined to get together, I fantasised.

I know this is a strange, almost weird, conclusion to come to after meeting someone briefly just twice, but I had an overwhelming sense that I might be right.

Praying sometimes works and it did that day. Billie called me the same afternoon, suggesting we meet for a drink that night. I might have been one Suzuki jeep down, but a phone call like that was worth ten of the things. And besides, I still needed Webbo as my wingman.

What a lot of people don't know about Bill is that she was originally an actress, not a singer. Her whole pop career was a happy, or unhappy – depending which way you look at it – accident.

Smash Hits had come up with the brainwave of finding a kid to be the face of their magazine, a visage that captured the very essence of what they wanted to convey. After scouring all the stage schools and talent agencies looking for their perfect pin-up, they struck gold when they discovered the enormous smile of a little girl called Billie Paul Piper, at the Sylvia Young Theatre School. She was an instant smash (forgive the pun) with the readers.

As I have said, Billie was an actress, but she could sing, and when it came to dancing she was like a little brunette female Michael Jackson – she really was that good. She had everything the magazine was looking for, and by the age of fifteen a record deal and the first of a string of number-one and top-ten hits.

Impressive stuff, and very time consuming.

From the moment Billie was spotted she had to kiss good-bye to what was left of her childhood. Show business doesn't do childhood. You wanna be a kid? Stay at school; forget about the bright lights and study. You can't have both.

It was our mutual alienation from the real world – albeit for different reasons – that would play a key part in us coming together, but not before my crash-course in how to date a pop star.

Our first date was a marathon, not for Bill but for me. She was recording an appearance at the BBC's Elstree Studios and suggested we meet back in town afterwards. By 'after-wards', it transpired, she meant 11.30 that night.

Two things here. Firstly, this was a week day and I had to be up at 5.30 am to host *The Breakfast Show* on Virgin the next morning, and secondly, I had usually been out drinking for close to ten hours by that time. Such indulgence would more than likely render me no use to anyone – especially a sparkly young ball of energy like Billie.

I hadn't had a sober afternoon for years. I had forgotten how to. I had tailored my life to suit my drinking and to all intents and purposes it worked, but that day my usual routine was going to have to change. I still drank, of course, and Webbo still accompanied me, but our usual routine had to be tempered.

Where we would normally sup and stagger, we stared and sipped, thus putting off getting drunk for as long as possible. Drink is a time killer rather than a time filler, and without our deadliest weapon 11.30 pm seemed an awfully long way off.

I've experienced some days that have dragged before, but this one was way up there with the most interminable of them all. I lost count of the number of times I looked up at the clock in whichever bar we had moved on to, only to witness time appearing to stand still before me, the opposite of what usually happened.

I've often thought we pass through time, as opposed to time passing by us and this was the strongest proof so far that I might be onto something.

The last half hour, post 11 o'clock, was like the last few miles of a marathon. If there was a wall, we'd just hit it. We needed Billie to turn up.

I've never been happier to witness the arrival of a Mercedes-Benz than I was that night. I am not the biggest fan of the Merc; for me they are all about practicality as opposed to passion but the midnight blue boxy E-Class that drew up that night was like Cinderella's carriage arriving at the ball.

Billie fairly skipped out, straight into the bar, where we just started talking – and never stopped.

Billie is unique in so many ways but most of all when it comes to her sensitivity and fragility, two qualities that are vital in order for someone to become a true artist. It's impossible to be any good in her business unless you are able to hear, see, touch and feel the poetry of the world.

Artists look at things in different ways to most people. Different things matter to them. What a thing it must be to know what moves people, and how to achieve that. This is surely the most powerful tool known to mankind. Where warmongers destroy, artists create.

And so it was with Bill. For the next five years I would experience what it was like to be close to one of these intriguing and complicated enigmas.

Before the end of our first date, I realised I was dealing with the human equivalent of platinum here. Billie simply shone, from the inside out. She was so magnificently alive, more alive than anyone I had ever met. I decided to go for broke. I would ask Billie Piper to marry me.

* * *

The next morning, the radio show that I was due to present came and went but I was not there to witness it. I woke up in a hotel bed, several hours after the show had ended.

And there was more. I was not alone. As I attempted to prise my eyes open, I felt the warmth of what was unmistakably the skin of another human being against my back.

'Shit, who the hell am I in bed with?' I thought.

I became instantly rigid, lying stock still.

'Think you prick – think.'

I was trying to do just that but my brain was more like a blancmange than the computer I needed it to be.

As I struggled with my total lack of recall, my body was in protest. It demanded to know whose skin this was against mine. My shoulders ached, my neck was hurting, my throat had dried out and my heart was pounding.

And then it hit me.

'Oh my God, I'm in bed with Billie. Shit, shit, shit.'

This was not what I wanted. This was not my plan. I didn't want a one-night stand, I wanted to marry this wonder of the solar system and live happily ever after, not have a quick bunk-up that I couldn't even remember.

I had begun to sweat, the cold sweat of absolute fear and loathing for oneself and one's situation. The more I tried to relax, the more the rivers of perspiration cascaded across my back. The sheets beneath were becoming damp.

'Jesus Christ, Evo, you're sweating buckets,' came a voice.

Not the voice of a teenage pop sensation, I realised ecstatically, but the voice of a hairy, rough and tough, tattoo-covered West Ham-supporting John 'Webbo' Webster.

'Webbo, you beauty,' I declared as I turned around, splashing in the sea of sweat that continued to engulf our shared berth. There to behold was one of the most beautiful sights a worried man can lay his eyes on – namely anything other than the woman who shouldn't be there.

Apart from my dad, I don't think there is another man I have ever loved more than I loved Webbo at that precise moment. It's a love that will last for ever.

Once I'd explained to my trusty pal the reason for my unfathomable delight, he suggested that we grab a shower – not together, of course. We were both still covered in sweat; unfortunately for Webbo, almost all of it mine.

After that I needed a debrief on what had actually happened the night before. There was also the small matter of proposing to Billie to attend to.

Webbo informed me that after we left the bar where we met, we went on to a rather famous but sleazy nightclub. That explained the headache that felt like several sledgehammers beating down on my skull. But I didn't care. There was work to be done. Within ten minutes Webbo and I were out on the street, hailing a taxi.

'Where to, guv?' said the driver. I'm not meaning to stereotype London cabbies here but a lot of them really do say that.

'Brompton Road, please,' I replied.

I was going straight to the Ferrari showroom. I had no idea whether or not Billie was a fan of the famous Italian marque, or if she could even drive (I later discovered she couldn't), but I wanted to stop this girl in her tracks, and how better than with the gift of one of the most magnificent sports cars known to mankind?

'Morning, Mr Evans,' said the salesman, trying to suppress a smile of expectant glee. 'What can I do you for?'

'I'd like that silver Ferrari in the window please, but I need to be able to take it now.'

'Of course you do, Mr Evans,' he laughed.

I was not laughing and neither was he when he realised I was deadly serious.

'Er ... right, well, that's not possible, it's gonna take a couple of days,' he went on.

'Well then, it's no deal. I need to drive it out of here within the hour, otherwise the moment will have passed, never to return. I will be loveless and alone, and you will be one car down on your monthly target.'

The salesman seemed to freeze momentarily while he had a word with himself.

'Alright Mr Evans, wait right there, I will make this happen,' he declared.

He was back no more than three minutes later.

'As long as we can confirm payment for the vehicle now, I have been assured by my superior that you can do what you bloody well like with it.' Er, his words by the way, not mine.

I don't think a Ferrari should ever be referred to as a 'vehicle' but not to worry; there were bigger fish to fry.

Coffee was had, calls to the bank were made and keys were handed over.

With Webbo by my side, I sped off in the spanking new Fezza, through Hyde Park, in the direction of north London. This is where I would deliver the world's most expensive envelope to my equally spanking-new and exciting little friend, but not before a visit to the florists.

'Hello, friendly florist,' I gushed with almost unbearable jollity.

'Hello, famous person,' he responded, wittily.

'May I purchase all of your red roses, please?'

His roses were actually crimson, with dark green leaves, and theatrically long stems. They were amongst the finest roses I had ever seen.

'How many do you really want, sunshine?' he enquired.

'No, I really do want them all. I'm going to propose, you see, and I need enough to fill up a car.'

We counted them together. There were one hundred and ten.

'Perfect,' I assured him.

One dumbfounded florist later, it was time to confront the porter at Billie's apartment block.

She had been advised to buy an apartment in a secure block of flats and it was the job of this smiling, avuncular gentleman, whom I was now facing, to protect her and all the other residents from whatever evils lurked outside. How, I'm not sure, but no matter. This man was my key to Billie's door.

'I'm here to deliver some roses and a message to Billie Piper that I would very much like her to read. It's on the front seat of that car over there, which is also for her.'

My proposal took the form of a handwritten note that I had slipped in amongst the roses. It read, 'I know you don't care about any of this and neither do I, but I had to stop you in your tracks. This car is for you. If you don't want it sell it and give it to charity. I think you're wonderful. Will you marry me?'

'The front seat of which vehicle, Sir?'

'Er, it's not a vehicle, it's a Ferrari, it's silver and it's over there.'

I hoped I hadn't snapped at him. He looked like a good man and one I was sure the residents must be fond of. I couldn't help feeling that he had probably witnessed many things he didn't understand and here was another one.

'Of course, certainly Sir,' he replied.

'Thank you so, so much,' I could have kissed him.

My delivery complete, I could do nothing more for the time being.

Whilst I had been depositing, Webbo had been on the phone organising transport back into town and was waiting for me over the road. I was about to exit the main gate of this mini fortress Billie called home, when a cry came from an upstairs window. It was my girl and she was screaming.

'Come back, come back,' she howled.

Two minutes later I found myself outside her door.

'What the fuck have you gone and done, you crazy guy?' she laughed.

'I have delivered a letter for you in a rather smart Italian silver envelope, no more, no less,' I said, trying not to sound too pleased with my efforts. 'That's what the keys are for – it's outside, waiting for you.'

'You've got to be joking!' Bill exclaimed, her mouth staying open for at least a good five seconds after she'd stopped actually speaking.

There, that was it, right in front of me; that snapshot. Exactly what I wanted to achieve – total shock and awe. Billie was gobsmacked. It was a home run, a slam dunk, six sixes in just the one over. She might not say yes to my marriage proposal but she would definitely never forget the bloke who'd given it to her.

The Ferrari-and-roses episode wasn't a money thing, it wasn't meant to impress Billie that way. But it was my one-stop-shop attempt to blow any competition out of the water. The roses and the Ferrari were my way of buying Julia Roberts a string of pearls and then flying her to the opera, as happened in *Pretty Woman*.

Over the years I've been lucky enough to have been in the position to purchase many things for people other than myself. There is a fine line between being generous and being perceived as a Flash Harry or a Champagne Charlie. I realised that the Ferrari-and-roses gesture was in severe danger of crossing the line but it was a chance I was prepared to take.

Whatever people's conclusions, let the records show that it worked. We became man and wife, for heaven's sake.

Bill and I had seen each other only the once, on our date, and then again briefly when I stopped off at her apartment that morning, so when she rang me on Christmas Day saying that she was coming round that afternoon, it was she who left me open-mouthed.

I mentioned that I was due to go on holiday to Madeira the next day.

'Brilliant,' she enthused. 'I'll come with you – if that's alright?'

Oh, OK then – if you must.

Bring on the big Merc again with the nice driver for one last time. Bill's trusty chariot would whisk her from her parents in Swindon to my house in Surrey that Christmas afternoon. She brought with her nothing more than a large brown leather bag stuffed with several rather cheeky outfits. When she arrived she flung her arms around me, gave me a smacker on the lips and said, 'Right, let's try some of these on shall we? I need to know what you think I should take on holiday.'

Happy Christmas everyone!

Madeira duly came and went but Bill moved in and stayed.

I had found my new friend. A friend with no agenda, in fact quite the opposite – Bill never asked me for a thing, which of course meant I wanted to give her the world.

As a result of our chaotic lives, we both needed fixing, and we had a suspicion we could fix each other. If anything, Bill's life was more of a mess than mine. She'd had years of success but had nothing of any real value to show for it. She had also been suffering from an eating disorder and was burned out and exhausted, emotionally and physically. She desperately needed out from a life she could no longer sustain.

With me she found the courage to say 'no' to people, something she would have to do if she wanted to survive. As our relationship developed, where I gave her experience and confidence, Bill gave me light and innocence.

Every day was like a breath of fresh air and saw us staying in the country more and more, even during the week, when I had to go to London to do my radio show. Finally, we had each found someone to build a few walls with to give us that independence from the rest of the world.

Conversation followed conversation, be it in the pub, lying in front of the fire or snuggled up between the sheets. With our new-found companionship, the days of not knowing quite what we were doing with our lives and quite why we were doing it, began to make way for a new dawn. Exactly what that new dawn might eventually become, neither of us knew, but for the moment the faint whiff of sanity was enough to keep us going.

With the security we gave each other, we slowly began to feel ourselves flowering back into life. I remember the relief as I woke up each morning to find Bill still there and not being able to believe I was going to get to spend another day with her.

Nobody understood what we were up to but we didn't care. In fact one national newspaper became so confused about us, they tried to convince themselves and their readership that Billie and I deserved to be buried from day one. They splashed us across their front page, alleging we were masquerading as a couple solely in a shameless attempt to halt my flagging career whilst also promoting Bill's latest single.

Poisonous, or laughable? You decide.

Nothing could have been further from the truth; the last thing on either of our minds was our careers. All we wanted to know was how could we keep the confusion of the last few years at bay for long enough to be able to breathe life back into each other.

Now, I don't know if you have ever seen the movie *Butch Cassidy and the Sundance Kid*, but in the final scene Butch and the Kid find themselves holed up in a derelict farmstead. They are surrounded by lawmen and various posses of bounty hunters. Vastly outnumbered, they have nowhere to go.

As they crouch down out of breath inside, wondering what few options they have left, Butch briefly looks across at the Kid as if to say, 'How the hell did we get ourselves into this unholy mess?'

A second later, they nod to each other as a signal to go out fighting. Sometimes it's the only way.

This was almost exactly the same scenario Bill and I were subconsciously heading towards. With me as Butch, Billie as the Kid, and airline tickets instead of guns. We would soon have to plan our own quick getaway but first of all I needed to back us into that corner.

TOP 10

FAB HOTELS I'VE STAYED IN

10 The Butlins Metropole in Blackpool – the first proper hotel I ever stayed in
9   The Berkeley in London – I lived there for a while
8   The Carnegie Club in Scotland
7   The Four Seasons in Las Vegas
6   The Hôtel du Cap d'Antibes (complete luxury but at a price – and what a price)
5   The Groucho Club
4   The Sunset Marquis in Los Angeles
3   The Chewton Glen in the New Forest
2   The Voile d'Or in Cap Ferrat
1   The Kurokai in Palm Springs

AFTER WE GOT TOGETHER, Billie almost immediately left the recording career that had been dragging her down for so long. She took some much needed time out whilst she figured out what she really wanted to do with her life. For my part, I was still doing *The Breakfast Show* at Virgin, but other than doing the minimum of turning up in the mornings, I wasn't paying attention to much to do with the world of work and broadcasting. This would go some way to explain why I had not the first idea that it was about to come crashing down round my ears.

TFI Friday had finished in December 2000. It had been a big success for over four years, but had come to the end of its natural life. And to be honest, it suited me. Billie and I were closing ranks with little regard for the outside world.

Having handed over control of the radio station and indeed my whole production company via the sale of the Ginger Media Group, I knew that my spell as a would-be media mogul was over. What I didn't know, however, was that my breakfast show was now under threat, too.

The Scottish Media Group had paid a lot of money for their asset and they were going to run it the way they wanted. When I was in control we had taken huge chances on ideas we believed in, whereas these guys were much more measured, and that's putting it mildly. They were intent on edging forwards slowly and surely, contemplating and calculating even the slightest move for what seemed like hours on end.

This is fine to an extent, but you're never going to take the world by storm with such a pedestrian philosophy, especially in a highly competitive market like radio and television production where you have to make big splashes to stay ahead of the game. Safety nets do not thrill the crowd.

However, this was never going to be the case with the new regime – the brakes were on from day one. A month or two after they took over there were a few uncharacteristic ripples coming out of the normally painfully placid executive ideas meetings. These mooted that my breakfast show was slowly going off the boil and needed to be freshened up. The consensus of opinion as to what to do to rectify the situation was even more surprisingly radical, inasmuch as it was suggested that the best way to move forward was for me to cut loose from my team and start afresh. The team in question being made up in the main by Johnny Boy Revell, Holly Hotlips, and Dan Dan the Soundman, all of whom I had been working with for the last five years since we got together to put on *The Breakfast Show* at Radio 1.

I couldn't deny that there was more than a grain of truth with regard to the state of the show, but to part company with these guys was something I had never even contemplated before. They were friends first and colleagues second, but in retrospect perhaps that was part of the problem. We had become too close to be professionally objective and that's always a mistake. We had lost perspective, along with the collective spark that used to make us shine so brightly.

Despite Billie's best efforts to reassure me, this most recent and unexpected shot across my bows sent me into an all-too-familiar state of uncertainty and paranoia.

My brain turned to fudge every time I gave a moment to the prospect of a split with the team. Could I ever go through with such a thing? How would I go about broaching the subject? Did all three of them need to go, or just one or two?

We had experienced so much together, the highs and lows, the laughter and tears, dirty beds and dirty bars. We had been an unofficial band of radio brothers and one sister. It seemed inconceivable that it could be about to end.

Uncertain and miserable, I resorted to another Evans disappearing act. Please understand I do not do this anymore, but back then it was my automatic default setting when things started to become sticky.

'Babe, can we go away for a while?' I asked Bill one early May afternoon.

'Sure, where d'ya wanna go?' she replied.

'How about LA?' I suggested.

'Alriiight!' she enthused. Bill adores LA.

Now, the thing was, I had asked Bill but I hadn't told anyone else; not my agent, not *The Breakfast Show* team, nor my current employers. I also hadn't informed anyone that Billie and I were going to get married whilst we were there. But that's probably because neither Billie nor I planned that either.

TOP 10 THINGS THAT MAKE A WEDDING BRILLIANT

10 The readings
9 The walk-in/walk-out music
8 The best man
7 The weather
6 The party
5 The location
4 A round of applause/cheering/whistling and general exuberant mayhem when you are pronounced married
3 Only inviting people who you really want there and who really want to be there
2 The bridesmaids
1 The bride

FIRST-CLASS LONG-HAUL FLYING is one of life's great pleasures. Basically, you sit in a huge airborne La-Z-Boy-type of affair, watching up-to-date motion-picture releases whilst extremely courteous ladies and gentlemen fetch anything you might desire. The most difficult thing about travelling at the posh end of the plane is therefore resisting total indulgence and grabbing some much-needed jetlag-busting sleep to help acclimatise yourself for when you land.

I remember climbing aboard a flight to LA once and spying the Who's Roger Daltrey a few seats in front. I was amazed when, as soon as we had taken off, he requested a large bottle of water, a blanket and a sleeping mask. That was him out for the next thirteen hours. What a waste, I thought, not taking advantage of any of the delights on offer. That was until I arrived at my hotel and could barely recall my name, I was so tired. Nowadays I limit myself to one movie, a few drinks, one meal and then some shut-eye but I am still not equipped with the same amount of self-control I witnessed from Mr Daltrey on that occasion.

After landing in LA Billie and I checked into the Four Seasons Hotel on Doheny Drive. There was a thick fog hanging over the city, so the next morning we rented a Ford Mustang convertible and headed south to Palm Springs, in search of the sun.

Palm Springs is situated a couple of hours' drive from central LA and started life as an Indian reservation. In the fifties and sixties it became an out-of-town resort in which Hollywood luminaries built their second homes, hence the scores of mouth-wateringly luxurious Art Deco hilltop houses that sell today for tens of millions of dollars each.

Kirk Douglas was early on the post-war scene, as was Sinatra and his good friend Bob Hope, who even became Mayor for a while – although these guys were just the second wave. The pre-war visits of Einstein, Roosevelt, Truman and Eisenhower sealed Palm Springs as a preferred location of the great and the good. If it was good enough for such an illustrious guest list, Bill and I concluded, it was good enough for us.

The first thing we saw as we drove into town was a visitor centre. Five minutes later, thanks to the perfectly cast, helpful lady behind the counter – everything's like a movie in California if you want it to be – we were knocking on the door of a very mysterious hotel.

This hotel, which looked like it had been fashioned out of wobbly white concrete, had no sign displayed outside and gave no impression whatsoever of being anything other than a private residence.

At first we thought we might have the wrong address but the big wooden door was slightly ajar, daring us to go in.

'You go first,' I said to Bill.

'No way – you,' she whispered. We both started to crack up.

The door began to open, seemingly of its own accord, like we were in an episode of *Scooby Doo*.

'Hi guys,' purred a drop-dead gorgeous woman, probably somewhere in her early fifties who seemed to appear from nowhere. 'How may I help you?'

'Er, is this the hotel?' I asked sheepishly.

'Well, it's *a* hotel,' she smiled.

It turned out to be the coolest hotel either of us had ever stayed in. She ran it for a guy who set it up in the late sixties. With more than a hint of the sixties' hippy vibe about him, he had been in the movie business but decided to quit and take his movie magic with him into the hotel trade. The Hollywood equivalent of a retired English lady setting up a tea shop in Devon. He really was a dude.

All the rooms were different shapes and funked up with rough, white stone walls, tiled floors strewn with funky rugs, dark wood furniture and wooden blinds. There were various areas in which to hang out, eat and relax, with communal dinners taking place in the evening followed by an invitation to sit on the grass to watch old movies being projected directly on to the painted garden wall.

The room we had been allocated was an artist's studio.

'This was Winston Churchill's favourite,' said the nice lady who had greeted us. 'It's where he came to paint whenever he was in town.'

The visitors' book in reception provided evidence of the great man's visits, as it did for those of Jack Nicholson, Humphrey Bogart and countless other Hollywood luminaries.

The more the magic of this oasis beguiled us the more we couldn't help feeling we had been guided there by fate.

Following a fabulous Moroccan dinner on our second evening, served in earthenware bowls and washed down with several rum punches, I woke the next day to find that firstly, I had a thumping headache and secondly, Bill was nowhere to be seen.

This was a little strange as Bill was not the earliest of risers. I stared at the ceiling for a while like you do when you are hungover and then, with still no sign of her, I hauled my skinny white arse out of bed, threw on some clothes and wandered down to breakfast to see where she might be.

Bill was already sitting at a table, coffee on the go and a glass of fruit juice standing by.

'Hi babe,' I said. 'Where have you been?'

'To buy this,' she replied, taking a notebook out of a flimsy carrier bag, along with some pens and a packet of coloured pencils.

'Brilliant,' I remarked, wondering what they were for. Billie couldn't wait to enlighten me.

'This is a book to make notes and draw pictures in whilst we plan our wedding.'

'Alriiight!' I whooped.

It had been decided, we were to get hitched in Las Vegas, only twenty minutes away by plane, with Billie overseeing the US side of arrangements.

'Babe, we can rent our own jet for just two thousand bucks!' I swung into action with a few phone calls back home.

The first was to Webbo, who said he would be wherever we wanted, whenever we wanted, although he was slightly taken by surprise to learn he needed to be in the middle of a desert in America in two days' time.

Two other friends of ours, Chris and Zanna, were next to be invited and with our guest headcount now up to a church-busting three, it only remained for me to call my best friend Danny Baker, who immediately declared himself both best man and stand-in father of the bride.

The jet was booked – private planes in America are inordinately cheaper than over here for some reason – and the future Mr and Mrs Evans checked into the ambassador suite at the Four Seasons. It was the plushest hotel I had ever seen but the suite was not a patch on the presidential suite to which, for some mysterious reason, we were upgraded less than an hour after we had arrived.

You know those hotel suites that you see in films about Vegas, with floor-to-ceiling glass windows through which you can see the whole city? Well, this was one of those. Not only that but the dining room consisted of a table for twenty people, there were two kitchens, a panic room and no fewer than five bedrooms. The view was one hundred and eighty degrees; sharing its panorama between downtown and the airport, it was almost as if we were hovering over the main runway.

After a whistle-stop outfit-buying trip to Banana Republic in Caesar's Shopping Arcade – stripy shirt for me, cute little pink skirt and white shirt for Bill, we indulged in the most amazing wedding-eve feast.

We ate and ate and ate; eating too much in Vegas is very infectious. We were surrounded by lots of large Americans who obviously didn't see anything wrong with not being able to fit both cheeks of their ever-expanding behinds in the same state. Bill and I, both in pretty good shape at the time, therefore felt like we had plenty of calories to spare, with their lard versus our lean only serving to convince us there was no need to hold back.

The next morning we awoke a good half-stone heavier but, hey, that just meant there was more of each other for us to marry. After a carb-tastic room service, it was time to see if our recently purchased new togs still fitted. They did, just about, but there was definitely more resistance than there had been in the shop the day before.

With now only a couple of hours to go until we became Mr and Mrs, the future Mrs E and I decided we needed some beer to soak up the food babies to which we were now threatening to give birth.

Poolside is the only place to drink a light beer during the day in Vegas, preferably lying on a sun lounger being periodically sprayed with a water mister by a dutiful and uncomplaining 'comfort attendant'.

Two happier and more contented souls you could not have found that day as Bill and I lay there without a care in the world, sipping freezing cold beverages out of those tumblers that have a layer of ice between the plastic to keep the liquid inside as cool as possible.

'We're getting married this afternoon,' we kept saying to each other, Bill in her bikini looking fabulous, me, in a long-sleeved shirt, chinos and floppy hat, sweating buckets.

Several chilled beers later our guests arrived, coming round the corner suited and booted straight off the plane and ready for their role in this adventure.

It was time for the party to start.

The register office in Las Vegas has to be the busiest in the world. When we turned up to register, the day before, a lot of those queuing were picking up their licences en route to wherever it was they had chosen to tie the knot, already dressed for the occasion. There was fancy dress, traditional top hat and tails, plus a few less predictable themes – half-naked gay cowboys, plus two hospital patients in their gowns with their drips still attached.

The queues, or lines, as they refer to them in the States, have to have been the happiest I've ever stood in. Almost everyone was beaming from ear to ear and for those not so sure, there was no need to worry, as divorces are just as quick to come by as most things in Las Vegas.

We'd been offered several marriage 'packages' but plumped for one of the simplest. Our actual wedding only cost us $179. The whole thing, however, was a little more than that on top. There were the four return flights to England, the private plane there and back to Palm Springs, the obligatory stretch limo – white with flashing lights inside and out, and champagne on ice (how could we not?) – plus the hotel and the seven-course banquet Bill had planned with the chef.

The ceremony was perfectly kitsch. Bill's first task was to go to the fridge and select her flowers; the higher the shelf, the more expensive the bouquet. Our 'priest' was one of those holy men who you can't help feeling is not really that holy; too much gold on his fingers and too much dandruff on his lapels. I couldn't help thinking that here was a man with the kind of secrets we might want to know.

We also had an inkling that he might well be enjoying an additional revenue stream, after several paparazzi photographers ambushed us just before proceedings were due to get underway. This suspicion was exacerbated by the fact that he wouldn't allow us to close the outside doors during the ceremony. He actually started frothing at the mouth at one point as we had a tug-o-door moment. No, this was definitely not a man of any God I had ever heard of.

Once the ceremony was over we piled into the limo and hit the strip, sunroof open, music full whack and fizz all round. After cruising round town, we had to get as close to the airfield as we could before our pals cottoned on to what was going on.

Driving straight through the gates and onto the runway, the driver delivered big-time.

'Aye, aye, what's going on 'ere then?' joked Danny, as we pulled up to the small but perfectly formed Citation executive jet waiting for us where we'd left it less than 24 hours before.

Following several enthusiastically appreciative comments, including the odd 'Fuck me' and 'You are having a laugh,' we piled on board, taxied towards the main runway and, in no time at all, were catapulting skywards to continue this most joyous day of festivities. Bill and I were beside ourselves. We took turns screaming, 'This is happening NOW!'

When we arrived back at the magic hotel in the middle of the Springs, twilight was on hand to help paint the perfect picture.

The hotel staff had laid on a candlelit spread to die for – an old wooden teak table by the side pool almost completely covered in the plentiful offerings that adorned it. There were brightly coloured bowls of freshly baked breads, rows of perfectly cooked fresh tuna steaks, plates dripping with strips of wagyu beef, bottles of wine and champagne, and a bucket of beers – anything and everything that we could possibly want, and far too much of it for just the six of us.

I don't think I have ever been as full as I was at the end of our wedding dinner but still, I remember doing that thing of sneaking some of the food under the table because I was so guilty about not eating enough.

The whole day was perfect, except for the business of – well, you can imagine. There was no way anything remotely energetic was going to happen in the bedroom after all that lot. How many people really do have sex on the night of their wedding anyhow?

Please tell me it's not that many.

The next day, with lots of yawning after the night before, our loyal wedding party was dispatched safely and semi-soberly back to London, leaving Bill and me alone to enjoy each other a bit more. But the clock was ticking and we couldn't stay away for ever.

* * *

My original week off had now already strayed into an unofficial second week. There were rumblings of discontent from my employers coming via messages from my agent. It was looking to them very much as if they were losing control of the former owner of the radio station for which they had paid over £200 million.

As far as I could see they needed to lighten up and go with the flow. I was their biggest billboard and generating a lot of press attention that could have been harnessed to promote our brand.

In my mind Bill and I getting married was a wonderfully positive story. Why didn't they get it? Perhaps it was because they didn't want to. Perhaps it was because they were dealing in black and white, whilst I dealt exclusively in colour. That was how I had always been and I couldn't change now, even if they wanted me to.

TOP 10

REALLY BAD CAREER MOVES THAT I HAVE EXPERIENCED

10   Making cat jokes

9   Wiping over really important interviews that haven't yet been aired

8   Setting fire to your radio station's outside-broadcast facility

7   Turning up for your first job as a BBC producer not wearing a tie

6   Declining to accept the highest award your industry has to offer (a gold Sony Radio Award in 1997 – because I refused to be abused as a pawn in a self-serving display of unashamed corporate promotion. A little too dramatically activist perhaps, as I have accepted several since and now actually host the awards each year. So much for my core beliefs, eh?)

5   Walking away from national breakfast shows for no good reason

4   Taking your ex-employers to court with a case no judge in their right mind would ever take seriously

3   Paying millions of pounds for the pleasure

2   Doing things for money alone when you no longer need it

1   Staying out when you know you should be home tucked up in bed

BILL AND I RETURNED BACK TO ENGLAND ready to write the next chapters in our new life together but the storm clouds were gathering apace over Golden Square, the home of Virgin Radio.

My first day back on the air was greeted with a distinct lack of enthusiasm around the building, not made any easier by the fact that I had begun the process of disbanding the team. I had already talked to John whilst I was away in the US, after which he had reluctantly – understandably so – agreed to leave the show, and I had sent word to Dan and Holly that we needed a serious chat. I had decided it was probably best if they didn't come in until after the show, when we would have a frank discussion about our future.

That was the first morning since I had begun appearing on national radio that I didn't have at least one of my old pals around me. With no explanation to the listeners, largely because I didn't know what to say, this must have sounded extraordinary but it was only the start of me burying my head in the sand when it came to facing the music, as far as my career was concerned.

With tears from Holly and mixed emotions from Dan following our meetings, they too were about to be cast aside. These 'chats' were highly uncomfortable affairs as the general theme was 'It's been a great ride, but now it's time to go off and do your own thing.' It was a predictably horrible experience for all concerned but I had resolved to remain steadfast and firm, and orchestrate a clean break.

It could be argued that there was more than an element of truth in what I was saying. It had been a great ride, and we had all had a great time and been paid handsomely into the bargain. But as we all know, nothing lasts for ever. This was a decision, however, that had been precipitated by others whom I had allowed to manipulate me and about three of the most important people in my life from the last ten years. If I did want to part company with these guys, it should have been one hundred per cent of my own volition. I owed them that, at least.

The parting with John, Dan and Holly was the turning point in the post-sale period of my Virgin Radio days. Things would never be the same again – in fact six weeks later, it would be all over for me, too.

Unless you can write a song, or paint a picture, or make a jumbo jet disappear it's very difficult to call yourself an entertainer. This is the perennial problem for a bloke whose job it is to be on the radio every day. You are in many ways a charlatan, piggy-backing off the talent of others. Radio shows that transcend this lowly status need things to happen to get them noticed.

The soap opera of the man behind the microphone was my way of doing this.

The adventure Bill and I had just experienced, with all the story of romance and escapism that went with it, was exactly the kind of energy that should have been captured and exploited by the people for whom I now worked.

If Bill and I could have married in secret we would have preferred it that way. To all intents and purposes that's what we thought we were doing until the paps in Las Vegas jumped out to greet us. Now that the news and images were out there, however, I figured we might as well turn the obvious intrigue and clamour for more information to our advantage.

To say this thinking fell on deaf ears would be one way of putting it but it was almost as if I were speaking a different language to anyone around me. *The Breakfast Show* was quickly becoming an island and I was about to be stranded.

Three incidents would seal my fate.

INCIDENT NUMBER 1

It was the 6th of June, the day the England football team were due to play against Greece in the away leg of their World Cup qualifier. Despite kick-off being over twelve hours away, on the show that morning I was already getting fired up.

As a result, listeners started contacting us to say the prospect of the forthcoming match was becoming almost too much to bear and they were finding it increasingly unlikely they were going to be able to focus for the rest of the day.

'Why shouldn't we be excited all day?' I enquired. 'How about we stay on air until tonight – and how about the whole country parties with us?'

It was a no-brainer to me. The papers would pick up on what we were doing and the idea would take on a life of its own. So the countdown to the end of the show continued, and I went on to suggest we hire a big screen, erect it in the square outside our studio and get bands to pitch up and play there throughout the day. How much fun could we have? How far could we go?

All I could see in my head was an all-round win–win situation, with listeners coming into London from all four corners and the station gaining masses of free publicity into the bargain. Yes, yes, yes, we would do this; we would stay on air for the good of the country, for the good of the human race, for the good of David Beckham's right boot.

But no, no, no, we would not do this; we would not stay on air for one second longer than we were scheduled to.

A junior member of management had been dispatched to tell us as much. This was embarrassing and infuriating – embarrassing because I had already announced our intentions on air with great aplomb, and infuriating because it was a good idea that could only reflect well on everyone concerned. To pour cold water on it, and from such a great height, just didn't make sense to me.

I didn't understand why the powers that be had reacted in such a hostile way to something that was so well intentioned and right at the heart of the kind of thing I was known for.

More messages arrived from the management floor, leaving me in little doubt that under no circumstances was I to stay on air over my allotted three hours. When it came to the end of the show, there were now several members of senior management waiting at the studio door poised, presumably, to stop me should I so much as even try.

This was all very incendiary stuff. What on earth was going on?

'Well, ladies and gentlemen, it appears our guitars are plugged in but we are not permitted to turn them on,' I said before signing off, frustrated and confused.

This was the first time since I had been at Virgin that I had been told I couldn't do something – without reason. (DC had once told me to immediately cease broadcasting my reaction to a lady revealing her brand-new boobs to me one morning at ten past eight.) Why wouldn't you want your biggest act staying on your station all day, at no extra cost, to pull off a positive stunt that had never been done before?

It was obvious there was something much bigger going on here and that this was not about my proposed idea for a pre-football match warm-up marathon on the wireless. This was about control and power. They were telling me and the public who was in charge; drawing a line in the sand, and spelling out that from now on things were going to be different.

INCIDENT NUMBER 2

A couple of days later I was taking a quick break to make a coffee during the 8 o'clock news. I wandered down the corridor to what we called the Zoo, an area for relaxing, with tables, chairs and a few sofas, plus a coffee bar in the corner.

In all the time I had been working at Virgin I rarely drank coffee. I am a tea man through and through, but for some reason on this occasion I fancied a change. Now the teabags were kept in the cupboard, whereas the coffee was kept in a jar on the counter. This would prove to be the crucial factor.

I stepped behind the bar to switch the kettle on, took a cup down from the shelf and went to scoop out a teaspoon of instant coffee powder from one of the glass jars. As I did so, I noticed that a notepad had slipped behind the jars, as if someone had rested it on top and then forgotten about it.

'What's this then?' I wondered, sliding my fingers behind the jars to retrieve it. Having done so, I began to flick through the pages to see whose it might be.

The book was about half-full with writing but it was not in a hand I recognised. None of the first few pages made much sense either so I couldn't tell who had written in it, but then as I turned to the next page all thoughts of 'who?' were replaced by much more distressing thoughts of 'what?'

Specifically what was now written on the page in front of me. It appeared to be an agenda for a meeting. The first line read: EVANS TO GO.

I took a beat, to make sure I wasn't imagining things, then read those three words again.

EVANS TO GO.

After confirming that those were indeed the words staring back at me, I gave myself permission to go into meltdown.

'Shit,' I thought. No wonder people were reluctant to interact with me. I was a dead man walking. The notebook suddenly made sense of it all; obviously there had already been meetings discussing my departure.

I scanned the rest of the page, which only seemed to confirm that the axe was suspended directly over my head. It read: HOW? WHO TO REPLACE? SOONER RATHER THAN LATER.

At that moment my world stopped. I was in total shock. As I continued to stare down at the page, the words started to grow and grow before beginning to career towards me like a steam train, just as if they were about to hit me.

'Chris ! Chr-i-i-s-s !!! Chr-i-i-i-i-i-s-s-s-s !!!!!' called Louise, my new programme assistant.

'What is it?' I suddenly felt like an old man who didn't know where he was or what he was doing.

'We're on the weather!' This time she was screaming.

Shit, I was in the middle of a programme. 'Er ... alright, the weather ... Yes, the weather.'

Within seconds I was back in the studio in front of the control desk, still reeling from what I had learnt only a few seconds before.

From that moment on, everywhere I looked, my fate stared right back at me. I was for the chop, there was no doubt about it, yet no one had uttered a word to me to suggest as much. Either I was dealing with a bunch of yellow-bellied cowards here, or they were going to wait until they were absolutely certain I could be removed as swiftly and as silently as possible.

I have since learned, however, that things are rarely that cut-and-dried, and that people often end up leaving simply because they don't have the confidence and self-belief to stick around and fight their corner. So many people jump before they're pushed, needlessly doing the job for their would-be assassins, often in a vain attempt to save face.

But if you choose not to jump, your detractors have to stand up and be counted, something they are often averse to doing. Those in charge often want change but don't want to be responsible for making that change happen – in case it goes wrong, of course. People like this try to safeguard their own position and often avoid confrontation. They are at their weakest when challenged and will often back down, so the lesson is never to offer your head upon a plate and save them the bother.

Unfortunately this is precisely what I was about to do.

INCIDENT NUMBER 3

Another show had finished – another show close to what was becoming the mere inevitable.

After my regular session at the gym and in the sauna, I pitched up with a gang for lunch at a restaurant called Zilli Fish in Soho, no more than three or four minutes walk from the radio station. Aldo Zilli, the proprietor, was a very good friend of mine and a man with whom I'd had many unforgettable experiences. Unfortunately, however, our relationship was not doing either of our careers any favours, as we were often having more fun than was perhaps good for us.

Six or seven of us sat down for lunch, ordered drinks and said we'd wait for Aldo to arrive before we ordered any food. Ten minutes later in bounced the crazy Italian.

'Allo everybody, 'ow nice to see you all!' he screamed. Energy was Aldo's birthright.

After much kissing, hugging and more continental salutations from Signor Zilli, Aldo posted our lunch orders through to the kitchen and then came over to me. He pulled up a chair and leaned over to whisper in my ear. He was currently working on a television idea and had just been at a meeting with Ginger Television, my former production company.

'I don't know what you 'ave done to upset them back at your place,' he said, 'but let me tell you – you are not a very popular boy with ...' He then proceeded to reel off the names of several people I considered friends, along with the word they had used to describe me (you know, the really bad one that rhymes with 'hunt').

I was stunned. The people that Aldo named had been to my house, come on holiday with me as my guests and profited handsomely from being associated with me, but more importantly, it was the fact that I considered them friends that hurt the most.

This was the excuse I had been looking for, or perhaps waiting for, the excuse to jump before I was pushed. Foolishly

I was about to give my detractors exactly what they wanted, by doing exactly the opposite of what I should have done.

'That's it, fuck them, I've had enough,' I said to myself, brimming with melodrama. I stared down into the serviette in my lap and tried to work out how I felt. I knew that I was feeling something but was it anger, or was it sadness? Did I want to scream, or did I want to burst into tears? Looking back I think it was probably the latter, but as it turned out I did neither. Instead, I gathered myself, looked up, smiled and decided to get drunker than I'd ever been before.

Brilliant, eh? Genius.

Those one hundred per cent wrong decisions just kept on coming. When your enemies presume you to be weak, then that is the time to be strong. But I was just about to play right into their hands.

The next twelve hours were not pretty. I drank heavily all through lunch and became uncommunicative and distant, though not enough to stop me from hiring two limos to take our group on to other venues where I would continue to do a comprehensive job of kissing my career goodbye.

By early that evening I was completely gone, no use to anyone. Billie and Webbo said later that they didn't recognise me as the person they knew and loved. They said I appeared possessed. People have asked me since why no one thought to take me home. Well, apparently they did try on several occasions, but I became belligerent and told them in no uncertain terms to leave me alone.

When we arrived at a bar closer to home, feeling the night closing in on me, I pretended to go to the loo but snook off and out the back to continue the darkest night of my life alone. Webbo and Billie didn't know what to do. They realised this was serious, but they had no idea where I might be.

The truth was I just wanted to be on my own. It was as if nothing mattered anymore, like nothing had any value. Drink has a cunning habit of making you feel that way. My life may have been a volatile ball of confusion yet it suddenly all seemed so simple. I was experiencing delusional clarity. 'Things only take on any importance because we give that importance to them,' I remember thinking over and over again.

A liberating thought, perhaps, but a dangerous one too, because it justifies the unjustifiable: the actions of the alcoholic, the drug addict, the warmonger. It wipes out the existence of both good and bad, and gives us permission to rewrite the rules that keep the human race afloat. It is the same thought that ultimately says, 'Life is only worth living if you want it to be,' which is only one thought away from the unthinkable.

It was 4 am when I stumbled through the door of our house in Wilton Crescent – not that I was aware of the time. Bill came into the room where I had passed out, took one look at me and went back to tell Webbo – who had stayed over – that I would not be taking part in very much that day, least of all a national breakfast show.

And that was it. I never went back to No. 1 Golden Square, the home of my very own radio station, ever again.

The building that had been the backdrop to so many of my adventures, so many wonderful and exciting experiences, within hours became a building in which I was no longer welcome. With guards even posted on the main entrance, just in case I attempted to gain entry. My goose was well and truly cooked. I had really gone and done it this time.

The following 48 hours continued to see some of the most ill-conceived decisions I have ever made.

The morning after the night before was Thursday 21 June. I know this because it was Ladies' Day at Royal Ascot, an event that Billie and I were due to attend, along with Webbo and his wife Lisa. Bill was so excited about the prospect of dressing up and having some fun around the gee-gees that she had bought a new dress, as had Mrs Webbo.

I had also contrived to push the boat out somewhat by hiring a helicopter to take the four of us there and back, but, seeing as I was still unconscious in bed, poor Billie had to forego her posh day out. She had to stay at home instead to look after her self-centred loser of a husband who had almost drunk himself to death in a nose-dive of self pity the night before. Webbo, however, was having none of that and, after seeking Billie's permission, kept his appointment with his wife and flew off to sunny Berkshire in the chopper.

When I did eventually rise from my pit, I was unrepentant and headed straight back to the pub, where I stayed until closing time. It was the same story the next day, by which time the ladies and gentlemen of the press outside easily outnumbered the customers inside. It was now very evident that this was becoming a very public professional suicide.

VIRGIN SACKS EVANS, shouted the headlines on the front pages of the newspapers come Saturday morning, and who could blame them? After ensuring all my bridges were not so much burnt as completely razed to the ground, I headed for the sanctity and security of my Surrey estate.

By the Thursday of the following week, things had settled down with the press beginning to lose interest and deciding me and my fragile out-of-control ego were no longer worth the train fare down to Guildford.

It was soon after this that I claimed to have discovered the perfect antidote to all my troubles.

'I am going to dig a pond!' I announced.

'That's nice,' said Billie, who had resigned herself to my temporary insanity, but was clearly glad that I was at least showing signs of wanting to re-enter the earth's atmosphere.

True to my word I marked out a pond and started to dig. I had read that physical labour calms the mind, and carries the added bonus of having something to show for it at the end. It was just what I needed. I dug and dug and dug, and it worked. As a result of my travail, cups of tea quickly became like well-earned trophies, my 11 am ham sandwich tasted like heaven and a simple five-minute break sitting on the grass brought a joy I had forgotten existed.

Very quickly I began to come round to what a complete arse I had been and, with guilt screaming in my ears, I apologised to my wife for the worry and distress I had clearly caused her over the last few weeks. I reflected on how close I had been to completely losing my mind and began to seriously ask myself why I had so willingly self-destructed in such a big way.

It didn't take a huge degree of introspection to see that I was deeply unhappy in my job and that whereas before Billie was around I had nothing else to cling on to, she had now given me the freedom to let go.

Performing on the radio was what I loved doing most, but for the last twelve months or so I had been doing it for reasons other than those that were perhaps good for me. Admittedly, I had not parted company with my employers via one of the most amicable separations the entertainment world had ever seen but nevertheless, I slowly began to realise that it was probably a blessing in disguise.

I suspect it was this conclusion that later stopped me from becoming embittered as well as reassuring me that I need never feel controlled by events again. I would still make mistakes – pretty huge ones at that – but I would always be able to delve down deep inside and figure out what those mistakes were trying to tell me and what I could learn from them.

In going over what had happened I began to see the bigger picture and to recognise the subtle difference between what drained my energy and what charged it. I realised that while I should always do my best, at the end of the day a job, no matter how glamorous, important or worthwhile, isn't everything and it is always the people you love who matter more.

TOP 10 REASONS WHY I LOVE CALIFORNIA

10 The mountains
9 The ocean
8 The planning laws
7 The standard of service
6 The fitness mentality
5 The positive mental attitude
4 The possibility to succeed
3 The confidence
2 The magic of its entertainment history
1 The weather

AFTER BOTH BILLIE AND I had now stepped away from the spotlight, we found ourselves with the time and means to do what we liked, whenever we liked, and wherever we liked. So once again it was 'California, here we come,' except this time we could stay as long as we wanted.

Bill and I skipped through Heathrow as if it were a field of tulips, stopping only to enjoy the delights of the first-class lounge and to buy a video camera. I don't know why we bothered with the camera; I've owned five in recent years, only used two of them – and then only once – and have no idea where any of them are now. Ah well, there you are.

Once aboard the big white bird, we settled in for another transatlantic movie, drink and food fest, along with the usual game of star spotting. There's always a good chance of seeing a few famous faces if you sit at the front of a flight to Los Angeles and today was no exception. Amongst the raft of lucky first-class passengers was the delightful Helen Field-ing, highly acclaimed author of the *Bridget Jones* books.

I had known Helen for a few years via a mutual friend and always found her a joy to talk to. I was also fascinated by how timid she was for a lady with all those clever words and funny ideas inside her. Words and ideas in such demand that the cinema tickets for the movie adaptation of her first book currently totalled $282 million and counting.

With the flight well underway, and a Bloody Mary and a few glasses of fizz inside me, I excused myself from Bill, who was ensconced in an episode of *Friends,* and went over to say hello to the lovely Helen. It transpired that she was not making the journey to the States to visit, as I had assumed, but was rather returning from Britain as she now lived in Hollywood with her partner, a writer on *The Simpsons.*

'Hold on a minute,' I thought. This was a whole heap of the type of information that is just too exciting for a person like me to take in without having to have a lie down in a dark room for a few days. Helen had been a lowly BBC researcher only a few years before and now she was part of the motion-picture cognoscenti, not to mention a resident of Tinseltown and the sweetheart of a guy who was part of the most successful TV show of all time.

'What are you doing in LA then, Chris?' she asked.

I almost forgot to answer, I was still so mesmerised by what she had just told me.

'Oh, er ... we're not actually sure,' I said, which was at least true if not exactly impressive.

'Sometimes it's good not to know,' said Helen with a kind smile. 'Here, this is our address, come for dinner one night,' and with that she handed me a card. What a perfectly all-round charming lady.

I couldn't wait to get back to Bill to tell her my Helen update.

'Wow,' she said, breaking off from her beloved *Friends* to hear more. 'She is so cool – and so normal!'

I knew exactly what Bill meant. Helen is proof that you don't have to be a hard-nosed ball-breaker to be the best.

'You should write more,' said Bill.

'What, in Hollywood?' I laughed.

'Sure, why not?' she said. 'You've never let anything stop you before.' I looked at her face, trying to spot the irony, but there wasn't any. She quietly put her headphones back on and returned to Rachel, Ross and the gang.

My mind began racing. I had always wanted to write and I had especially always wanted to write a movie. Now, here I was on a plane going to LA having met Helen who had done exactly that, and my brilliant and beautiful wife was telling me I should do the same.

I tapped Bill on the shoulder.

'What is it babe?' she asked, removing her headset so she could hear me.

'If I did do that – you know, become a writer in Hollywood ...'

'Yes?' she replied encouragingly.

'What would you do?'

'Oh,' she said, without missing a beat, 'I'd go back to acting. It's all I ever think about.'

And there it was in a nutshell – our immediate future for the taking. We had the money, we had the time and most importantly, we had each other. As Bill returned to *Friends*,

I felt fit to burst with excitement. It was time for me to have another beer – for everyone's sake.

As I drifted off into a deep and happy sleep, I started to dream our dreams of tomorrow, and Hollywood. When I finally awoke I heard the pilot announcing that we only had half an hour more of our flight to run. Billie, far brighter eyed than I could possibly hope to be, had already eaten breakfast and was now transfixed, staring out of the window, looking down over the vast Grand Canyon, which was beneath us.

As we touched down, my mind was already racing once again. I wasn't sure what our next move should be exactly, but I could feel something rather big looming on the horizon.

As we prepared to disembark, Helen came over.

'Oh, hi Billie,' she said. 'It's lovely to meet you and Chris. Here's the card of the guy who found our house for us. He knows all there is to know about getting you into the hush-hush houses that aren't officially for sale. You never know when you might need him, good luck and don't forget that dinner.' And with that she was off.

'You didn't mention that you were talking to her about us buying a house here,' whispered Bill as she stood behind me in the aisle.

'I didn't,' I whispered back.

'So why did she give you that card then?' Bill enquired.

'I'm not quite sure.'

'Would you like to live here then?'

'Actually, I think I would – would you?'

'Hell, yeah.'

* * *

The next morning over breakfast I dialled the number of the real-estate guy. We weren't seriously thinking of shelling out several million dollars for our very own LA pad, but we had already decided on an extended stay, and thought renting a house for a few months might be fun.

There was no answer from the guy's cell phone but we noticed from the address on the card that his offices were just down the road. We decided it would be just as easy to drop in on him and so five minutes later we found ourselves in the reception of a swish set of LA offices. We were greeted there by a young lady busy answering the telephone in between taking sips of water from the designer plastic bottle that was sitting on her desk. It's obligatory to drink water in LA, I think it might be the law. Everyone does it all the time.

'Hi, may I help you?' she asked.

'We're looking for a Mr McGeachy,' I said, reading the name from the card.

'I'm sorry, its Gordon's half-day today. He's out of the office until tomorrow. May I leave a message or get him to call you back?'

I was just about to reply when someone walked in behind me.

'I'm Gordon,' he said. 'How may I help?'

We looked around to see a man who was probably in his forties but who, at a glance, looked a good ten years younger. Dressed in white shorts, white sleeveless T-shirt, white socks and white trainers he was handsome, tanned, fit and at a guess probably gay, but in a very LA, almost macho way.

'Hello, my name's Chris, this is my wife Billie and we're interested in renting a property.'

'I'm sooo sorry but I don't do rentals, you'll need to talk to a colleague of mine.'

He was about to turn away, but Bill had other ideas. 'Really? You came highly recommended by a good friend of my husband's ... Helen Fielding.'

This stopped Mr McGeachy in his tracks. He paused and then smiled. 'Any friend of Helen's is a friend of mine. I was just going home but I popped back to pick up my cell. Come into my office – I'll point you in the direction of the people you'll need to talk to.'

'Alright let's see what we can dooo for youooo twoooo,' he announced as he plonked himself down behind his desk and started to flick through his Rolodex. Bill and I smiled at each other in that typically couply fashion.

'OK let's see-dar-dar-dar-deee, what we have here ...'

Gordon was completely in the zone, like a mad chemist looking for the ingredients for his next concoction, blissfully unaware of anyone or anything around him.

After a few more tum-tee-tums and the frantic scribbling of several numbers on a Post-it note, he paused.

'Heck, how well do you really know Helen?'

Bill glared at me.

'I, er, I worked with her at the BBC, when Bridget was still just a daily. Her diary, she used to read it to me.' That was as big a lie as I could come up with at such short notice.

Gordon howled, 'Oh – my – God, are you serious! Don't you just love that woman?'

Where was this going?

'Look guys, I'm looking at some rentals on Tuesday that are yet to go to market. Admittedly three of them are porn locations, but that only means the decor has to go. You can be sure they will have views to die for. You are very welcome to "come with", if you wish. I like you guys, you're cute.'

And that's how we met the great Gordon McGeachy, ironically Glasgow born and bred but now totally LA, and with enough energy and chutzpah to take on this world and the next any day of the week.

Tuesday arrived and Gordon picked us up in his black Range Rover, the calling card of the successful gay Los Angeles realtor, accompanied by his gorgeous golden retriever, Belle. It's important to point out at this juncture that American realtors bear little or no resemblance to British estate agents. They are superstars, as are the lawyers, the plastic surgeons and the doctors in Los Angeles. Realtors are also among the top five richest professions in California, way ahead of actors. There are so many astronomically expensive houses in LA and Malibu – and all the way up Highway One towards Santa Barbara, Carmel and Monterey – that these guys can earn millions of dollars a week. And they do.

They also have a much more sensible way of marketing houses than we do, with regular 'open-house' days being held every Wednesday and Sunday. This system allows everyone who's buying and selling to do so at the same time. Balloons and flags are put up outside the properties for sale, and the doors are flung open to all and sundry. Everyone knows where they stand and there is no hanging around waiting for buyers who might not turn up, whilst the buyers that do, get to see a whole host of properties in just one afternoon. Tuesday is also an open-house day but exclusively for the realtors to recommend potential properties to their clients. Helen had been right about Gordon. He was the man to help us jump the queue.

As we set off east down Sunset Boulevard and turned right to go up to the Hills – not Beverly Hills, which is in fact a rather sedate, very flat suburban affair, but the Hollywood Hills, the real McCoy, overlooking the whole city – Bill and I were about to receive a masterclass in how to conduct a day of house-viewing, Gordon-style.

From our hotel there had appeared to be no more than a couple of hundred of idyllic movie-star-style cribs perched up on these hills, but once we were up there we were amazed to discover there were literally thousands upon thousands, and almost all of them beautiful.

The narrow access roads just kept on spiralling skywards and what we thought was one hill led to another and that in turn to another, and so on. With every corner we had to catch our breath as the next piece of glorious architecture or jaw-dropping vista revealed itself. If someone says they don't like Los Angeles, ask them if they have ever seen the Hollywood Hills.

If Gordon was trying to sell his adopted homeland to us, he was doing a damn fine job. But he had a question.

'Hey guys, do you know anyone who may own three rather large 4x4s?'

'No, why?' asked Bill.

'Because they've been following us for close to the last hour.'

Ah. That would be the paparazzi, then. The British paps are almost more prevalent in LA than they are in London. No doubt because a lot of British stars go there. Plus, it's much sunnier than it is in the UK, so people spend more time outdoors and with fewer clothes on, which makes it easier to get a more sellable picture. They'd been tailing us on and off since we'd arrived.

We explained to Gordon whom it might be, to which he replied, 'Who the hell are you guys?'

Now for someone who had no idea, this was potentially a long story. But we gave him the short version, which seemed to suffice.

'Well shit, I wish you'd told me before – I look a mess today!' he exclaimed.

What a perfect reaction. We were both falling rapidly in love with Gordon.

The potential rentals he proceeded to show us were the best three houses I had ever seen. One of them was definitely a porn location, as Gordon had forewarned. The cameras were still set up and the 'director' was still in residence. The second house really did belong to a rock star and the third was empty but had a bedroom that hung magically over the infinity pool below. Suddenly, Britain seemed a long way away – even with the paparazzi in tow.

'Alright, you two troublemakers, I need to take you back to your hotel now, unless you wanna stick around for the afternoon session?'

Bill and I couldn't imagine what could be more fun than what we were already doing.

'Do you think we could stay with you?' Bill asked.

'Sure, why not? Belle and I are sick of the sight of each other anyhow, but the deal is you buy the coffees, OK?'

That wasn't a deal, it was a steal as far as we were concerned. When we arrived at the Coffee Bean coffee shop on Sunset, two doors down from the world-famous Mel's Diner, I volunteered to get the drinks while Gordon and Bill found a table outside. Armed with three skinny grande lattes, along with various pastries and muffins, I went back out into the dazzling sunlight. But when I spotted Bill and Gordon, there was clearly something untoward going on. Gordon was looking to one side, tight-lipped, as if refusing to divulge a secret, while Bill looked like she'd seen a ghost.

'What's the matter with you two?' I said quietly out of the corner of my mouth.

'Don't look now,' Bill whispered through gritted teeth. 'But Matthew Perry's sitting at the next table.'

Suddenly I got it. If Matthew Perry – Chandler Bing from *Friends*, Bill's favourite television show ever – really was behind us, Bill might well pass out at any moment. I looked over to Gordon.

'Is it him?' I mouthed.

Gordon gave an almost imperceptible nod, as if he were a member of the CIA identifying a potential assassin in a crowd.

Holy shit, this wasn't such a big deal for me, but Bill really was a *Friends* fanatic. She looked like she was about to cry. I handed the coffees around and tried to pretend that everything was normal but it was impossible. We were no more than six feet away from one of the six people in the world Bill actually wanted to be. And here he was simply minding his own business, reading a newspaper, totally unaware of the stress he was causing a young girl at the next table. Until, that is, the paparazzi who had been following us reappeared.

'Oh fuck,' I thought, as I saw Matthew spy them out of the corner of his eye. Not that it was difficult; they were descending on us like a herd of elephants.

Seconds later they attacked, their cameras like guns. Bang, bang, bang, one shot after the other. Matthew was about to launch into a counter attack of Hollywoodesque proportions, when he suddenly realised that the lenses of the offending mercenaries were not pointing at him but at Billie and me instead. He looked at us, totally baffled.

'It's alright, Matthew,' Gordon said, as we made a hasty exit past his table. 'I have no idea who these guys are either, but if it's any consolation, she thinks you're just the best.'

Back in the car and back on the road, Bill screamed. 'Can you friggin' believe that?'

Even super-cool Gordon was not immune to the irony of it all. 'I have to admit, that was quite fucking funny. He needs to lighten up by the way and have a drink!'

Not the most sage advice to hand out to a recovering heavy drinker, but I knew what he meant. Now if someone had told the three of us at that juncture that our encounter with Chandler Bing from *Friends* was not going to be the highlight of our afternoon that day, then we wouldn't have believed them but LA just never knows when to stop surprising you.

And it hadn't finished with us yet.

TOP 10

CELEBRITY ENCOUNTERS

10   Michael Jackson on stage at the Brits
9   Madonna in one of my favourite pubs after one of
     her gigs
8   Bill Clinton at Elton John's house
7   The Queen at Radio 2
6   George Harrison at Jools Holland's 40th
5   Clint Eastwood at a private screening of his new movie –
     none of us had any idea he was coming
4   Dennis Hopper in the back of a minibus at St Andrews
3   Mick Jagger wearing a blue track suit at 3 am in Chicago
2   Michael Douglas in a meeting room at the Celtic Manor in
     Wales
1   Half of the cast of *Friends* in my new kitchen

WHAT GORDON HAD PLANNED FOR THE AFTERNOON was different from the morning. He was previewing several houses for a specific client of his, a major player.

'Alright guys, now here's the deal,' he began. 'I am Scottish, everyone knows this, and for the purposes of avoiding a whole croc of shit that I won't bore you with, you two are my relatives from London. Chris, you are my cousin, and Billie, you are his child bride – goddit?'

'Goddit,' we both concurred.

The houses we had seen in the morning were about to be exceeded tenfold.

The first dwelling of the afternoon's agenda was the former property of Frank Sinatra, and before him, silent-movie star Buster Keaton. It was both ostentatious and gorgeous at the same time. The second house was hidden from view by its own grove of palm trees. A much more understated plot. It was like a rich man who still chooses to dress in jeans and a ripped T-shirt, whilst driving his old pick-up truck to and from work – which is exactly what Ralph Lauren does, by the way. Don't you just hate him?

Inside this disguised palace were dark wood floors and furniture, which looked wonderful against the white walls. It was the home of a record producer. 'He doesn't really want to sell but says for the right cheque he would consider moving on.' Gordon sighed, as if he heard this line all the time, which he probably did.

I had to ask. 'How much would the right cheque actually be?'

'Twenty million,' announced Gordon.

Twenty million dollars – and this was ten years ago! Bill and I were awestruck.

'Hey, come on you two – this is Hollywood, what do you expect? Besides you ain't seen nothing yet.'

An hour later we entered the gated estate where Sylvester Stallone and Denzel Washington lived. These were no longer houses that stood before us, they were vast edifices, monuments to the success of their owners.

'Surely this is the top of the pile, Gordon?' Bill enquired. 'Please tell me it doesn't get any sillier than this.'

'OK, you can breathe again now – this is about as silly as it gets,' he conceded, 'unless you take into consideration the fact that Sly and Denzel both bought the houses either side as well – for security purposes.'

After the Sly-and-Denzel stop-off it was time to hop back on the tour bus.

'OK, one more to go and then we're done,' Gordon announced triumphantly.

The drive to the last viewing of the day was the lengthiest so far, as we had to come all the way down from 'Stallonesville', which was set way up high on top of a small mountain range (I'm not kidding) back to what they call the Bird Streets, off Doheny Drive looking over Sunset Boulevard.

'This is it guys,' said Gordon, as we pulled up to the end of the quiet lane. He turned to us, dropped his sunglasses down his nose and declared, 'I love this house. If I had the money, this is the one I would live in, no question. Stand by to pay homage to the former home of hit maker and all-round cool dude, Mr Lionel Richie.

'This house is what LA is all about!' he enthused. 'Now, we have to be on our extra best behaviour here guys, although I can't actually tell you why – you're just going to have to go with me on this one.'

Why would we not? Gordon had brought us nothing but entertainment and education since we'd met him. He was the boss and we were more than happy to comply with any conditions he felt the need to impose. That's not to say, however, that we weren't intrigued by his little speech.

Just as we were about to alight from the Range Rover, a black Jaguar saloon with blacked-out windows rumbled up the lane before grinding to a halt in a cloud of dust behind us.

'Ah no, this is what I was alluding to,' muttered Gordon under his breath as he looked in his rear-view mirror. 'Just hang back a sec, I need to sort this out.'

Bill and I looked at each other and shrugged – we'd been doing a lot of that today. What was going on now? As Gordon stood beside the car, the darkened glass slid down and a conversation commenced. Gordon nodded a few times before flashing a brief smile, replacing his sunglasses and making his way back.

'Alright guys – we're good to go, they're fine with us.'

Keen as we were to know who was in the car and why they might be 'fine with us', it was plainly obvious that Gordon was not about to let on, so we turned our attention back to the house. It was difficult to see much at all from the outside as the entire property was surrounded by a stone wall, ten foot high in places, which extended for at least half of the street. This, we discovered, was to accommodate the basketball and tennis court, and the olive grove. The main entrance to the property consisted of a huge stone archway that led up a dozen or so stone steps to a vast, ornate front door opening onto a hallway. This looked fairly ordinary at first, until one rounded the corner to behold a sight I will never forget; a sight that may cause me to weep as I type these words of fond recollection.

For laid out before us was a huge, triple-height living room littered with various items of oversized furniture, which included one of the most substantial dining tables I have ever seen. But that was not all, in fact that was not nearly all.

Dear Reader – one of the walls was missing!

The whole of the back wall, some forty feet wide and fifteen feet high, was simply nowhere to be seen. It transpired it was made up of two enormous sliding doors that disappeared at the flick of a switch to reveal a perfectly framed picture of LA. Except it wasn't a picture, it was for real.

'Jesus bloody Christ – would you look at that?' Bill said.

'What did I tell you?' smiled Gordon.

This place really was incredible but it didn't stop there. Between us and the city of Los Angeles was a black-bottomed swimming pool running the whole length of the garden, with an invisible raised channel churning out gushing white water at what must have been hundreds of gallons a minute. No ordinary pool already, this pool was about to get even better, for this was Lionel's pool, with yet more surprises in store. Like the fact it stretched from outdoors all the way into the house.

If he wanted to, as I'm sure he did, Lionel could get out of his bed in the morning and, without setting foot outside the perimeter of the master bedroom suite, dive straight into the cool dark water, swim out into the open air, across the garden and into his kitchen. Wow bloody wee! You don't get that in St George's Hill.

Now I know materialism is not for one second what life is all about, but Lionel's pool was something else. In addition to the above, there was, of course, the obligatory cinema, remote-control flame fires in every room, electronically activated sky lights, his and hers everything (bathrooms, dressing rooms, etc.), plus a four-bed guesthouse at the rear of the property, just for good measure.

In short this house was the nuts. So what do you think we did next?

Bill and I called an emergency secret meeting in the corner. This time it was our turn to whisper and Gordon's turn to wonder what was going on. After no more than a couple of minutes, I had some breaking news for our new real estate man on the inside.

'Gordon,' I declared. 'We would like to buy this house.'

'Yeah, baby,' he said, smiling. 'I know, wouldn't we all?'

'No, really,' I repeated. 'We really would like to buy this house and we would like to buy it now.'

Gordon stared at us. Only the slight twitch in his left temple betrayed the fact that he realised we might actually be serious. At that moment the doorbell rang.

'Guys, I don't mean to be rude but we need to hold that thought because if that's who I think it is, there's something you need to know.'

The people at the door were also here to look at the house. That's the first thing Gordon had to tell us. The second thing? The fact that those people were Jennifer Aniston and Brad Pitt!

As I am sure you can imagine, Bill went into apoplexy. 'You've got to be joking,' she said immediately, starting to shake as these two names came out of Gordon's mouth.

'Is that who was in the car?' I asked, putting two and two together.

'Actually no, that was Courtney Cox, who was waiting for them. She'll be coming with.'

It was turning out to be quite a day for Bill. Half of the cast of her favourite show in one day, with a bit of Brad Pitt on the side. But there was more. As the volume of voices grew louder, here is a list of the people who came into view:

- Jennifer Aniston
- Brad Pitt
- Their assistant
- Courtney Cox
- David Arquette – Courtney's husband and the producer of *Friends*
- Their interior designer
- And, last but not least, bringing up the rear, Rosanna Arquette

I promise, promise, promise you this is true.

Here's what Bill and I had to do next. We had to pretend that this was not in any way a big deal for us and continue looking around the house as if it were the most normal thing in the world. The famous people had us surrounded and there was no escape.

I bumped into a bearded Brad in one of the guest bedrooms.

'Excuuuuse me,' he smiled politely as he squeezed passed. Bill had a similar moment in the kitchen with Jennifer, she told me later. Out of all of them, Courtney was the busiest of the bunch; just like her character in the TV show, she was almost hyper with officiousness as she and her designer eagerly scribbled and sketched away on big yellow pads.

'They're all like this,' whispered Gordon. 'Stars never shop for houses in groups of less than five. I have no idea what they think might happen to them if they did.'

Though it broke Bill's heart, we eventually had to leave these famous friends – forgive the pun. We'd run out of things to look at and were beginning to hover a bit like star-struck out-of-towners, which is exactly what we were.

Back in the car, Billie was the first to speak, slowly and emphatically.

'That ... was ... the ... greatest ... half ... hour ... of ... my ... life!' she exclaimed.

Ten minutes later, we were back at the hotel.

'I need a drink,' said Gordon.

'We all need a drink,' said Bill.

And we really *did* want to buy the house, a conversation we now resumed with Gordon at the bar.

'Guys, are you sure you want to come and live here? Don't get me wrong, I love it and I'm presuming you have the cash but ...' I stopped him mid-flow.

'Gordon, find out what they want for the house and offer it to them, the full asking price, not a cent less and tell them we are cash buyers.'

It was true, we were cash buyers. For a good few years after the Virgin deal, I was a cash buyer for most things although it might have been better otherwise. Banks tend to take time to lend you money and like to know what you might want it for, which would probably have helped me to cool down where future, less sound, purchases were concerned.

Now it was Gordon's turn to be on the back foot. He hesitated for a moment, took a big slug of his Dry Martini before flashing that big, white, gleaming LA smile we were now becoming accustomed to.

'What the heck – you guys sure are crazy, but let's do it!'

It transpired that the Friend who was interested in the property was not Jennifer Aniston, as we'd first thought, but the more industrious Courtney C, which explained why she'd been so busy during her visit. This was, apparently, a house that she had been stalking for several years and she had almost bought the last time it had come to the market.

If we wanted to get in on the action we would have to lodge our offer the next morning and, in Gordon's opinion, get it accepted and signed off by the end of the day, as there was no way Courtney was going to let this pad slip through her fingers a second time if she could help it.

'The asking price is $7 million,' Gordon told me on the telephone that evening.

'Then that's what we'll offer,' I replied.

I have learned over the years that one of the few really useful things money can do is give you the ability to make a decision quickly and act on it. If we genuinely wanted the house, this was no time for penny-pinching. Gordon made the bid, got it accepted and two days later Chez Richie had become Chez Evans. We moved in within the week and made LA our new home town. But we never saw any of the cast of *Friends* again.

How mad is that?

TOP 10

GREAT THINGS TO DO WITH YOUR MONEY

10 Bid for stuff at auctions (exciting and usually a good investment)
9 First-class travel (the joy of not queuing is immense)
8 Top-class restaurants (my absolute favourite night out)
7 Buy cars for people you love (a brand-new car for someone who would otherwise never be able to afford one can change their life)
6 Send people on holidays they've only ever dreamed about
5 Employ a full-time driver (anyone who can afford to do this and doesn't is insane. It is the ultimate luxury – except for a full-time assistant)
4 Employ a full-time assistant
3 Pay off people's mortgages
2 Buy your mum a house
1 Pay for life-saving private medical care

OUR LA RESIDENCY WAS A ONE HUNDRED PER CENT platinum experience. So many weird and wonderful things happened to us whilst we were there, we absolutely loved every second of it. Take the day we ended up watching the first episode of a new television show that MTV were piloting by the name of *The Osbournes*. Nothing strange in that, you might think, except that we actually watched *The Osbournes* at the Osbournes' *with* the Osbournes.

I was walking down Sunset earlier that morning, soon after we moved out of the hotel into our new home, when I spied a familiar face over the road. Actually, it was more the gleaming bald bonce that I recognised at first. If it wasn't me old mate Adrian, the taff from Epic Records, a lifelong mate of Ozzy's and an all-round music-biz nutjob.

'You gotta come along to Ozzy's tonight for the first episode of this TV show,' he said. 'Ozzy's fucking mad and they think it might make a good one of those fly-on-the-wall reality shows.'

I said we'd love to and that evening, there we sat, in Ozzy and Sharon's living room. Ozzy was out of town but Sharon, Jack and Kelly were on hand to give us a running commentary on what we were seeing.

As the credits rolled there was a victorious round of applause – the show was like nothing any of us had ever seen before but no one could deny it was most highly entertaining for any number of reasons. Adrian suggested we leave the kids to party and invited Sharon to join us for dinner.

'What did you think?' she asked, as we sat down in the restaurant.

'I thought it was hilarious, to be honest with you,' I replied.

'Well, MTV have filmed six and they're going to see how the ratings are,' she volunteered. 'It'll probably come to nothing, but it was fun to do.'

Over the course of dinner, Sharon asked how Bill and I had got together and had now ended up as her neighbours. Compelled by our tale – at least I like to think she was – she concluded that she wouldn't have done a thing differently, had she been in our shoes. She also told us that she was as nosey as anyone when it came to having a snoop at other people's houses and that she would love to see our new place.

We extended an invitation and she came over the next day with a very tired-looking Jack and Kelly in tow.

'Mum, methinks you and Dad bought the wrong house,' said Jack, when he saw the view from our new lounge.

'This is amazing,' said Sharon. 'Really amazing.'

'Who are these people?' said Kelly. 'Why are we here?'

'Shut up Kelly, don't be so rude,' snapped her mum.

Shortly after this contretemps, Sharon excused herself to answer her phone. It was the producer of their new show from MTV. The overnight ratings had come through.

'Ohhhh – myyyyy – Godddd!' screamed Sharon. 'It's the biggest ratings they've ever had for anything since MTV began, even bigger than the *Video Music Awards*.'

She was delighted, they were delighted and the rest, as they say, is history. *The Osbournes* went on to become an instant worldwide phenomenon, a break-through hit in over a hundred countries, making the loveable Los Angeles lunatic family tens of millions of dollars in the process.

It was also Sharon who gave Bill and me our first lesson in how to shop LA style, specifically how to furnish your house in the manner of a true Angelino. She told us there was little point in spending all that money on buying a property and then skimping when it came to furnishing it. She said that her 'stuff' was worth more than the house it was in. 'The feathers are always more than the nest,' as she put it.

And so we went shopping.

There is no place to shop on earth that comes close to LA. You don't have to wait – for anything. You want a mattress? Dial 1-800-Mattress and the mattress of your choice will be delivered to your door within the hour. If not, there will be a ten per cent discount for every hour it's late. Ten hours late and it's yours, for free.

When you're in some of the bigger stores, you are offered whatever it may take to keep shopping, whether it's a pizza or a pint of beer, a massage or a mojito. As long as it keeps you in the store, it's yours, but whatever you do, if you do see something you like don't go away to think about it.

Bill and I did just that with several items of furniture to begin with, returning no more than an hour later to find they had disappeared, sold, packed off and on their way to their new owners. The LA way is to choose and pay or risk disappointment. That's it, there's no in between. If you snooze, you lose.

LA also does big very well, even when it comes to vermin, with rats the size of small dogs somehow finding their way into your kitchen cupboards. An exterminator is a must, and again ours was a revelation.

'Hi Chris, hi Billie – it's Ray here from Western Exterminators,' he would buzz cheerily through the intercom every Wednesday. Ray was the happiest rat catcher in the world and, like everyone in this town, he wanted to be the best.

People say to me, 'Los Angeles is all so false.'

I say, 'No it's not; it's just that their very nature is "Let's make this the best it can possibly be." Positivity rules, what's wrong with that?'

Of course it doesn't do any harm that the weather is always absolutely beautiful over there. Although the sky is a perfect blue and the temperature is hot, very hot at times, it never actually feels too hot thanks to the welcome relief of the onshore Pacific breeze. As the LA day then gets ready to say goodnight, the temperature cools but not so much that you can't sit outside comfortably until the early hours.

In the whole time we lived in Los Angeles I can only recall it raining once and that was for no more than a couple of hours in the middle of the night. This didn't, however, stop the 'freak' rain shower becoming the lead story on all the local news channels. They showed non-stop rolling footage all morning of the overnight rain 'as it fell', interviewed eye-witnesses who had 'seen the rain' and went on to list the countless road-traffic accidents as LA motorists failed to cope with these 'adverse weather conditions'. Hilarious.

The jet flight-path is another big factor of LA life, whether you live below or above it. Our house was above it, which meant that incoming jets to LAX were below our line of sight on their approach – apparently this is quite a big deal, almost as important to a property in LA as having a sea view would be to a flat in Brighton. The television traffic helicopters, on the other hand, buzzed no more than a few hundred feet over our rooftop on a daily basis. In fact KTLA's Jennifer Shriver of 'Skycam 5' could be seen as clearly from our garden as she could on our television screen.

Having completed our initial internal nesting, we needed some wheels to get about. A task I was very much looking forward to, as I set out in search of a sixties Mustang convertible. After an interesting induction into the Californian classic car market, I hooked up with a character called Reuben, who had more Mustangs than he knew what to do with. He kept the majority of them in single garages all over the Valley area, a little suspicious but that was no concern of mine, as long as he could provide me with what I wanted.

After spending most of a day following him from one seedy lock-up to the next and inspecting seven of his surprisingly immaculate babies, I plumped for a 1964 1/2 convertible model – the first of the Mustangs ever made. Black, with white leather, she was a beauty, complete with original white electric hood and an FM radio, the first to be fitted as standard to any car in the world.

Bill, on the other hand, had her eye on a rather wonderful Land Rover V8 ragtop that she had spotted for sale. British by birth but with an American twist, this left-hand drive limited edition automatic version of the world-famous powerhouse was the mirror image of my Mustang to look at, with white exterior body, black roof and black leather inside. We came across this magnificent specimen of engineering in the far more traditional surroundings of a classic car dealer, one of the many that serve to satiate the tastes of the Beverly Hills car nut. Back home in our garage these two icons of automotive design complemented each other perfectly and with our wheels now sorted our temporary materialistic madness was almost complete.

New wardrobes were towards the bottom of our to-do lists but flying visits to Melrose soon sorted these out as well. This was the least expensive of all our forays into the retail world, until that is, I picked up a pair of combat trousers that I thought were $110. I'm embarrassed to tell you that there was another naught involved somewhere. I still look at those trousers with contempt today.

For anyone who is sceptical when it comes to the gene and environment theory, I would urge them to take a month out in Los Angeles. I have never eaten more healthily or been fitter than I was when Bill and I lived there, but without having to give it a second thought.

The famous Farmers Market, which is a fitting testament to the past in the almost space-age setting of what is now the Grove precinct, is almost the opposite of our food shops, inasmuch as it's nigh on impossible to buy anything that is bad for you. Everything looks good, tastes good and is good.

As Bill and I let nature take over and just lived how we felt was right, the weight fairly began to fall off us and as for drinking too much alcohol – forget it, wasn't going to happen. The whole weekend social scene is based around outdoor physical activity, interspersed with long, healthy lunches or early diners with no more than the odd glass of wine or perhaps one or two freezing-cold beers.

The beach is littered with volleyball courts, the gyms are more like theme parks than sweatboxes, and then there are always the hills for hiking up or mountain biking down. Oh, and don't forget the lakes, will you?

Bill and I were in love with each other, in love with our new home and in love with Southern California. With a new-found vigour and the zest for life once again coursing through our veins, it wasn't long before Bill and I were chomping at the bit to do more with our days than just join in the LA scene.

We were both ready for fresh challenges, and for Bill it was back to acting. After a few false starts with various acting groups and creative classes, she chanced upon a quiet genius by the name of Sabin Epstein, an acting coach of fine repute who lived in a modestly hip four-storey house in the hills of West Hollywood.

He was like an acting Buddha who lived upon high, ready and waiting patiently should another worthy student come within reach. I used to drop Bill off at Sabin's three or four times a week and then go and hang in one of the coffee houses nearby. Here I would read, mostly about writing and how to do it. I found the subject of writing fascinating and could feel myself being drawn closer and closer to perhaps having a bash.

These were very happy times. I was happy, Bill was happy and together we were ecstatic.

Each time Billie came back from Sabin's she was more inspired than the last, now more certain than ever that her future lay in the world of theatre, television and film.

Whilst she continued to study, I had decided you can only read so much about writing before it becomes an excuse not to write. It was time to put down the books and power up my computer. Would I be any good? I was about to find out. Right from the start I wrote all day and every day about anything and everything. I wrote poems, short stories and even a comedy drama. I also wrote the first hundred pages of my original autobiography, a very angry book that would have been neither use nor ornament to anyone, full of little more than bile and unashamed self-aggrandisement.

It was during one of these early writing sessions – when I was staring out over the pool searching for inspiration – that the house phone rang. It was Michael, my agent back in England.

'What are you doing?' he asked.

'I'm writing,' I replied.

'Writing. Why?'

'Because I want to.'

'Oh I see, well forget that for now. ABC Television want you to go and see them. They've heard you're living over there and they want to offer you a job.'

'Really?' I said.

'Yes, really. Now here's the number, write it down and don't lose it.' I did as instructed.

I told Bill the second she arrived home.

'I'm not surprised,' she said. 'You're bloody brilliant, why wouldn't they want to give you a job?'

Billie was always encouraging and full of confidence on my behalf, so with these words of support still ringing in my ears, I picked up the phone to find out what the legendary American television network wanted with an old has-been like me.

TOP
10 VISIONARIES

10   Marcus Aurelius
9   Leonardo da Vinci
8   George Orwell
7   Gandhi
6   Sam Goldwyn
5   Jim Henson
4   Charlie Chaplin
3   Lennon and McCartney
2   Walt Disney
1   Jesus Christ

ABC TELEVISION HAD EVOKED MAGIC FOR ME ever since I read a book about Walt Disney. Walt didn't believe in money as a concept and firmly believed it was just a phase we were going through that would eventually pass. He was convinced we would one day revert back to the system of bartering, moving away from what he referred to as 'this ridiculous system of paper with cash sums painted on to it.'

Although how he supposed people would gain entry to see his much-loved films by offering a sack of potatoes up to the cashier bemuses me. In fact, lots of his ideas lead me to suspect he may well have been away with the fairies for much of the time but then again some of the best people are.

[Ahem – author clears his throat nervously.]

This doesn't, however, make me worship him any the less. I think he is the most innovative and fearless force enter-tainment has ever seen. His story is one of the all-time great tales of overcoming adversity. Not that any of it would have happened without his big bro' Roy and the aforementioned ABC TV.

Due to Walt's rather original take on money, Walt's brother Roy, the financial brains behind the outfit, declared him bankrupt relatively early on and stripped off any financial power or responsibility whatsoever. Not in a dastardly *Dallas* kind of way, as JR might have done to Bobby, but merely to protect Walt and allow him to keep doing what he wanted.

One day, however, Roy marched into his kid brother's office. It was 1951 and the Disney Corporation were $11 million in debt.

'This is serious,' said Roy gravely. 'We are $11 million in debt and the bank is about to foreclose on us.' There was a moment's silence and then ... Walt laughed.

'Why on earth are you laughing?' asked Roy, not exactly enamoured with his bro's reaction.

'Because I can remember when the bank wouldn't lend us a hundred dollars. Have they really gone and lent us eleven million?'

I have a suspicion that this story is the source of that rather brilliant and beautiful line, 'If you owe the bank a thousand dollars that's your problem, but if you owe the bank a million dollars, that's their problem.'

Regardless of whose problem it may have been it was clear to Roy, and now Walt, that if they wanted to stay in business they would have to make some gesture to pacify the banks. Financial ruin was no longer knocking on their door, it was about to break it down. As a result, Walt agreed to do something he had hitherto been dead against, despite his brother's many and varied protestations to the contrary.

For years ABC TV had been begging Disney to allow them to buy the franchise to Mickey Mouse for a television show. Walt was super-protective of his first and biggest animated motion-picture star, and the last place he wanted to see his famous mouse was on a small glass screen in the corner of every living room in America. But now he had no choice, if he wanted to keep his company afloat, Mickey had to go to make-up and get in front of the camera week in, week out to entertain those kids.

And so it was that the world witnessed the birth of the unstoppable Mickey Mouse Club on TV.

Now, I hope you know me well enough to have figured out that I wouldn't be telling you this story unless there were more to it than just a brief lesson in survival. The twist in the tale is that the Mickey Mouse Club, via the global medium of television, was so successful that it catapulted the Disney name into a stratosphere that even the great visionary himself had failed to imagine was possible. And here's the best bit. As a result of the programme Walt never wanted to make, Disney went on to accumulate enough money to realise all his dreams, with enough cash left over to actually buy out ABC TV.

Now that's a result.

What exactly this Disney-owned company wanted with me I had no idea but I was looking forward to climbing into my delicious drop-top and finding out. When I arrived at the

Disney lot, there was a barrier, a very big barrier, and out of a brightly painted hut strutted a man, a very big man.

'How may I help you, Sir?' The man may have been very big, but he was very polite – Disney-polite, to be more precise.

'Hi, my name's Evans.'

The very big man looked down at the clipboard he was holding.

'I'm here to see a Mr Lloyd Braun.'

As I uttered these secret words, the need for the very big man to look at his clipboard any further seemed to vanish.

'Ah, certainly, Sir. Mr Evans, if you would like to drive up to the main building and park in space 001, there will be somebody to meet you.'

Wow, this was cool.

Space 001 was no more than a few feet away from the front doors of the six-storey glass-fronted structure that housed the American Broadcasting Company.

'Mr Evans, so good to see you, and nice car, if I may say so,' chirped a small, smiling brunette. 'If you'd like to come with me, I'll take you in.'

'Thanks and thanks.' I tried to sound snappy, relaxed and up to speed. The truth was, I was none of these things, but I was excited, very excited.

As we waltzed past the reception desk and stepped into the elevator I noted it was full of various people of differing demographics. Not only that but when the small brunette lady pressed the button for floor 6, they all looked round to see who it was that she might be taking there.

It suddenly struck me that there was a pecking order going on here to do with which floor you worked on. As the elevator stopped at each level there was a silent competition to see who had to get out and who would make it to the next round. Those that survived each time nodded respectfully to each other in a display of mutual congratulation. After the 5th-floor stop, the small lady and I were alone – we gave each other the nod. We had won.

With the number 6 now illuminated, we had arrived at our destination and as the doors parted I was given the next insight on my crash course in American corporate structure. Whereas the previous five floors had looked like normal offices, this floor looked more akin to the inside of a country club. The walls were oak-panelled, expensive rugs lay over shiny parquet flooring and antique leather chairs lined the walkways.

'Welcome to the executive floor, Mr Evans. Mr Braun will be ready for you shortly, if you'd like to take a seat. What can I get you to drink?'

I ordered tea, more to be British than because I wanted one, although as I've already told you, I do love my tea.

Lloyd's office was exactly as you might imagine the head of a US television network's office should be. At least, it was exactly as I thought it should be. It was very masculine, in a hunting, shooting, fishing, Harvard kind of way and there were so many shelves! Awards and pictures of his family battled for pride of place; I wasn't sure which was winning so I turned my attention instead to the seating area. Yet more leather furniture to be witnessed here and then there was the obligatory bank of six televisions – a must-have for a network president – all on, all showing different channels.

But where Lloyd had done best was with his view. The office was situated on one of the four corners of the top floor and the double aspect afforded the spectator a one hundred and eighty degree panorama of the San Fernando Valley. It was inspiring, to say the least.

A smiling Lloyd welcomed me, after which we were joined by an equally smiling – though altogether more beautiful (sorry, Lloyd) – Andrea Wong, his vice president. She was hot, hot, hot, dressed perfectly in a pink power suit, consisting of skirt and jacket. She also wore black stilettos, with black stockings to match – meow! That's the way to do it.

There were two additional human beings present but other than say 'Hello', they barely spoke the whole time I was there. I think their presence was to 'meat the room', as they say in the States – a strange American concept designed to give a meeting a greater air of importance simply by increasing the number of attendees.

'Chris, I'll be up front with you,' said Lloyd, after a couple of minutes of small talk. 'We want you to work for us, and we want to pay you $1 million a year.'

It was a good job I wasn't drinking my tea at the time, or I would almost certainly have spat it out all over Lloyd's executive designer everything. $1 million wasn't the most I'd ever been paid, but it wasn't a bad opening offer from someone I'd never met before, who was yet to tell me what he actually wanted me to do. Did they want somebody killed, perhaps?

I decided it might be a good idea to find out.

'Er, right Lloyd, wow, that's fantastic. What exactly would you like to pay me that fabulous amount of money for?'

Lloyd laughed, then Andrea laughed. The other two guys thought about laughing but were a little too late, so opted for a nod and a quick grin instead. Lloyd explained that he and Andrea had a plan for me. They were both familiar with my TV work in the UK and wanted me to be a consultant to their entertainment department.

'We will provide you with an office here ... on the 6th floor.' Lloyd paused for dramatic effect whilst everyone smiled in unison. 'We have already earmarked an assistant for you and of course you will also be allotted a parking space. What we would like you to do in return is watch our entertainment output, along with that of our rivals, and simply tell us what you think.'

'That's it?' I said, waiting for the catch.

'That's it. No curve ball, that's all we want you to do. Just tell us what thoughts you have concerning what we and others in our business are doing.'

'Can I work from home?' I joked.

'Sure, why not? Whatever suits you best,' said Andrea, without missing a beat.

I was impressed but I'm always brutally honest in these circumstances as it's a fast-track to knowing where you really stand. I had to push them to tell me more.

'I'm not sure I would be worth the money,' I volunteered.

'Sure you would,' enthused Lloyd. 'Let's give it a go now. What show has most caught your eye since you've been over here?'

'Well I love *Live with Regis and Kathy*, I watch it every day.' It was true; I was a big fan of their daily mid-morning talk show, which conveniently happened to be on ABC.

'Sure, sure, but that's been there for years, it does what it does – it works, we know, yada yada yada. Name another one.'

'Alright then,' I said, beginning to enjoy our little game. 'How about *The Bachelor*?'

'Another one of ours again.'

I hadn't even realised. I'd just said it off the top of my head. This was going far too well.

'See, you're a company man already,' said Lloyd, making himself laugh. 'So tell us, what do you think of the show?'

Now here's the thing; I did have a problem with *The Bachelor*. Because I've worked with such formats most of my life, it really irks me when I see a lazy flaw, or something that could easily be made better. Whenever I see this, I automatically try to figure out what's wrong or what's missing. My ego and professional pride were pleased I had something to say.

'Well ...,' I began, as my audience leaned forward expectantly, 'the bachelor gets to pick one girl to be with out of fifteen women after a string of dates, dinners, kissing and basically whatever he wants – that we know.'

Everyone nodded.

'So the girls spend the whole time fawning over him and trying to get him to pick them. Now for me, this is perfectly acceptable at the beginning, but as the numbers get pared down there is no jeopardy, it's too one-sided.'

'So what do you propose?' asked Lloyd. I wasn't actually sure what I proposed but I was too far in to stop now.

'Well, how about, when the guy names his final five, there is a power shift where the girls then assume control and can decide what happens next – if the bachelor has been a good boy and can stay, or if he has abused his position and so must leave? If he stays, fine, but if he goes, then a replacement is called in – his best friend say, or perhaps even his arch enemy.'

I surprised myself with the second half of this solution. It wasn't mind blowing but it showed there's always somewhere else to go, even with an idea that's already working. It doesn't have to be bad to be better.

There was a pause. Had I passed the test?

'See, there you go, that's exactly what we want. That's it, isn't it Andrea?' Lloyd asked.

'Precisely,' Andrea confirmed. We talked some more but I was mindful that I had probably peaked and it would be a good idea for me to quit while I was ahead.

I couldn't wait to get back home to tell Bill about my exciting parking space and elevator journey all the way to the exec floor to meet my new friends at ABC. But when I arrived Bill had some breaking news for me that was a little more important.

'Hascombe Court is finished, the builders rang today,' she informed me.

Blimey, I had almost forgotten about that gorgeous old 170-acre estate that I'd bought a few years back and the renovation that was due to be completed any time now. This was a project that had consumed me for a good year or so before I met Billie. I was on site most days and was involved in every decision. The former seventeen-bedroom mansion was undergoing a no-expense-spared transformation into a six-bedroom wow house, complete with pub, cinema, library and games room – in many respects, the British equivalent of Mr Richie's LA pad we were currently calling home.

After Billie came on the scene my priorities changed, with Hascombe Court slipping several places firmly down the list. But I still held the house close to my heart, having spent so long designing it. I knew that when it was finally finished it would be spectacular but that always seemed like such a long time away. Not anymore.

'They called and said you need to fly back as soon as possible to sign it off, whatever that means,' Billie said.

To be honest, I had no idea what it meant either. Apparently certain documents needed to be signed and agreed, due to the size of the project. Both Bill and I began to feel apprehensive.

'Does this mean we have to go back to England?' she asked.

'It looks like it,' I said. 'We only need to go for a few days though. I could go on my own if you like and get back even sooner.'

'No way, we go together or not at all. I'd rather we didn't have to, but we both know all the work you put into that place, so let's just get it over with. Do whatever you have to do and get back here before anything happens.'

This last phrase, 'before anything happens', may have sounded a little dramatic but I knew exactly what Bill meant. Our lives had changed immeasurably since we met and even more so since we had been in Los Angeles, a fact that neither of us was about to take for granted. We knew that what seemed so permanent here – our changed mindset, our more positive outlook on life and the infinite potential opportunities – could so easily come crashing down if we allowed the madness back in. That madness, as far as we were concerned, resided exclusively in the UK.

We were wary to say the least. However, once we got used to the idea of a quick jaunt back home, we decided it was probably more sensible to embrace the potential of the trip, as opposed to fear the anticipation of something going wrong. Rather than make this a smash-and-grab job, staying in England for the least time possible, we would book two first-class return flights, with the return scheduled for ten days later.

That seemed a reasonable length of 'safe' time for us to survive away from our newly beloved Los Angeles.

But as it turned out, the date of the return flights didn't matter, because we would never use them.

TOP
10 THINGS I LOVE ABOUT BRITAIN

10 The people
9   The weather
8   Winston and William (Churchill and Shakespeare)
7   A village green
6   The BBC
5   St Andrews
4   A Sunday roast
3   A fry-up
2   The Lake District
1   A good country pub

THE FIRST THING THAT TOOK US BY SURPRISE when we arrived back in Surrey was the house. It was simply magical, a masterpiece of craftsmanship and attention to detail.

All the hard work and planning had paid off. The forty-seven acres of garden had been dug over and replanted. It was resplendent during the day and brought to life at night with hundreds of outdoor lights. The interior was simply stunning. I had made a deal with myself when designing the layout that no one room would outshine any other. I was not to be disappointed. The hand-built kitchen, complete with a fifteen-foot long, nine-inch thick worktop, led through to the main hall; a sixty-foot by thirty-foot limestone-floored, oak-panelled, double-height reception area with a huge fireplace at the far end. This in turn led through to a more traditional games room, off which could be found an exact replica of the bar from the local pub down in the village.

Along the corridor from the bar was a curved glass wall, behind which lay the open-plan library, flanked by a waterfall on one side, lit with different colours, against a backdrop of blue slate. Upstairs the six bedrooms were all unique in their own way, from the no-holds-barred master suite through to the RAF-style dormitory, where ten single beds lay in wait for a mass sleepover. The master suite was complete with floor-to-ceiling windows, limed oak floors, vaulted ceilings, four-poster bed, leather sofa and flat-screen telly. To the left of this lay an open-plan wet area with his and hers showers, a steam room constructed of stone, glass and steel, with yet more oak around the limestone sinks and finally the centrepiece of the whole show, a 1.7-tonne limestone bath that I'd imported from Italy, via two lorries, a ship and finally a thirty-five tonne crane to haul it precariously over the roof and into position.

The story of the bath was an epic in itself. It was originally the winner of a 'block of stone beauty competition', as I'd been sent various photographs of several different stones from a quarry just above Rome and asked to make my selection. From the very stone I chose, my bath was fashioned and it was now here in situ, so thick that the hot water had to be double temperature in order for it to stay warm when it hit the stone surface.

Once in my new bath, the now-relaxed bather could settle down to music from the sound system or watch the waterproof flat-screen telly, while for the more adventurous bathroom guest, the glass doors on either side of the tub could be opened by remote control for that 'oh so fresh' al fresco bathing experience.

Linking the bedrooms on the first floor was a mezzanine area that I had created after dispensing with four of the old bedrooms to provide a wide-open space. Flooded with light, it featured a galleried balcony looking back down into the hall, along with a glass and stainless steel spiral staircase leading up to the cinema.

'Wow,' said Bill as we drove through the gates and the garden lights faded up. 'Wow,' she said again, open-mouthed, upon entering the hallway. Jackie, our housekeeper had lit the whole place with church candles; there were over fifty in the fireplace alone.

'Wow' again, as we rushed from room to room, laughing hysterically. This wasn't a house, it was a playground that had been dragged, kicking and screaming, into the 21st century. Now bristling with pride once again, as it woke up to a new beginning, borne out of a respect for its past, but with both feet firmly in the future.

The house was wonderful, so wonderful it was about to present us with a major problem. When couples are close there are many things that are felt before they are said. Bill and I both knew we faced a dilemma. What America had given us was the very thing that now meant we no longer needed to go back there. If Lionel Richie's house had been the reason we stayed in LA, this house was now our reason for moving back.

After we'd examined every nook and cranny and ran around screaming a bit more, we went to the local pub. Not the one in our new house, but the real one.

'Babe,' I said, after we'd settled in a quiet corner.

'It's alright, I know what you're going to say and I agree,' Bill interrupted.

I laughed. 'How do you know what I'm going to say?'

'It's easy,' she replied. 'You think, the house is to die for. It's so you and therefore it's so us, and you've put all that time and effort into it, and life's not really about where you are but who you are with. Plus, we both feel so much better now than we did when we left, so why don't we stay here and make a go of it? And before you say anything, that's what we're doing.'

Well, that was about the size of it I suppose. Bill had nailed it, with very little left for me to add. It didn't matter where the house was, we just wanted to be there.

Calls were made to LA. I declined ABC's kind job offer, our belongings were to be packed and shipped over to England, and Lionel's house was to be put back on the market. Courtney Cox was about to get yet another shot at it, and this time we both hoped she'd get a move on.

People heard we were back home and all shiny and new. I hadn't been this healthy for years, and Bill was looking tanned and terrific. Not only that, we were brimming over with optimism. Where once there had only been thoughts of doom and gloom, the future was now looking brighter than it had ever been.

We were back but did Britain want us?

TOP 10

TURKEYS I HAVE BEEN INVOLVED IN

10   *Lock, Stock* – the TV show (Channel 4)

9   *Live with Chris Moyles* (chat show for Channel 5)

8   *Live with Christian O'Connell* (same as above)

7   *Live with Richard Bacon* (BBC Radio 5 Live)

6   *One Man and His Hob* (cookery show)

5   *Tee Time* (golf show for Channel 4)

4   *Boys and Girls* (game show for Channel 4)

3   *Terry and Gaby* (daytime show for Channel 5)

2   *OFI Sunday* (chat show for ITV)

1   *Johnny Vegas: Eighteen Stone of Idiot* (Channel 4)

IT WAS TIME TO THINK SERIOUSLY about getting back to work. As I still had my agent, I asked him if he would consider representing Billie as well.

'What, as an actress?' he protested.

'Please, just do it Michael,' I said. 'I promise you, she's amazing.'

He's still her agent today.

Michael started to send Bill scripts and got her a small part in a movie alongside Orlando Bloom, a boxing flick entitled *The Calcium Kid*. Bill was thrilled to work with the young Bloom; she said they spent most of their time talking about sword fighting as he'd just been cast in a new movie, some lame old no-hoper by the name of *Pirates of the Caribbean*.

More work came Bill's way when she was given a co-starring role in an ensemble piece called *Thirty Things to Do Before You're 30*; not a huge film but again, more valuable experience. She was clearly loving it, and with every day she was growing in confidence.

After this the word began to get around the industry that there was more to Billie Piper than just being an ex-pop star. Her next part confirmed this and banished any lingering doubts anyone might have had about her ability. Bill was cast in a harrowing television drama entitled *Bella and the Boys*, where she turned in a blistering performance, to rave reviews.

Billie's star was most definitely in the ascendant and next came a call from the mighty BBC Drama Department.

They were going to film six stories from *The Canterbury Tales* and wanted Bill to star in the opening episode. This was the job that would take Billie's acting career to a whole new level.

'Babe, this sounds amazing,' she said, after being offered the role.

'It is,' I agreed.

'But there's one thing,' she said, wearing the frown I had come to recognise meant she was unsure about something. 'They want me to play opposite Dennis Waterman.'

'So, what's wrong with that?'

'Well, isn't he a record producer, you know, in Stock, Aitken and Waterman?'

Obviously, reruns of *The Sweeney* and *Minder* had completely passed her by. Once I'd stopped laughing it was time to go out and get a few DVDs.

Luckily there was no need for any explanation about her other co-star, that lovable Northern Irish rapscallion James Nesbitt. And, yes, he would get to jump her bones – the devil.

The Miller's Tale from *The Canterbury Tales* was another big hit for Bill, as well as a critical feather in the BBC's cap. Once again Bill had nailed it, and this time before an audience of millions. The viewers' eyes had been opened and a new star was born.

In the meantime I wasn't sitting around doing nowt – promise. I too was back working in television, after a call one day from an old acquaintance who was now running Channel Five, for his sins.

Kevin Lygo had been my boss on various channels a few times over the years and had been charged with the task of lifting Britain's fifth terrestrial broadcaster out of the shadows and into the sunshine. But it was not going to be the easiest of challenges.

Kevin asked me to a breakfast meeting in the Berkeley Hotel, in my old stomping ground, Belgravia. He explained that he was looking for a live show that would make the channel more relevant and give it energy. This was my home territory, as 'live' was my thing. Excited at the possibilities, we began to discuss the most important aspect of this kind of show, namely the key talent.

I always believe that if someone already has a following then – budget allowing – buy them and you get their flock at the same time. The two guys with the biggest untapped wells of followers were the country's two biggest DJs: Terry Wogan at Radio 2 and Chris Moyles at Radio 1. And neither of them had been on television much in the previous few years. By the end of the meeting I had agreed to produce two new daily live shows; the first, a mid-morning show starring Terry along with Gaby Roslin, the second, an early-evening show starring Moyles.

Bruce Forsyth Enterprises Ltd.

Chris Evans Esq.,
Ginger Productions.
131-151 Great Titchfield Street,
London, W1P 8DB.

2nd March, 1998

Dear Chris,

Thank you so much for being so kind to me on your show. You
made the interview so easy and the dressing room with the
two bowls of fruit, chocolate biscuits, cups of tea and a
bottle of champagne, what more could a 'Super Star' want!

I hope your trip to Dubai was successful and if you would
like to come to Wentworth in the summer for a game,
preferably June, July or August, please give me a ring and
be my guest.

Thank you again for being so gracious to me.

Yours sincerely,

BRUCE FORSYTH

Clockwise from above: Happy Birthday Sir Terry, only 13 years to go 'til I take over your show;
Bruce Forsyth, Strictly the Gentleman; Me and the *Drivetime* team after we won Sharleen Spiteri
in the annual Sony Awards raffle.

Clockwise from above: For the red one to stay, the black one has to go – sometimes life's like that; 'Now son, there's a film called *Ferris Bueller's Day Off* I need to tell you about…'; Excuse me, can you tell us the way to the Pope's house please; Senor di Montezemolo, I love all your cars – will you adopt me please?; Me and the Breakfast team 30 seconds before our last show: 'Don't panic'; Hey, let's point some fingers; And save the best for last, cue Alex Jones, you're on.

Evans 'boosts Wogan audien

Clockwise from above: Mad Dad strikes again; Big sis, little brother; 'Please, give me just 4 more weeks on the breakfast show – I promise I'll get better!; Quick, cut to another camera – I can't hold my stomach in much longer! Me on *Friday Night with Jonathan Ross*.

Ross turns off 360,000

Listeners desert his Radio 2 show in droves after the storm over lewd phone messages

Clements
Business Reporter

JONATHAN Ross has lost 360,000 listeners from his Radio 2 show in a year.

The desertion of almost a fifth of his audience will be seen by many to his lewd calls veteran actor Andrew Sachs.

But the BBC put it down to 'seasonal fluctuations' in listener figures, which were released yesterday by the industry body Rajar.

His falling audience comes as listening as a whole has hit an all-time high.

And many of those who tuned into three-hour Saturday morning show appear to have reached for the off-switch following the lewd messages he and fellow radio presenter Russell Brand left on Mr Sachs's answerphone last October.

More than 45,000 people complained after the obscene messages were broadcast on Brand's Radio 2 show. In the furore that followed, Brand resigned and the BBC was fined a record £150,000.

Ross, 48, was suspended from the BBC for three months without pay but resisted calls to resign. His quarterly listener figures show he is continuing to lose fans after his weekly audience fell by 50,000 from January 1 to March 31 from 3.08million 3.03million.

At the beginning of 2008, 3.39million people tuned in to his show.

A Radio 2 spokesman denied the Andrew Sachs scandal was behind Ross's drop in listeners, adding: 'It's just a seasonal fluctuation.

'A lot of the figures are very slightly down now, but it's not part of a trend or anything.' Ross is not the only Radio 2 presenter to lose listeners.

Sir Terry Wogan's weekly audience fell from 7.96million to 7.77million between January 1 and March 31. He had 8.1million a year ago.

Sir Terry, who has presented his two-hour weekday Radio 2 show, Wake Up To Wogan, since 1993, has already revealed he would rather quit than be forced to retire.

He said: 'You really will have to leave before they shut the door on you. It is rather like the Eurovision Song Contest. I gave up Eurovision because it was time.

'You have to get out the exit before someone starts leading you towards it.'

The spokesman said of Sir Terry's falling audience: 'It's seasonal. Terry has stated publicly on many occasions that he is very happy where he is and we're very happy where he is.

'He still has the biggest music breakfast show in the country.'

However, the Rajar study shows that he is in danger of losing the crown to Radio 1 DJ Chris Moyles whose listenership increased by 400,000 to 7.7million between the end of 2008 and March 31.

Radio Ga-Ga – Pages 26-27

Clockwise from above: Please hand Daddy the microphone; 'So Noah, here's how it's going to be, w
both do exactly as your mother says, otherwise we're toast'; How to stare your Dad out at 4 weeks.

Clockwise from left: Natasha marries Steve Davis; Seven beauties that are no more; The only thing I still own is the number plate.

I set up a brand new company in order to produce both shows, and only weeks after landing back in Blighty I was once again steeped in the process of casting, writing and creating, whilst also searching for office premises, staff and studio facilities. Sadly it was to be a slow and painful realisation, over the next two years, that I was never meant to produce anyone other than myself.

The *Terry and Gaby* show sank without a trace, as did the Moyles show, which was so weak that when the host decided to slip off quietly and wait for the next television bus to come along, no one even noticed.

As if I hadn't already spent enough British broadcasters' money, I sealed my production fate with another live show, this time a much bigger and more expensive one. *Boys and Girls* was a concept I had dreamed up whilst lying by my pool in LA. The format was simple – one hundred boys, one hundred girls and one hundred thousand pounds. By the end of the show there would be one winner, the twist being that they would win the jackpot but have to spend every penny of it in the next seven days. After that they had to come back and try to keep what they had bought. If they failed, everything would have to go back to the shops.

The problem with this show was that the pitch was far better than the actual show. Even reading it again now, it sounds like it might play, but alas it bombed like a plane without wings. When the show hit the screens it didn't know whether it was a dating show or a game show, and as a result, nor did the viewers.

That was it – I had scored a hat trick of high-profile, expensive flops; huge, big belly flops into a bottomless pool of dismal ratings so low they barely managed to register. Not that I ended up being down on the deal. I was paid a set fee for producing these duds and so did fairly well out of the experience financially, as did everyone involved but of all the things I have ever done professionally, those are the two years I would ask for back first.

No one's fault more than mine, I hasten to add.

TOP 10 THINGS TO DO WHEN THE SHIT'S ABOUT TO HIT THE FAN

10   Be aware it's going to happen

9   Figure out from which direction it's likely to come

8   Figure out the worst-case scenario

7   Figure out how long will the stink last for

6   Analyse whether it's your fault

5   If it is – accept it

4   If it isn't – stay cool but don't react, yet

3   Figure out whose fault it really is

2   Warn anyone it may affect

1   Buy some deodorant

TO HEAP IGNOMINY ON TOP OF FAILURE, a year or so after Bill and I moved back from the States, I faced my former employers, the Scottish Media Group, in court, and lost. Well, when I say I lost, it was more like I was annihilated.

After I left Virgin, angry and hurt at realising they wanted me out, I stupidly attempted to sue them. The case took two full years to come to court, finally arriving before the Honourable Mr Justice Lightman in June 2003.

Gather round, everyone, as I share with you the story of how not to win a court case, via a little tale, also known as:

CHRISTOPHER EVANS

versus

THE SCOTTISH MEDIA GROUP

My gripe was that out of my original payment for the radio station and production company, I had agreed to accept forty per cent in cash, and the other sixty per cent in shares. The same shares I foolishly refused to sell to the nice man from Goldman Sachs. These shares were to be paid over three years at a rate of twenty per cent per year, but because we had parted company before the third year, the final third I argued was outstanding.

My lawyers and I then spent £2.2 million – and two years of our lives – working up some argument as to why they might still want to hand these babies over to me.

A couple of days before the case was due in court, I was encouraged to go to arbitration to try to settle things before the case went public and the costs really started to go into hyperdrive.

I found myself sitting around a table in an office, somewhere in the City, face to face with the very gentlemen who had previously almost begged me to sell them my company. And where once we had been allies, we now found ourselves on the verge of the almightiest of legal and financial ding-dongs.

The man in charge of arbitration was a qualified QC and a professional peacemaker. Everyone else in a wig and gown was out for the kill, but all he wanted was for the two sides to agree to disagree, shake hands and move on. He quietly advised me to walk away from any further proceedings and expense. He suggested that if I were willing to do that, he was fairly sure he could make the other side see sense and walk away too. He wanted us to shake hands, bury our bad feelings, swallow our legal bills and move on with our lives.

At this juncture, I was in for around £2 million in legal costs and I think SMG were in for almost double that.

'I have come this far and I am not about to walk away now,' I said – or something equally as predictable and unconvincing. The nice man rolled his eyes.

Why, oh why, oh why didn't I listen to him that day?

Aaaaaaaaaaaaaaaaaaaaaaaaaaaaaaaaaaaaaargh.

The next time I saw the boys from SMG was in the High Court, where Mr Justice Fingers, in all his wisdom, ruled very much in their favour on all counts, in front of the entire nation's media. Mr Justice Fingers also referred to me as a liar, a bully and a whole list of other nice names in the process, just in case anyone hadn't quite grasped his point – which, of course, they very much had. In my opinion the judge may have been wrong in some of the things he said. But that didn't change the fact that I should never have embarked on this ridiculous and self-indulgent course of action.

I swear to this day that I did not lie in court, but what I should have done was wake up and get the hell out of there before we ever got to court. No one wants to hear a multi-millionaire asking for more, trying to squeeze the last dregs of dirty dishwater out of a sponge that once contained liquid gold.

I had been at the centre of the deal of a lifetime and for doing something I loved – it doesn't get any better than that. I should have had the grace to quit whilst I was ahead. And I was well ahead. On the day we went to court, I was worth £83 million. Give or take a few pounds either way.

I used to be a newsagent, for goodness sake. I used to be a paper boy before that and supplement my wages to the tune of £1.50 by collecting the bills every Friday night. I was a kissogram for a year or so, for £6 a time. When and where did I lose the bloody plot? Of course the judge was going to rule against me – I would have ruled against me, for crying out loud!

As a consequence of the verdict my final bill for this whole fiasco would hit £13 million, as on top of my legal bill I had to pay SMG a fair chunk of money. That's £11 million more than the day the nice arbitrator whispered in my ear that I might want to reconsider my position before going ahead.

Though I was worth a lot of money on paper, I didn't have enough ready cash to pay the lawyers, which resulted in me having to sell my much-laboured-over wow-house, the Surrey house, the one it took me a lifetime to buy and two years to refurbish, the one on which I had lavished so much attention and energy, the one I had turned into a dream house with its Italian stone bath, waterfall in the library and replica pub bar. Bill and I had lived in it for less than a year.

And painful as that was, I hadn't finished with my financial self-flagellation.

After the sluice gates of my bank account had finally closed again, I was left with a couple of more modest properties and a piece of land in Portugal, but the majority of my personal wealth was held in the remaining ten million shares I still retained in SMG. I know, I thought, I'll hold onto these shares and watch their value soar and as result I will mitigate my recent losses without having to lift a finger. And everything will be alright.

Sadly I was wrong. Just how wrong, I would learn to my cost.

At the peak of their value my shares were worth £3.76 each, so that's £37.6 million in all. What I should have done, as we now know, was sell them there and then, because soon afterwards they began to slide and they didn't stop. The all-powerful market began to sniff that this company was no longer what it had once been, or indeed promised to be. A couple of years later my shares had fallen to a new all-time low of £1.30. 'What a silly boy,' I thought to myself. £13 million, where there had once been £37.6 million. I felt sick. But not as sick as I did a few months after that. The price was now down to 60 pence. I couldn't think about it, and yet, of course that's all I did. But still I didn't sell – I was in total denial.

A year later they were down to 27 pence.

'What do I do now?' I thought. I tried to find a way out, one which could be construed as my snatching victory from the salivating jaws of defeat. And then I saw a car, a car that was both beautiful and may well go up in value in the future, but the point was that it was something as opposed to pieces of paper that were increasingly becoming worthless.

'Why don't I cash in my chips now, after I pay the tax I'll have just about enough money left for this thing of beauty. And then I can look at it every day and think – well, at least I got that for all my efforts from the deal of a lifetime.'

But no, surely the shares simply had to go back up. Isn't that what share dealing is about, not losing your nerve? I put the idea of the trophy car on the back burner.

So with my shares now down to a value of just over £2 million after tax, I still didn't sell. Can you spot a pattern here? When they slipped to an unthinkable eleven pence, the car was no longer an option. When they tanked to five pence, I was beyond incredulous. Whereas a few months before I wouldn't have thought twice about my shares fluctuating by a million, I was now literally losing sleep over a few thousand pounds. It was time to set myself free.

The day I instructed my accountant to sell, my shares were worth just over three pence each.

Ha-ha, ha-ha, ha-ha, ha-ha!

Boo-hoo, boo-hoo, boo-hoo!

Out of the original deal in which I made £83 million, I had successfully lost £74 million of it. And you know what? It was all my fault – period. I have been blessed with a sharp mind and more than my fair share of good fortune. There is no reason, no reason on this earth, why I couldn't have bitten my tongue, put my head down and finished my contract.

After that I could have made a clean break, sold up and headed out of town. Instead I decided to fight, for all the wrong reasons. And I ended up worth less than the day I had bought the station from Richard Branson.

But here's the thing, as I sit here today, I am genuinely happier. I look back and think, what a fantastic story, what a load of stuff and nonsense, what a clever and silly boy you have been, all at the same time. And if I achieved all that without even really trying, what can I achieve in the next ten years now that I know a thing or two?

I have friends who live in the past and talk about what might have been and I have to say they're really dull, sappers not zappers; in fact I've dropped most of them. The past is gone, it's dead. Learn from it or forget about it, but whatever you do, don't dwell on it. Such thoughts will only hijack the present and cast the future into doubt. Athletes don't save energy for races they've already run.

When it comes to money, I've always had a very simple theory. When we are asleep we are all as rich or poor as the next person. When we are having sex, or writing at our computers, having a pee or watching telly, money is of no importance whatsoever. It's only possible to actually *be* rich for a very small percentage of each day, and that's usually when paying the bills.

So yes, I do still confess to having nice things in my life but if they all had to go tomorrow, it wouldn't bother me in the slightest.

By definition, if you win, you will eventually also lose. It's not a probability, it's a fact.

TOP 10 SATURDAY NIGHT TELEVISION TREATS

10 *Generation Game*
 9 *Mike Yarwood in Persons*
 8 *The A-Team*
 7 *Stars in their Eyes*
 6 *Only Fools and Horses*
 5 *Blind Date*
 4 *Match of the Day*
 3 *Jim'll Fix It*
 2 *Noel's House Party*
 1 *Doctor Who*

THE FIRST TIME I HEARD THE WORDS 'Doctor Who' come out of Bill's mouth was in the kitchen of our cottage.

Though we'd had to sell the big house to a very private Russian man, after the nice QC tried to tell me not to go to court because I would get my arse spanked by the long-suffering Scottish chaps, we still managed to retain almost three-quarters of the estate.

The very private Russian man, you see, the one who turned up to view the place in an armour-plated vehicle with a car either side and two motorcycle outriders, had only wanted the big house and the nice Gertrude Jekyll gardens. He wasn't remotely interested in the farmland over the road and the various buildings thereon, and I was not about to quibble over such a trifling matter. He had the cash, I had the house and we both coveted each other's booty. Besides, I was very much aware of the strange-looking bulges underneath the jackets of his four bodyguards – always a useful negotiating image to bring to the table.

Having said that, I have never come across anyone straighter to deal with. He was polite to my staff, paid up on time and was never any bother thereafter. In fact I've never set eyes on him since; you can't be less bother than that.

In the middle of this remaining land were several buildings, one of which was a three-bedroom cottage, officially called the Pump House but known to Bills and me as Christmas Cottage, as it's where we got it together on Christmas Day when we first met. It was small but perfectly formed, and it was here that we now resided. We may have come down a peg or two in terms of square footage – from 12,000 square feet to less than a tenth of that – but what we had lost in floor area we had gained in acres. Our little love-nest was set in a 120 acres, to be precise – so we were by no means slumming it.

In the whitewashed interior of the Pump House, Billie and I were joined by four dogs: our two mad little lurchers, Percy and Epstein, an ex-racing greyhound called Rita and my faithful German shepherd, Enzo. It was a tight squeeze but we were all friends, the fur and the flesh rubbed along fine together.

One afternoon during this harmonious idyll Bill arrived back from a meeting in London. She ran in breathless and stood in front of me looking like she was about to burst. 'Babe, they're remaking *Doctor Who* and they want me to audition for the part of his assistant,' she said.

'Wow, that's fantastic,' I replied.

'Well, what do you think?' she asked.

'I think yes is what I think, yes, definitely.'

The more Billie told me about the new *Doctor Who*, the people involved in it and their plans for the show, the more it sounded like the dream job she'd been waiting for.

Bill was, however, apprehensive about a number of things, because it was a sci-fi show and a long-running franchise. Sci-fi could be notoriously nerdy and with a franchise comes the potential to be typecast. But we both knew these were minimal downsides when compared with the potential upside of a successful primetime dramatic hit.

Bill was trying not to be excited – one of her many charming traits – but her disobedient smile was betraying her.

'I'll go for the audition and take it from there,' she said, attempting to play it down. It wasn't working; we both knew this was a very big deal. But I don't think either of us realised then that it would cement Billie Piper as one of the most successful television actors of her generation.

Two auditions and a screen test later she was offered the part of the Doctor's assistant, Rose, playing opposite the new Doctor, Christopher Eccleston. It was a huge break and we were both thrilled, but as is so often the case, success was to come at a price.

TOP 10

MOMENTS WHEN YOU KNOW YOU HAVE TO LET GO

10 Before the rest of the world tells you
9 Before you begin to hurt each other
8 Before you have any children/any more children
7 Before you stop having sex
6 Before arguing becomes your sole form of communication
5 Before one of you has an affair
4 Before you begin to forget why it was you got together
3 Before you fall out of love
2 Before you stop seeing the good in each other
1 Before you stop being friends

BILL'S HEAVY FILMING SCHEDULE required her to move to Cardiff for the majority of the time, early starts and late nights meant it could be no other way. We discussed the situation, of course, and how it might affect our relationship but I, of all people, knew that when this business of ours calls, it very rarely rings back to ask again. Bill had to do whatever it took to get the job done.

The producers rented her a lovely pad in the same building as the Welsh songstress Charlotte Church. 'She's crazy,' Billie said, in one of our first telephone conversations after she'd headed West. 'Good crazy, but really, really crazy.'

Over those first few weeks, filming went well, in fact better than well. The word from everyone was that Billie was not only a real star but a joy to work with – no surprise to anyone who really knew her, yet lovely to hear nevertheless.

Filming takes for ever though and you have to be a certain breed of individual to cope with that, especially if you're an actor.

Bill would hang around for hours, or even days, in full wardrobe and make-up waiting to deliver a single line. Here's where the skill lies. How do you retain the same mood, voice and energy when your lines might be two days apart? I could probably cope with directing because the director is always busy, but acting – no thank you. I take my hat off to anyone who does it.

This wasn't the first time Bill had been away on location. She'd made a couple of movies, one of them a horror movie in Romania. I flew out to surprise her one night and ended up getting smashed with the crew whilst watching England in the quarter-finals of the World Cup. At least I think that's what it was – I can't quite remember.

But while previously she'd been away for a few weeks at a time time, the shooting schedule for *Doctor Who* was to last for a whole nine months. This is a considerable length of time to spend apart from someone who you got together to be with, rather than without. Not only that but I have to confess to not being the missing type, I never have been. I suppose this could be little more than the thinly veiled veneer of a much deeper self defence mechanism. When situations change I tend to change with them, rather than sit there wishing they hadn't and questioning why they had. Moreover when I see further inevitable change upon the horizon, it's the waiting for that change to arrive that I can't bear, often causing me to precipitate and even expedite that change sooner rather than later.

Could I sense us drifting apart or had it already happened, with geography now being the excuse for us doing something about it? I think this is more likely the case. Age gaps can be sustained in relationships when the two parties are older I think, but when a young girl has her prime years ahead of her, it is a foolish older man who chooses to deny rather than admit the potential for calamity all round. When I first met Bill even though she was so much younger, we had more things in common then than we were beginning to have now. We were less about ourselves and more about each other. We had met coming from opposite directions but at the same crossroads and now it was time for us to turn and go our separate ways. To pretend it was otherwise would have been to delude ourselves and each other, as well as putting at risk everything we'd gained from being together.

There was no question that our falling in love and the fixing of each other, was entirely a good, beautiful, wonderful and exciting thing for both of us, but in simple terms our work was done. We were ready to move on. Bill was already off and running. She was becoming her own person once again, for the first time in a long time; maybe even for the first time in her life.

Therefore, all things considered, it's no surprise there was no flashpoint, there was no blazing row, there was no screaming and shouting and declaration of a mutual love now lost. There was just one night after dinner, when I made a trip to Cardiff to spend a night with my wife.

Bill and I went out for dinner and came back at around half nine. She had been her usual wonderful self throughout the evening, and I couldn't help thinking that she looked particularly beautiful.

We settled down on the sofa to watch the telly. The golf was on. It was the final day of the Masters.

'Oh goody, golf,' she joked. 'I love it when you watch golf, it's so cute.'

I believe she genuinely did love it when I watched golf because she knew it was something I'd had a passion for since I was a little boy, when I saved up for months to buy a second-hand five-iron from the local junk shop.

Bill fell asleep whenever we watched anything on television, but she did so particularly quickly when it came to golf, and seeing as she had an early start the next day I couldn't help feeling that I was inadvertently doing her a favour. Minutes, maybe even only seconds later, she was fast asleep, her head in my lap.

And that was the moment.

That was the moment that I knew, whether it was today, tomorrow, next year, or in five years from now, Bill and I would one day have to part. It was inevitable. I sat there with tears streaming down my cheeks, filled with memories of how we'd met, saved each other from our demons and embarked upon our magnificent adventure together.

And that's exactly what it was. A magnificent, magnificent adventure.

The next morning, after a fitful night's sleep, I awoke earlier than Bill and wandered into the kitchen to make us some tea, feeling sick at the thought of the conversation I knew we had to have. While I was still messing about with the teacups and teabags, Bill shuffled in behind me. I felt even sicker.

'Babe, I need to talk to you,' I said.

'What's the matter?' she asked.

'Can we go and sit down?'

'Sure, what is it?

We went into the living room and sat down on the sofa. Bill suddenly looked terrified. She began to clutch her cup with both hands, her knees tight together under her chin, her shoulders hunched.

'There's something I have to say ...' I began.

'Go on, tell me.'

As I looked at her I noticed there were tears in her eyes. Did she know?

I paused and took a deep breath. I wasn't sure if I had the courage to get the words out. It felt as if they were still hiding somewhere in my stomach.

'I think we're about to start not being "us",' was as close as I could get to what I wanted to say.

Bill didn't say anything, but her eyes were sad and afraid.

'I can't believe I'm about to say this, but whatever we had together, I think we're about to lose ...'

As Billie started to fight the tears it made what I was saying all the more difficult. There had been no rows, there was no animosity, no jealousy, we loved each other completely and unreservedly, but we both knew that our love had evolved into a deep and sincere friendship and was no longer that of a husband and wife.

As I continued talking, Bill began to sob. She was just extremely sad, as I was, and am again now writing about it.

Bill and I both knew that whatever we had was dying, right in front of us, as we sat there hand in hand feeling helpless.

We were like two little kids being pulled apart by the grown-ups, and we were both devastated.

When I think about the worst moments of my life, this was second only to the moment my mum told me, when I was thirteen, that my dad was going to die. The feelings of hopelessness and despair were exactly the same.

The more Bill and I talked about our situation, the more we both cried, like two people consoling each other over the loss of a loved one. Bill had begun to nod in agreement at what I was saying. 'I know, I know, I know ...' she kept repeating, although she said she would rather have stayed together than bring the conversation up herself.

We hugged, we kissed and we held each other tightly, like we never wanted to let go. Billie and I had never planned anything, so how could we possibly plan for what was happening now? We were lost and confused. It hurt so much but there was no turning back, life was moving on and we had no choice but to move on with it.

By the time Bill's car arrived to take her to work, we were both a puffy-faced, snotty-nosed, red-eyed mess – and we still hadn't said goodbye.

'So, are you going to go then ... is this it?' Bill asked.

'I suppose I should,' I said. It all seemed so horribly final.

'Oh. OK then. I love you.' Bill began to sob again, silently this time.

As I turned to walk away, she looked every inch the lost little girl I had first met five years before, but I knew she was different now – and stronger than she had ever been.

Pulling out of the car park in my old man's silver Mercedes saloon, I burst into tears myself. The best friend I'd ever had was back inside the building I had just walked out of and I knew that if I turned around and went back, we could both stop the misery immediately. But I also knew that if we did that, the pain would be back one day and we would end up making each other unhappy. Breaking up was our best chance of staying friends for life.

And we have. Other than my wife, Bill is still the best friend I have and she always will be. When I think about that morning and all that sadness that went with it, I cry the same tears that I did that day; they feel the same, they taste the same, they are the same.

I love you Bills ... I really, really love you.

PART THREE

THE RETURN
OF RADIO BOY
– TAKE THREE

TOP
10
THINGS I'VE GOTTEN
AWAY WITH

10 Walking out of grammar school after clumping a teacher over the head with a chair

9 Losing all my records as a mobile DJ the week before Christmas

8 Dropping a three-and-a-half tonne fat-fryer, when I was a forklift-truck driver, onto my boss's brand-new Rover Vitesse

7 Setting fire to the outside broadcast truck at Piccadilly Radio

6 Taping over an interview with Sir Bob Geldof yet to be broadcast only a week after Live Aid

5 People still believing in me when they must have been close to giving up

4 Not becoming an alcoholic

3 Not going broke

2 Not being dead

1 Being given one last chance, both professionally and personally

SO HOW DID I END UP HOSTING the biggest show on British radio, the Radio 2 *Breakfast Show*?

Initially two things happened:

In September 2004 a very nice lady called Helen Terry who produces the Brits every year (despite also saying every year that she's never going to do it again), called me up to ask if I fancied a third pop at presenting our national musical gong show, following my first two efforts in the mid-nineties.

She said the Brits always needed a twist and bringing me back to telly after such a long layoff would get them at least half the way there.

I was flattered and surprised, not to mention a little apprehensive. But I wasn't going to let any of that stop me. After all, what did I have to lose? I was completely out of the loop and this was as fun a way as any to get back in, or to fail trying.

Before Helen had the chance to come to her senses and change her mind, I instructed my agent to do the deal. A week later, a press release went out and a few hours after that I found myself in a swish London bar, on a Wednesday morning, answering questions to various assembled members of the nation's media.

'So Chris, what albums have stood out for you these last twelve months?'

Ah, now here's the thing. I hadn't been listening to anything new musically for three years. I had been in self-exile from all things radio and musical. I could feel myself going red from the ankles up as I looked at all the journalists who were wondering why I had lost the power of speech.

'I believe technically anything I say may be taken down and used in evidence against me and seeing as I am the host and really ought to be impartial – I am going to pass on that one, I'm afraid.'

I just about got away with it. And the first thing I did, after I left the launch, was order twelve months of back issues of the *NME*, *The Word* and *Q* magazine.

'Time to bone up, bonehead,' I chastised myself.

Everyone involved with the Brits was kind to me and seemed genuinely glad to have me back on the scene. I was excited and, more importantly, I felt like I cared again. I don't know quite how well I did when it came to the big night, but I was OK enough to be asked to do it again the following year.

It was because of this Brits-induced blip in my profile that my next offer of work came in. On Boxing Day 2004 a tsunami had devastated thousands of square miles of Asia and claimed hundreds of thousands of lives as a result. In response to this, early in 2005, the UK independent radio network decided to join forces for the first time in a twelve-hour fund-raising simulcast on behalf of the victims.

It was a noble, brilliant and ambitious idea, and when I was asked to be part of it I jumped at the chance – it would be the first time I'd been on the radio since I walked out of Virgin almost four years earlier.

The organisers paired me with the lovely Kate Thornton and asked us to host the main 8 to 10 am slot. I was going to be back on a breakfast show! This felt a little strange at first, but I wanted to do it. Tony Blair was to be our guest, there was as much tea as we could drink and it was all for a worthwhile cause.

'Good morning, it's five past eight and you're listening to UK Radio Aid ...'

I was back on the air, and two hours later I was back under the spell of the one thing I'd wanted to do for as long as I could remember.

Radio Aid went well, in fact it went very well, raising over £2 million and it won a special Sony Radio Award two months later. The one thing that struck me above everything else that day was how blasé a lot of those involved had become about being on the radio.

'I'd kill to have any of their jobs,' I thought, and then realised this was how I must have been for the last few years of my previous radio incarnation. It had become the norm for me then, as it was for these guys now. But being on the radio should never be the norm. It's a great privilege to be able to do something you love for a living, especially when it involves being allowed into people's lives via the wireless. I too had come to take that for granted, I could see that. But now everything had changed and suddenly I felt like the spotty teenager I once was back in Manchester, the kid who would do anything to get on air. I remembered the words of my letter to Tony Ingham, the boss of Piccadilly Radio, begging for a job:

> ... I will do anything, for nothing, for ever, to be able to work at your radio station ...

I made a vow to myself that I would never take being on the radio for granted again – if I could ever get back on the radio in the first place, that was. And I was going to give that my very best shot, one last time.

I was a big fan of Radio 2 during my time away from the business and especially of Jonathan Ross's show on a Saturday morning, but I felt that following on from him the listeners needed a wall of fantastic music, after all that chat.

I made up my mind to pitch this idea to the controller of Radio 2, a lady by the name of Lesley Douglas. I had heard a lot about Lesley. There were few who knew the station better, as she had climbed all the way up from being a secretary to the number one job, some twenty years later. She lived and breathed Radio 2, but would she even be willing to see me? What I was about to request was akin to a former Premiership footballer asking for a meeting with Sir Alex Ferguson, to see if there was any chance of the odd game.

To my great relief, the word came back from Lesley's assistant; the meeting was on, and a date and time agreed. We were to meet at my agent's office over a cup of coffee.

Lesley is a larger-than-life Geordie, and as soon as she arrived at Michael's that day, it was clear from her energy and enthusiasm just why all the big names wanted to work for her and why her station conveyed so much vision.

Radio 2 had always been successful, of that there was no doubt, but over the years the gap between Radio 1 and Radio 2 had become a chasm as Radio 2's original audience grew ever older. Lesley had arrived in the controller's job determined to reverse this process.

It wasn't a difficult task, simply one that needed someone with the balls to do it. Radio 2 needed to be repositioned before it was too late. Lesley saw this and, while respecting her older listeners, she had the good sense to revitalise the output of her station in order to attract Radio 2's next generation.

After a few pleasantries, I put my idea to Lesley.

'Well, that was the last thing I expected you to suggest to me,' she said. 'Chris Evans coming back and hosting a Saturday afternoon music show on Radio 2. I have to tell you I'm very pleasantly surprised. As much as I was intrigued to meet you, I thought you were going to offer me more of what I already had, but this sounds a lot more original.'

Lesley had assumed that I would be after a show not dissimilar to Jonathan Ross's, which was the last thing she needed, but once I had focused on the idea of playing great tunes and lots of them, Lesley smiled and there was an ever-so-mischievous twinkle in her eye. The type of twinkle that alerts the rest of the world to the fact that the one doing the twinkling may well be hatching a plan. I was in, only just, but I was in and I knew this was my last chance. If I messed up at Radio 2, then Radio Boy was dead, once and for all.

Lesley has many attributes but more than anything, she is the queen of spotting talent and knowing what to do with it. She is also a highly astute operator.

She suggested that rather than suddenly appear on air as part of the weekend schedule, it would be useful for every-one concerned if I first covered a couple of Bank Holiday relief shifts. She would slip me in under the radar and that would be that. It was a subtle tactic but one that worked perfectly. After a couple of successful holiday fill-ins, it was announced that I would be taking up a regular Saturday afternoon slot.

Whether Lesley thought she was taking a risk with me, I cannot say for sure, but of course it had to be. Maybe this was why she put me together with a producer by the name of Helen Thomas.

'She's as mad, if not madder than you,' Lesley informed me. 'But she's tough and I have a feeling that's just what you need. She's in China at the moment, though, so you'll have to talk to her on the phone. Let me know if you think you can work with her, but I think you'll be perfect together.'

Lesley, as usual, turned out to be right. I have always had the creativity, but I had also been handed the control. This was not a risk she was prepared to take.

Not only did the live-wire from Hull turn out to be as mad as had been promised but she was also very, very loud. She may have been in China but I swear I could still hear her five minutes after I'd put the phone down. When I finally got to meet her, I couldn't believe how small this almighty force of nature was, and in the flesh she was even more unbearably enthusiastic than she had been on the phone.

We clicked immediately, not least because Helen was prepared to stand up to me from day one, letting me know that, although she would do everything she could to facilitate the kind of entertainment I wanted to create, there would always be limits to how far I could go.

My Saturday afternoon show kicked off in September 2005 and went well straight from the get-go. We started slowly, sitting on our hands. We were both bursting with ideas but we knew we had to let the audience get to know us before we dared invite them on a more original date. Lots of music was the order of the day, plus a few fairly quiet features but most of all we had to have the patience and the good sense to stand back and let the show grow of its own accord.

It felt very, very good to be back on the wireless, and on a great station to boot. I promised myself that, whatever happened, I wasn't going to blow it this time.

So, with my radio rehabilitation under way it was time for me to try to sort out the rest of my life back in the real world.

TOP 10 FRUITCAKE MOMENTS

10 Trying to pay for things with bananas
9 Flying to Ireland for one drink
8 Flying to Cape Town for one drink
7 Playing one hole of golf for €247,000
6 Spending $12 million on a car I'd never driven
5 Spending £7 million on land I'd never seen
4 Forgetting I'd bought an £8 million house
3 Paying lawyers £2.3 million to lose in court
2 Waiting for 10 million shares worth £37 million to go down to £250,000 before selling them
1 Thinking for one second any of the above is remotely important

'ONE LIFE FOR SALE – ONE RECKLESS OWNER' read the headline on the front page of the *Independent* newspaper.

I had decided to sell most of my belongings so that I could start afresh. I had hundreds of items in storage from houses I no longer owned – my house in LA, the six-floor house in Wilton Crescent and the rock-star mansion in Surrey. It was costing me a small fortune to hang onto these things, most of which I would never need again.

I know, I thought to myself, I'll hire a market stall and sell them off.

A fun idea? No, a really bad idea, as it turned out.

Camden Market, where I had decided to set up shop, was a very cool place to hang out generally. So I took a six-month lease on a big lock-up there, in one of the old railway arches.

I also enlisted the assistance of my friend and housemate at the time, Big Pete, and together we set about repainting my new premises in time for our grand opening nine days later. By the end of our first day of decorating our style was beginning to attract a bit of attention, to say the least. Against the backdrop of the white, curved tunnels, we were splattering random colours all over the walls, all over us and all over anyone who happened to get too close or was too nosey.

We embellished this with what we felt were deeply meaningful statements such as 'Nothing in this store has a price – like life.'

Not only was this sentiment hopelessly idealistic but it didn't make any sense, when it came to retailing. I had the idea of letting people pay what they wanted for items, hoping any potential customers would feel the whole karma vibe and pay what they thought was fair. But within minutes of opening on our first morning it was evident that any potential customer wanted everything as cheaply as they could get it and, as far as they were concerned, any karma could go take a running jump.

Upon realising this, price tags were hastily added, but alas to no avail. I had paid fortunes for some of the items on offer, $30,000 for a sofa, for example, but our asking price of £5,000 had people walking away as soon as they saw the second zero. Although we probably had more footfall that day than any other market stall in the western world, we barely sold a thing.

Still, we'd met some very interesting people and had a day out in the fresh air into the bargain. A fact we intended to celebrate, as we headed off to the pub once we had shut up shop for the day.

With a raging thirst, Big Pete and I hit the bar, shoulder to shoulder with our new colleagues from the market. They had enjoyed the extra publicity my new enterprise had created and were happy to share a few drinks with us – far too many, as it happened and enough to ensure that it was going to hurt come the morning.

This was a pattern that would repeat itself for the next six months. Pete and I continued to flog off the accumulated detritus of my life, whilst also learning a few harsh truths about the selling game, namely:

1. Regardless of hangovers, fines were imposed for anyone opening up late.
2. Our prices would have to be dramatically reduced to stand any chance of covering the £950-a-week rent we had to pay come Sunday evening.
3. We would never see the £14,000 cost of transporting all the items out of storage in the first place, let alone make any profit.

In short, the market stall was a disaster whilst also being evidence that the crazy bulb was still burning brightly somewhere deep in my ever-fading ginger head. For heaven's sake – the house I had recently bought cost over three million quid, yet here were Pete and I freezing our knackers off and sacrificing a large chunk of our weekends for precisely bugger all. In fact, minus bugger all. But it was my own fault for buying all this nonsense in the first place.

I once asked a wise old owl friend of mine what one piece of advice he would pass on. This is what he said: 'Whenever you think you might want to buy something – don't.' As he took another drag on his pipe and then a sip of his beer and looked out of the window I waited for him to finish this pearl of wisdom, but he said no more and I realised that was it.

Stuff and the owning of stuff is a nightmare, a needless headache. It's the ball and chain of consumer addiction that we all fall for.

Nowadays when I drive past a high street on a Saturday afternoon and I see all those hard-working people spending money they might not have on things they might not want and disappearing under countless bags in the process, I want to jump out of the car and scream, 'STOPPPPPP! For your own sakes, take it all back and go out for a nice meal instead, or save up for a holiday, or anything – but just stop.'

Having said that, I still own more cars than any one man ever needs, a house big enough to be a small hotel and a garden the size of a small county. Never mind, I suppose it's a work in progress for us all.

However, let's finish this section with a smile. I live very close to the house where John Lennon wrote the line, 'Imagine no possessions.'

And his place was twice the size of mine with 80 acres out the back. So what the fuck was he going on about?

TOP 10 TV/RADIO JOBS I HAVE TURNED DOWN

MY SATURDAY AFTERNOON SHOW ON RADIO 2, which continued to prosper, was well into its first year by now and there was soon talk of a more full-time position, but it was not to come from within the BBC.

'There's a man who wants to see you,' announced my agent over the telephone.

'That's a bit vague, Michael,' I replied. 'Can you give me a bit more to go on?'

'Don't you trust me?' he snapped.

'Of course I do.'

'Then be in my office this afternoon at two o'clock.'

Since I spent most of the week trying to stay fit, stay out of trouble, find a girlfriend and wait for the Saturday show to come round again, this was not going to be a problem.

'I'll see you then,' I confirmed.

Michael was waiting for me in the boardroom of his agency, the same room where I had met Lesley Douglas almost a year earlier.

'There's a gentleman coming in to see you in a minute and he wants to offer you a job – for a lot of money. It's a job that's already done by somebody very well known but this gentleman with the offer wants you to do it instead. Although he says if we ever talk of this meeting after he has left, he will deny it ever happened and will allude to the fact that you and I are mere chancers attempting to kick up a fuss and increase your market value as well.'

Fair enough, I thought. I love a clear brief and they don't get much clearer and briefer than that. Where I had been intrigued, now I was excited.

I fixed myself a cup of tea and waited in the boardroom. After a few moments Michael returned with the gentleman and his offer.

For the sake of this gentleman, who is still very active in the business of radio, I am now going to give only the bare minimum of detail of the proposal he brought to us that day. In a nutshell, he wanted me to take over the reins of something that was once great but was currently fading, in an attempt to make it great again.

I thought about what he had said for all of a second before informing him that though I was honestly flattered, I was very happy working for the BBC and although I was only appearing on a weekly basis, I hoped it would lead to more. It wasn't about the money so much as the platform.

Unpeturbed, he then told us about the money. Suddenly it did matter. No wonder he had been cocksure, with that showstopper up his sleeve.

'Bloody hell,' I said. Michael burst out laughing.

'I need to have your answer within forty-eight hours. This is a one-off proposal in an attempt to get us back to where we want to be. If I don't hear from you, I shall take that as a no. Good day, gentlemen.' And with that he was off.

Now here is the thing. I loved my Radio 2 show. I'd received more-than-favourable reviews and I could feel the audience beginning to forgive me my mistakes of the past. I also felt a deep loyalty to Lesley for believing in me, not to mention a growing bond with Helen, who had given up the chance of working on much bigger shows to help me with mine. But the job the man was offering was one of the best in the land, and for a truckload of cash.

I had to talk to the girls.

I spoke to Helen first and when I told her she said she had to admit she would completely understand if I felt I had to take up such an unexpected and lucrative opportunity. Having said that, Helen assured me she was certain Lesley would not want to lose me, and suggested she talk to our boss before I did.

No more than an hour or so later, Helen called me on my mobile. 'Lesley is totally up to speed and says that she feels there is definitely a conversation worth having before any drastic decisions are made. She says give her twenty-four hours and come in to see her tomorrow after-noon.'

Twenty-four hours was all we had, but was it going to be enough?

The next day in her office, Lesley was eager to put me at ease.

'Wow Chris, there's no doubt this is an amazing offer you've received and I will understand and support you if you decided to go, BUT ...'

To say this was the biggest BUT that I was ever going to hear in my life is not overstating the issue.

'How about if we offer you a daily show?'

I was blown away, but there was more.

'And after that we'll see ...'

What the heck did that mean? A daily show, and after that we'll see!

There was that twinkle in her eye again.

The show Lesley had in mind for me was *Drivetime*, the slot currently occupied by the legendary Johnnie Walker. Johnnie would move to weekends as well as deputising for Terry Wogan on his breakfast show, *Wake Up to Wogan*, Lesley explained – something she'd had in mind for a while anyway.

But there was something else.

'Terry will want to go at some time and I have a feeling that time is not awfully far away. How about you move to *Drivetime*, let the listeners get to know you a little more there and then when Terry says enough's enough – on you go.'

On you go! On you bloomin' well go!!!

'Lesley, what are you saying? Have you just offered me the breakfast show on Radio 2? Is that what just happened here?

'No – not yet, that's not what I'm saying. If and when it becomes available, and if you've behaved yourself and things have gone alright on *Drivetime* – who knows?'

What a meeting that was. I would happily stay on *Drivetime* for a hundred years if it meant I had a shot at the big one. There was no need for any other discussion. Phone calls were made; the man with the offer would have to make other plans. I was staying firmly put.

A daily show on Radio 2.

'And after that we'll see ...'

Five words I will never forget.

TOP 10
THINGS I'VE LEARNED ABOUT MARRIAGE

10   It does not have to happen every time you have a romance

9   It does not have to happen every time you fall in love

8   It is not a game

7   Your marriage is more important to your loved ones than you might imagine

6   Your wedding is your wife's most special day ever (other than childbirth) and she must be the star – willing or not

5   Don't invite anyone you don't want there, no matter what the fallout may be

4   There will always be someone who is not happy about it

3   It should be for ever

2   It doesn't have to be for ever

1   Wives are sexier

WITH THINGS ON THE PITCH HOTTING UP, as it were, it was time for things off the pitch to get cracking.

I hadn't had a steady girlfriend since I separated from Billie and frankly it was getting to me. I was running out of places to look until those two lovely telly favourites Ant and Dec came up with the bright idea of putting celebs playing golf back on the box.

The All*Star Cup, as it was to be called, would be an amateur golfer's dream come true; three days of televised competition with two teams – one from Europe and the other from the USA – battling it out head to head, Ryder Cup-style, at the Celtic Manor Golf Resort in Wales. There would be team outfits and team bags, crowds of tens of thousands and ultimately victory, not once but twice, for Team Europe.

Already good but what Ant and Dec didn't put in their programme proposal was that this golf-fest would also introduce me to the goddess who would become my wife.

Other than my mum and radio, golf has been the longest and most positive force in my life. My cousin Brian competed in the Open Championship and was my hero as a kid. He looked like a surfer, had a car I'd never even heard of before and was always somewhere else in the world other than Warrington, where I was.

Brian gave me my first half-set of clubs when I was nine, along with a few old, scuffed balls, and I played for four years on the field at the back of our council house before I could even think about affording to play on an actual course.

I can't tell you how much I still look forward to a game of golf. I remember the time when losing the ball was not an option as it was the only one I had, and I am constantly aware of how lucky I am when striding out on to courses like St Andrews and Wentworth with as many brand new balls as I need, which is usually quite a lot. So having been asked to join the European team – the term 'bit their hands off' would not be out of place in describing my reaction – I was asked if I could spare the time to play a few holes at a course near London a few weeks before the tournament, so that the production company could make a short promo film.

This I was more than happy to do. I was always glad of any excuse to get out on the course, especially when they told me the filming would take place at the magnificent Stoke Park Golf Club in Buckinghamshire, a stunning course, and the location for James Bond's infamous match against Auric Goldfinger.

When I arrived I was told that I would be joining my All*Star team-mates Jodie Kidd and Ronan Keating to make up a friendly three-ball. We played nine holes all in all, with lots of stop-starting and interviews. It was all about the telly programme rather than the golf, with the three of us laying down a challenge to the Yanks to 'Come and get us if they dared!' After we'd finished, Jodie flew off in a helicopter – she does that kind of thing a lot – while Ronan and I ordered a sandwich and a soft drink on one of several colossal terraces that flank the majestic clubhouse.

Whilst we awaited our order, Ronan looked up and did a double-take.

'Here, Chris, come and meet a friend,' he announced, jumping up.

I followed him to an ornate, low stone wall behind which, teeing off, were two men and the most beautiful creature I had ever seen, dressed in a skimpy pink top along with an almost illegally short black skirt, white ankle socks and a pair of super-cool golf shoes.

Who the bejesus is she? I wondered. She's bloody gorgeous. And she was. Dark skinned with long, slender legs, so toned they looked as though they'd been carved, rather than grown, and a classically pretty Persian Princess face, with brown eyes and masses of thick brunette hair gathered cheekily into two bunches.

This, it turned out, was Natasha Elizabeth Annahid Shishmanian, or the Golf Nurse as she was known to thousands of readers of *GolfPunk* magazine. The Golf Nurse was a fictitious character that Natasha had brought to life as every male golfer's fantasy; a beautiful woman who not only played golf, but who was on hand to help the ever-frustrated reader with his golfing worries. All this I was yet to learn. For the moment I just stood watching her, filled with wonder.

'Hi Ronan,' she said, seeing your man on the other side of the wall, before running over to give him a kiss.

'Hi Tash,' he replied. 'This is Chris, we've been filming for the Ant and Dec golf thing.'

'Oh yeah, I've heard about that,' she said.

'Hello,' I gestured.

'Hi, pleased to meet you,' she returned politely.

After this brief exchange, Ronan and Natasha shot the breeze for a few more moments before one of Natasha's playing partners called her over to take the shot.

'Time penalty, nursey, if you're not quick,' quipped one of them.

'I have to go Ronan, please don't look, I'm bound to mess it up with you watching,' she said, before skipping back to join her game.

Alright, I thought to myself. She's stunning, but is she any good?

After carefully selecting her club of choice and standing back to eye up the challenging par three hole, Natasha the Golf Nurse paused before taking her practice swing. Focused, she took the club head back and powered through on the down swing, her hips perfectly locked into place to create maximum power. As she made contact with the ball it rocketed skywards.

I was in love.

'I love golf,' I mouthed. 'She loves golf.' I suddenly came over all queer, as if I had five lottery numbers with only one to go for a £14 million jackpot. I tried to keep my cool.

'Ronan,' I whimpered.

'Don't say it, we're all thinking the same thing,' he interrupted.

And with that we walked back to our seats and our sandwiches.

I never expected to see Natasha again. I'd never met her before, so I could only assume we moved in different circles, but I was wrong.

The night before the first day of Ant and Dec's tournament there was a huge party and guess who was propping up the bar with the best of them? As good as she'd looked on the golf course that day, the Golf Nurse looked even more sizzling when she had her fun boots on.

'Oh hi,' she shouted over to me. 'Nice to see you again.'

She talked with a permanent smile, a big, wide, diamond white smile. I still hadn't actually said anything.

'Would you like a drink?' she offered.

Not only would I like one, I needed one. I wondered if she was aware of the effect she had on the male species.

'Yes please, what are you having?'

'Champagne and shots!' Natasha declared triumphantly.

'Guinness instead of champagne for me,' I said.

'But you'll have the shots, right?'

'Right!'

I spent the rest of the evening attempting to stay glued to her side, exclude everyone else from the conversation, go to the toilet as few times as humanly possible, and be funny and engaging while trying to keep up with her on the drinking front.

All of the above I did reasonably successfully – successfully enough to find myself, at the end of the night, in the lift with Natasha. She had agreed to come to my room.

'I cannot believe this', I thought to myself, fearful my thoughts might be heard out loud. This woman, this creation of perfection, with all the right bits in all the right places, this woman who is fun and smiley and energetic and generally wonderful, is gonna be in my hotel room in less than a minute from now, providing there isn't a fire or a war or some such disaster in the next few seconds.

The lift doors opened.

'Don't turn the wrong way out of the lift and forget where your room is,' I was telling myself. One drunken slip now could be crucial in the grand scheme of things.

But I needn't have worried.

'I'm sorry Chris, I can't do this,' Tash said suddenly. 'I don't do this. I'm not doing this.' And with that she ran off down the corridor in the direction of the stairs.

'Noooooooooooooooooooooooooooooooooooooooooooooooo ooooo!' screamed the voice in my head.

That was so close to being one of the best nights of my life, right there, right now, yet, with Natasha's swift exit, I had been transformed into no more than a lone and drunken ginger man merely swaying back and forth in an over-carpeted hotel corridor, pathetically waving my room key around like a magician whose wand no longer worked.

The next morning seemed to arrive in a second. I opened my eyes to see the thick brown goo of hangover dribble that was currently sticking my right cheek to the pillow.

As I staggered across the room and opened the curtains, the last thing in the world I felt able to do was swing a golf club. Then I remembered I was here to play golf, and according to my watch I was due to tee-off in fifteen minutes.

This was not a casual game on a Saturday morning with a couple of pals, this was a multi-million pound television production and I could already see the crowds gathering down below from my window.

My heart pounding, after half brushing my teeth and barely saying hello to a shower, I made it to the tee box with seconds to spare. All thoughts of what had gone on the night before would have to be put on hold, for the time being.

'Ah, Mr Evans,' said one of the organisers. 'I believe you know two of your playing partners. However I am delighted to introduce you to the fourth in your group, Natasha the Golf Nurse.'

'You have to be joking', I almost said out loud, hoping this was some kind of sick joke set up by the other lads.

But no, there she was, all golfed-up again, except this time with knee-length tartan socks into the bargain, and managing to look miraculously as if she hadn't been anywhere near a bar in years, let alone drunk me under one just a few hours before.

What could I do but take it on the chin and attempt to clear the air.

'Hi, I'm the loser who tried to get you into bed last night,' I whispered out of the corner of my mouth.

'Hi, I'm the loser who almost said yes,' she whispered back. I was in love all over again.

We enjoyed our round together, playing to the crowds and cameras whilst clearing our hangovers. But alas, I would come no closer to securing the affections of this golfing goddess during my visit to Wales. For the second time Natasha disappeared back to wherever it was she came from, whilst I returned to my usual pattern of going out and staying out in the hope of coming across someone equally gorgeous who might also like the odd round of golf and who would be prepared to put up with a geeky, slightly pink and podgy ginger bloke for the rest of their lives. Natasha had raised the bar.

Time now to tell you about the Once a Month Club. This little ruse involved me and two pals meeting up once a month to discuss anything that might be on our minds, whilst enjoying a few decent ales. Our get-togethers would often be infiltrated by guest members, either invited or chanced upon as we visited various pubs and bars.

One such night, following my return from Wales and the golf, we bumped into a couple of girls, one of whom was single, and I found myself buying a drink for her at the long bar in London's Soho Hotel.

I was waiting to order when I felt a tap on my shoulder. I assumed it was one of the others requesting further refreshment, but I was wrong. It was Natasha.

'Oh my goodness, hello to you,' I guffawed.

'Well, hello to you too,' she said. 'Is that your girlfriend?'

'No, I've just met her tonight.'

'Good.'

'Why?'

'No reason.'

Within five minutes Natasha had joined us, whilst also making it very clear to the other two girls that they might want to move out. Half an hour later they were gone, and a couple of hours after that, Natasha and I found ourselves in the back of a taxi, on the way to my flat in north London. Three strikes and I was in? Please God.

The first night Tash stayed she slept on the sofa – Scout's honour. The next morning when I woke up, the Girl on the Sofa had vanished into thin-air.

'Not again,' I mused through bleary eyes. I hadn't even managed to acquire her phone number.

This last fact hit me as I staggered back to the bathroom.

'She was gorgeous, you idiot,' I said out loud whilst taking a pee with one hand against the wall to provide much-needed balance. Things had calmed down on the drinking front but I was still happy to put a few away if the occasion called for it.

As I gently swayed back and forth, whilst also humming – something I do a lot when I'm in love – I could have sworn I heard the familiar creak of my front door opening. I looked up and cocked an eye. Next there was a loud clunk followed swiftly by the thud that always shook my walls as if they might fall down at any moment. Someone had gained entry to my humble abode.

'Hiya,' piped up a crisp, energetic voice.

No, surely it couldn't be.

Hastily I threw on my dressing gown and stumbled down the three stairs which led to the kitchen. The Girl on the Sofa had returned, and not only had she returned but she had brought gifts of fresh milk, orange juice and other very welcome consumables that come criminally over-priced from the 24-hour shop round the corner.

Within seconds the kettle was boiling, bacon was sizzling under the grill and the toaster was whirring away in the corner. Not since I'd taken up residence had my city-slicker kitchen seen such a frantic assault before midday.

'Plain bread or toasted, red or brown sauce?' enquired the chef.

'Er, plain always – and red please.'

'Red always?'

'Almost always. You?'

'Both, red and brown, on the side – always.'

This response alone prompted me to consider a proposal of marriage.

As much as I adore bacon sandwiches and fry-ups generally, I couldn't remember the last time I had enjoyed such a treat midweek.

'You go and sit in the front room, and I'll bring it through.'

This was contentment porn.

I lay on the sofa and clicked on the telly.

Within seconds a mug of strong tea was plonked in front of me.

'Won't be long, just waiting for the bacon to crisp up.'

Crisp up? Yeeeeeeeees. This got me thinking about whether we should have a big or a small wedding.

There's making bacon sandwiches and then there's getting them right; an entirely different discipline.

After joining me to eat these masterpieces Tash disappeared back into the kitchen and began tidying up. I lay in the living room, listening to the sound of dishes being rinsed, wondering if all this was a dream.

'Oh Lord, please tell me this is really happening and I promise to be good for the rest of my life.'

I waited with bated breath. Footsteps were heading in my direction. I could hear bare feet on the oak floor.

'May I have a shower now?'

We were married eight months later, in August 2007, on top of a mountain in Portugal.

I hit the jackpot when I met Tash and with God's good grace I hope I'm going to be counting my winnings for years to come.

For some reason Tash loves me to death. She's my biggest fan, my fiercest defender and my most candid critic. She also has me by the balls on a daily basis which, quite frankly, is exactly what I need.

TOP 10

JOHNS/JONS/JOHNNYS/JONNYS/ JOHNNIES/JONATHANS I KNOW

10 Jonny Lee Miller (actor)
9   Jon Bon Jovi (rock star)
8   John McEnroe (tennis player)
7   John Inverdale (sports presenter)
6   John Morgan (Ferrari dealer)
5   John Collins (Ferrari dealer)
4   Jonathan Ross (TV personality)
3   Johnny Saunders (sports reporter)
2   Johnnie Boy Revell (entrepreneur)
1   Johnnie Walker (disc jockey)

IT SEEMS WHENEVER ANYONE TAKES OVER A SHOW AT RADIO 2 there is a backlash. The listeners love their DJs where they are, and change is seldom welcome. And so it was with *Drivetime*. When I took over from Johnnie Walker, the BBC message boards exploded with calls for me to be thrown in the Tower for the rest of my days. How dare the BBC presume I could possibly replace such a legend of the airwaves?

There was no arguing with the status of Johnnie on the radio and in the hearts of his fans, but he was on the move from *Drivetime* anyway, whether I stepped in or not.

The natural reaction is to want to defend yourself, but I was advised to keep my head down and get on with racking the hours up. 'The more you are on, the quicker people get used to you and the more you can relax and start doing your own thing,' I was told.

Solid advice, which I followed, and the objections very quickly started to fade away.

'How you getting on?' asked Steve Wright one afternoon.

'Oh, I'm doing alright now that all the fuss has died down,' I said.

'You got off easy mate,' he laughed. 'I had two thousand complaints a day for a good couple of weeks when I started, my old son.'

Now he tells me!

I continued to mention Johnnie's new weekend show at every opportunity and read out the odd anti-me email, just to underline the fact that both the team and I knew our place and were respectful for the chance we had been given.

Jeez, I remember thinking. If it's like this when you take over *Drivetime* from Johnnie Walker, what the heck is it going to be like if you ever take over the breakfast show from Terry?

This was a notion that filled me with such dread and nausea that I decided never to think about it unless I absolutely had to.

Drivetime didn't hit its stride for a good few months, perhaps even as long as a year. The show was as good as we could make it, but to be honest it was still a very conscious process for us and quite a rigid experience for the listener. The best radio shows tend to just happen, or at least sound that way, but it's not something you can force, it's something you just have to wait for.

As the show eventually did begin to feel right, the tension lifted and everyone involved relaxed a little more. And the more we relaxed, the more organic and natural the show became.

Our conscious philosophy of being positive was also having the desired effect, as was evident from the correspondence we were receiving. People said we were the tonic they needed after a hard day's work, and before a cosy night in or a special night out. It was a similar story when it came to our decision to focus on passionate real people as opposed to less passionate famous people only interested in self-promotion. We began to discover 'real' stars on a daily basis and often had to ask them to come back, due to public demand.

With our consistently strong content came our first volley of awards – another sign that we were winning the battle, if not quite the war.

Lesley, however, had already seen – or should I say heard – enough. She had found the apprentice she needed to take over her flagship show, and just in the nick of time, as somewhere in deepest, darkest Buckinghamshire the proud elder statesman of British broadcasting had decided the time was right to hang up his headphones.

It was January 2008 when Sir Terry Wogan, the most respected broadcaster in his genre, decided to call it a day. We all knew that once it was announced there were bound to be tears, not to mention uproar and outcry as to who might replace the King, but while everyone would begin to speculate and put forward their opinions about a worthy successor, a select few of us knew that the task would be down to me.

Contracts had been signed and the decision had been made, but those of us in the know were sworn to secrecy. Terry would announce that he was stepping down on the

Monday after that year's *Children in Need* on 20 November. Until then, none of us could say a word about anything. This was the biggest secret of my life concerning the best job I would ever have, but I would have to pretend it didn't exist – it was the only way I could trust myself not to say anything. I felt like an unexploded bomb.

Assuming that this would be our last year on *Drivetime* and that come January 2009, *Wake Up to Wogan* would be the sole right of Lady Helen Wogan, our plan for the next twelve months was to make *Drivetime* the best it had ever been. We would throw everything at it during our third and final year, to ensure we went out on a high.

What we didn't know then was that it wouldn't be our final year after all. Everything would change when the dynamic duo of Russell Brand and Jonathan Ross decided to get together for a late-night radio programme and make a breathtakingly distasteful telephone call to much-loved actor Andrew Sachs. Not only would this call mean that the secret I was already having trouble keeping would have to be kept for an extra year, it would also change the way the BBC was run, for ever.

TOP 10 THINGS I WANTED AS A KID

10 Striker
9 Gat Gun
8 Minolta camera from the Argos catalogue
7 A dog
6 Carbon-fibre fishing rod
5 Two zebra finches
4 Raleigh Arena 5-gear racer bike
3 Eddy Merckx 10-gear racer bike
2 Yamaha FS1E motorcycle
1 Ferrari 328 GTS

ONE OF THE MANY THINGS I LEARNT LISTENING TO TERRY is how to break up a year on the radio to provide it almost with seasons of its own. Although he claimed to just turn up and turn on the magic, he was of course much cleverer than that.

Four major events gave Terry's show its shape: *Eurovision, Proms in the Park, Children in Need* and his abnormally lengthy holiday entitlement. All were fair game for his listeners to comment on, usually to the detriment of their beloved host.

Terry would spend the weeks approaching each of these events decrying and belittling his own involvement in them, for the amusement of his listeners and as a beautifully subtle way of building their profile. After each event took place, he would spend the next few weeks reading out emails about what happened as a result, and once again taking on the role of the reluctant fall guy who perhaps should not have been there in the first place. It was a simple but brilliant formula and one that endeared him to his legions of fans.

Taking a leaf out of Terry's book, we started to spike our year on *Drivetime* with similar key high points to build up to and climb down from, the biggest of which was our annual *Children in Need Drivetime* Dine and Disco, and for our last year with Added Drive.

The Added Drive was to come from seven Italian stallions in the shape of seven of the finest motor cars ever to take to the road. The successful bidders in our auction would get to drive seven fabulous vintage Ferraris over two days and a whole heap of money would be raised for Pudsey and his pals in the process.

The collective value of the cars was over £10 million, they were all mine and part of a collection instigated by my wife's love for a Saturday morning cappuccino. As long as we are all happy and healthy, there is little Tash desires in life other than the odd nice frock and her beloved treat of a frothy coffee on a morning, especially at weekends.

And thereby hangs the tale.

Just before Tash and I got together I had sold some land I'd had in Portugal for a while and decided to reinvest the money in a farm back home. Tash and I moved into the farm together just in time for Christmas 2006. Tash wouldn't let me come home until she had lit the whole place up with candles and decorated a fabulous tree in the hallway.

The farm was small but perfectly formed, consisting of fifty south-facing acres, a bluebell wood, a tennis court, a stream, a swimming pool and a helipad. Yes, I'd done the helicopter thing as well; bought one and learned to fly it – forever the cliché, I know.

One thing we didn't have, however, was a frothy-coffee machine. This meant that a frothy coffee, the weekend must-have consumable, was only available via a car ride, either to the local pub, which we had also bought (that's another story) or a trip to our local Waitrose in Godalming.

Now marriage, as most of us are aware, is about making a situation work for both of you, rather than one of you having to put up or make do while the other one gets their way. Tash and I have lived by this credo from day one, and so it was with Tash's coffee cravings. We had a deal that whenever we went into the village for a coffee, I was allowed to drop into the classic car shop nearby – to have a browse.

My car-buying days had been curtailed somewhat in recent years and whereas I had once owned over twenty – don't ask – I now owned only three: the old Mark II Jag Tash and I drove off to register our marriage in before flying to Portugal, a Land Rover Discovery (dog wagon) and a Merc 500 for me for work – I know, it's a Merc and I hate them, but it was a bargain and very practical and blah, blah, blah. Alright, guilty as charged.

So while I still loved cars, I had very much been there and done that, or at least I thought I had.

Coffee purchased, we walked over the road from the car park towards the huge plate-glass windows that had some seriously classy old motors glimmering behind them.

'Morning Chris, morning Mrs Evans,' said the kindly, smiling, silver-haired proprietor as we walked in. 'You might want to take a look at that little lady in the far corner,' he added, pointing toward the front of the showroom. 'She's proper special, that one.'

Tash nodded encouragingly and having been given the all-clear, I fairly sprinted over to see what Graham was getting so excited about. Graham and I had known each other for years but he normally just left me to mooch. This was the first time he'd ever seen fit to steer me in the direction of a particular car.

When I set eyes on the work of art before me I could see why he had felt it appropriate to change his tactics. There in all its splendour, was an immaculate rosso-red Ferrari 328 GTS. She was perfect and looked brand new.

'Isn't she a beauty?' he smiled, with the satisfaction of someone who knew they had hit the spot. 'Fourteen hundred miles from new, original tyres, not a mark on the paintwork, probably the best in the world.'

He wasn't kidding. This car had to be over twenty years old and yet it looked as if it had just been driven out of the factory gates in Maranello. It was love at first sight.

'How much is it?' I asked.

'Forty-nine, nine-fifty.' Graham had hooked his catch.

'Forty-seven and you change the cam belts and give it a service?' I countered.

'Done,' said Graham, knowing it was a win–win.

And that was it, she was mine. And now a disclaimer.

I just need to explain that although this may have seemed like an impulsive purchase, it was actually two decades in the making. This is because when the Ferrari 328 GTS came out, I couldn't afford one for a couple of reasons:

1. I was only fourteen at the time
2. I was on £1.80 a week wages as a paper boy

Four days later she was in our drive back at the farm, but as I've said, that wasn't the end of my Ferrari-purchasing days. She was only the beginning – there were more to follow in her wake, including the most expensive car ever to be sold at auction anywhere in the world.

TOP
10

THINGS I LOVE ABOUT FERRARIS

10	The aspiration
9	The rarity
8	The outrageousness
7	The history
6	The power
5	The speed
4	The smell
3	The noise
2	The engine
1	The curves

WITH THE PURCHASE OF MY NEW LITTLE TOY came all the memories and dreams of a childhood that had seemed to vanish into thin air. The more I thought about it, the more I became sad and angry.

I began to reflect on all the days, weeks, months and years that I had wasted, slumped in dark and dingy pubs and bars, paying good money to do nothing more than pickle my liver and addle my brain.

I made a promise to myself. From that day on I would fall back in love with my dreams and I would hunt down the greatest Ferrari of them all – a work of utter perfection that goes by the name of the 250 GTO.

At the same time Tash announced that she wanted us to have a baby. 'Alright,' I agreed. 'Let's go for both and see which arrives first. The race is on – may the best man win.'

Not so fast though, sonny. After some fairly basic research it was evident that the baby would almost certainly arrive before the beast, as Tash and I were able to undertake all that should be necessary to procreate, whereas I would have to rob several banks to lay my hands on enough cash to buy a GTO.

Blimey, I had no idea they had become so expensive; they were now changing hands for upwards of £15 million! The GTO, it seemed, was simply never going to happen.

'Bums,' I thought, as I recalled a guy once bringing a GTO onto *The Big Breakfast* back in 1994. It was billed as the most expensive car in the world – a mere snip at £2 million.

Why hadn't I taken all the money from the Virgin deal and spent it on classic Ferraris? If I had I would own every single important classic Ferrari in the world and I would have been sitting on a profit of almost ten times the value. And even if the cars had gone down in value, I would still have had them in my garage to look at – unlike the useless pieces of paper which stated I once owned millions of shares that were now worth literally nothing.

How could I right this wrong? The fact was, I couldn't. That particular ship in my life had sailed, I had to accept it. However, there were other Ferraris in the world.

'This came through the post yesterday babe,' Tash said one morning when I was sitting in the kitchen, aimlessly stroking the dog, still stewing on what might have been. 'I think it's the brochure for a car auction – something to do with Bernie Ecclestone selling off a load of his collection.'

Tash was right and there were lots of them. Where I had messed up, Bernie had lucked out and been buying classic cars for years. The rumour was that he had hundreds and it was time for him to thin his crop a little.

I studied Bernie's collection but I didn't understand it. It was all over the place. There were fifties Cadillacs and seventies BMWs and the odd Roller, there was even a VW Beetle. I already thought he was a strange, albeit brilliant, little man but looking at his car collection, or at least some of it, he seemed even stranger.

None of them were for me, not by a long shot. There was, however, another collection also up for sale, the majority of which were emblazoned with the infamous badge of a black prancing horse against a yellow background, the calling card of Signore Enzo Ferrari.

Tash and I went to the auction which was being held in London's Battersea Park in a huge purpose-built marquee. It was more rock and roll than gavel and hammer, with dry ice and spotlights all over the place. It was exciting, which I suppose was the intention, and immediately I eyeballed a bright yellow 1967 Ferrari 275 GTB4 that was on offer. Sure, it was no GTO, but it was also £15.25 million less expensive.

'You don't want that, do you?' gargled a gravelly Scottish voice behind me.

Blow me, if it wasn't the guy who had brought the GTO on to *The Big Breakfast*.

'JC, how are you?' I smiled back at him. 'Sweetheart,' I said, turning to Tash, 'this is John Collins, Ferrari dealer extraordinaire and one-time handsome, hard-drinking womaniser.'

If John was pleased to see me, which he seemed to be, he was even more pleased to see my wife. I won't go into John's history, other than to say he's been there and got most of the

T-shirts, and even though he's nearly sixty now and a little craggy around the edges, you wouldn't trust him with your worst enemy's wife.

John said he had been out of the market for a while, having sold up and bought a polo team instead – well, you would wouldn't you? But if I wanted a serious car he would be happy to find one for me, for his usual finder's fee, of course. We talked about GTOs for a while and how he'd had not one but six of them go through his books.

After a few minutes, John suggested we grab a drink.

'John, we'd love to but Tash only likes the bubbles and I really fancy a cold beer.'

'Leave it to me,' announced John.

It turned out that he had been a shareholder in the company that was running the auction and had a special supply of booze in their production office. He also had ciga-rettes and it was very much a cigarette night.

John asked me how serious I was about getting into high-end Ferraris. I replied that I was deadly serious but had a limited budget that sadly would no longer stretch to a GTO. He said, no matter, GTOs come and go and if it was meant to be then it was meant to be. John suggested I think about a 250 Short Wheel Base, the predecessor of the GTO and the car Sir Stirling Moss described as the best car he'd ever driven.

Four weeks later, there was one in my garage – and a few months after that she'd been joined by a few friends, all Ferraris, and all absolute classics: an F40, a 288 GTO, a 275 GTB4, a Dino, a Daytona Spyder and a Lusso. A very tidy collection indeed, beautiful to look at, thrilling to drive and only ever going up in value – I hope. But there was another roller-coaster ride around the corner.

In the spring of 2008, Tash and I were invited to Italy, to the home of Ferrari motor cars in the village of Maranello. It was a two-night trip, including a factory tour and dinner at Pavarotti's old restaurant on the Saturday, followed by a second dinner in the ancient town of Modena on the Sunday. In the middle of all this was another auction, this time featuring only Ferraris and Ferrari-related merchandise.

The price for the whole trip was less than a thousand pounds a head. I told Tash I would love to go and she said she would be more than happy to come with me. Once on the plane, a privately chartered jet, the talk was only of cars, since all twenty people on board were on the same trip. JC was there, of course, having now jumped back into the market fulltime after kissing his polo-playing days goodbye.

Everyone was already excitedly talking about the auction and what they might or might not bid for. Some had deeper pockets than others, but they all sounded like they might be up for something. And of course there was lots of discussion concerning the 'lead car'.

The lead car at an auction is the car they put on all the posters and the front of the catalogue to promote the sale, and when it comes to an auction like this one it has to be something very special. The auctioneers were in no mood to disappoint; they had somehow acquired the former property of Hollywood legend James Coburn – his stunning black Ferrari 250 Short Wheel Base California Spyder.

I knew this was some car, but not for a second, sitting on the tarmac at Farnborough airport flicking through pictures of it, did I think I would come to own it by Sunday evening. I wasn't even considering bidding on any car, let alone that one! All I wanted to do was have a couple of days away with my wife, enjoy some nice wine and food, and see the factory where dreams come true.

I'd like to say the next forty-eight hours were a blur but I remember almost every second. The factory tour was fascinating for me and just about bearable for Tash, as she became the main attraction for many of the young Ferrari mechanics. Pavarotti's restaurant, where we adjourned afterwards, was so typically Italian it was brilliant, with shiny tiled floors, big tables and mountains of food. Italy began to work its magic on us – after a late night and a lie-in of course! And I suppose that was the point of the whole trip.

It was almost midday on Sunday by the time we made it down to the foyer to grab a taxi back to the factory where the auction was being held.

I don't know what happened to me in the next few hours but it was as though I had been possessed. As soon as we arrived back at the gates of Maranello, I began to think about the Coburn Car. Whilst Tash went to grab a much-needed coffee – not her usual frothy white but rather a fuel-injected double espresso, I crept off to have a quiet drool over the black beauty.

The California Spyder has often been described as 'the most beautiful car ever made' and now I could see why. Inspired by the sunshine of America's West Coast and designed by the descendants of da Vinci – and with a whole heap of horsepower under the bonnet – this car combined the best of all possible worlds for a Ferrari fanatic like me.

As my inspection melted into admiration and then into love, I began to have a serious word with myself. I might not be able to afford the mighty GTO but I could probably just about afford this little belter – at a stretch. A very long stretch, as proved to be the case come hammer time.

I had to apply some logic to justify what I was about to do (I don't know why – I just felt I should). The logic I plumped for was that I had once been able to buy a GTO but could no longer do so. Therefore, if I didn't go for the Cal Spyder now, what if they too went the way of the GTO? Plus – if I needed an additional argument – they always say buy the best of the best and forget the rest and the Coburn Car had a history to die for. James Coburn had owned this car for over twenty-five years, after his good pal, renowned car nut and subsequent frequent passenger Steve McQueen, recommended he buy it.

The estimate for the Cal was between $4 million and $6 million. JC had reserved us three seats on the front row but still had no idea I was going to bid for the car. I leaned over, in between other bids from earlier lots, to inform him of my intention.

'You've got to be joking,' he said. 'It's due up in ten minutes. Why the hell didn't you tell me, we could have prepared a strategy?'

'I've only just decided,' I whispered.

'Chris, nobody decides to bid for the lead car in an auction like this without thinking about it for at least a few days beforehand, usually a month or two!'

Most of the big decisions in my life, as you've probably worked out by now, have been the result of impulse rather than planning.

'So what do we do now?' I whispered again.

'Fuck! Give me a minute to think.'

John suggested we go in high and try to knock any other bidders out straightaway. It was a high-risk strategy, but one he said had paid off in the past. Pick your second-best bid, go in with that and have one more up your sleeve if you need it. If bidding carries on after that, you were never in with a shout anyway and you're none the poorer for it – at least that's the theory. The thing I have since learned about auction strategy is that once you've decided what yours is going to be, it's important to stick to it.

It was time.

'Alright, the James Coburn California Spyder. Who will start with a bid of two million euros?' barked the auctioneer. The figure two million euros flashed up on a huge red screen behind the car, followed by its equivalent in sterling and dollars.

'Four million,' shouted John. There was a gasp from all around us.

'Four million?' exclaimed the auctioneer.

'Four million euros,' he repeated.

There was a deathly hush in the room as over a thousand voices fell silent. Something big was going down here and everyone in the room was about to witness it. This was the gamble, this was the moment. There were several other bidders in the room, plus perhaps seven or eight people participating via international telephone lines. Would this first bid – double what the auctioneer had asked for – be enough to scare them all off in one fell swoop?

The silence gradually gave way to a growing chorus of mutterings, as everyone tried to figure out what was going on.

My heart was already thumping like a bass drum. JC, on the other hand, was in the zone, his eyes fixed on the auctioneer like an assassin waiting patiently to squeeze the trigger. It had been a good few seconds now, maybe ten, maybe even twenty, and still no one had proffered a counter-bid.

I looked over to where the phone lines were. I could see the various auction company assistants trying to explain to their frustrated clients that the first bid had been double what the auctioneer had asked for. Many of them were already hanging up, conceding defeat. A minute had passed and still no counter-bid was forthcoming.

'Ladies and gentlemen, what am I to bid next?'

'Just put the hammer down,' shouted John. He wasn't joking; he was prepared to use every tactic in the book, including heaping pressure on the auctioneer.

For that first minute, it really looked as if we had pulled it off. A few seconds more and the auctioneer would have been forced to close the lot, but then ...

'Four two-fifty,' shouted a voice from the back of the room, almost instantly followed by, 'Four million, five hundred thousand.' With the deal almost in the bag, two bidders had woken up to what we were trying to do and were not prepared to be railroaded.

'Fuck it!' said John. 'We're done.'

And we were – according to our plan. The story had now moved on and the bidding was very quickly at five and a half million euros.

'Can you lend me £2 million?' I asked him.

'Fuck, I don't know,' he answered. 'I could probably get it. Why?' I didn't have time to answer but that was all I needed to hear. When you've borrowed £85 million in the past, £2 million is a drop in the ocean.

'Six million euros,' I shouted. From nowhere, I was back in.

John almost passed out. Tash had long since turned pale, which is not easy considering her dark Persian complexion.

I had upped the stakes yet again, in a final attempt to get my hands on Mr Coburn's baby.

'Are you crazy?' hissed John under his breath.

We could see that the third bidder had now come off the phone, so where there had been two rival bidders there was now only one.

'Ladies and gentleman, this car is now at a new world record for any automobile ever sold at auction,' declared the auctioneer triumphantly. This solicited an almighty cheer and much applause from the crowd. We were now in a movie, but we were not alone.

'Six two fifty!' countered my nemesis, who was clearly as crazy over this car as I was. At this moment I knew the end was nigh and I remember suddenly feeling eerily calm and peaceful in a room verging on hysteria.

'Alright,' I said to myself. 'How much do I want this car? I know I don't have the money but I also know I can probably get it.'

The auctioneer was now looking at me as I'd taken over the bidding from John, who wanted no further part of it. This was my call now – what was I going to do?

Honestly, I had no idea.

'Mr Evans, would you like to give us one more bid, or ... are ... you ... done?' the auctioneer asked me directly.

And then I thought to myself, How often in life does a person get to buy a car like this? Sure, I don't have the cash but that's never stopped me before and who's gonna want to know about the afternoon we 'almost' bought the most beautiful and expensive car in the world? That's not a story I wanted to tell.

I made up my mind to go one more time.

'Six million four hundred thousand euros,' I said.

'Six million four hundred thousand euros is Mr Evans's bid and that, I believe, is his final bid.'

And it was, I promise. If the other bidder had gone just one hundred thousand more, to six and a half million, I would have bowed out gracefully. But they didn't and, as the hammer came down, the car was mine.

All I had to do now was figure out how I was going to pay for it.

TOP 10 THINGS THAT CAN HAPPEN WHEN YOU FAIL TO CONFRONT AN AWKWARD SITUATION

10 High blood pressure
9 Panic attacks
8 Ulcers
7 Over-eating
6 Sex addiction
5 Insomnia
4 Alcoholism
3 Depression
2 Self-loathing
1 Self-destruction

THE COBURN CAR WAS EVENTUALLY PAID FOR, SORT OF. Actually in many ways I am still paying for it now. 2008 was shaping up to be some year.

By now Tash and I had sold our farm in Surrey for a small profit and had found ourselves having to live in a caravan, of all things.

This state of affairs came about because, having sold up expecting to move straight into our new house – the one I'd been having built for the past couple of years – we were duly informed that the builders were still very much in residence and it was going to be a good few weeks (or even months) before they moved out.

'I know,' I said. 'Let's live in one of those swish American silver bullet things.'

And for once, I made the right choice. It was fun and it was romantic and, as it was on our own land, it couldn't have been more quiet and peaceful. It also helped remind me and Tash how little two people need to be happy and content.

Having said that, we still had the helicopter parked outside – I wasn't ready for total sanity just quite yet.

Inside our temporary accommodation, the Airstream was as luxurious I suppose as a caravan can get. It benefited from not only a power shower but also had air conditioning and a flat-screen telly in the bedroom, which was a real treat as we'd never had a telly in the bedroom at home. But it is for an entirely different reason that I will remember our time in the field.

'Sweetheart,' Tash said one morning while I was still in bed, listening to the sound of the birds and staring up through the skylight at a God-given clear blue ceiling. 'I know something you don't.' This was the stock phrase we used when either of us had a surprise for the other.

'What is it?' I asked eagerly.

She looked coy but excited. Tash took a deep breath and then said, 'I've done two pregnancy tests and they both say we're going to have a baby!'

I jumped up, arms aloft, screaming like a madman and ran straight out of the caravan completely butt naked into the field – which, thank God, we owned and was surrounded by trees. I was cock-a-hoop, pleased as punch and over the moon – all at the same time. Little did I realise, however, that it was a bloody good job I reacted with such sincere glee as I was under surveillance of the severest kind.

Tash had prepared herself to judge my reaction in the finest of detail to make sure I was really as pleased as I was obviously going to say I was.

'Your reaction was a ten out of ten,' she told me later. 'There was absolutely no delay in your euphoria, so well done. There was no way you could have been faking it, it was too quick, so it had to be natural. I one hundred per cent believe you were really happy.'

Phew, guys, be careful, it's a jungle out there.

Having passed Tash's celebration polygraph it was safe for me to suggest we now do what all expectant couples do and figure out the famous count back to see exactly where and when the magic happened. After a few minutes of elementary maths and a lot of giggling, we were thrilled to conclude that the Coburn Car was not the only thing we had acquired on our flying visit to Italy. *Bellissimo*.

I was genuinely thrilled that I was going to be a dad. But of course this would be for the second time. Quickly my thoughts turned to the first time, but I also knew I could only really do this properly if I first made an effort to rebuild my relationship with my daughter, the one thing I had failed at even more spectacularly than anything else.

'It's not about me anymore,' I thought to myself. 'I have no choice; this is something I have to do. After all, Jade is about to have a kid brother or sister. She needs to be part of this and I need her to be part of my life.' I talked to Tash and she gave me her full support. In fact she actively encouraged me to do something about the situation.

I was aware that Jade was fast approaching her twenty-first birthday and was now a young woman. I also knew she was in a relationship and had been in the same job since she left school, working with a husband-and-wife team who ran their own jewellery business. She still lived at home with her mum, and by all accounts was a fine young woman. But it was time to find out more.

Whereas there had been trepidation on my part before concerning this hugely important and unresolved aspect of my life, I suddenly felt the nerves and the fear begin to disappear. I suppose lack of choice does that to a person.

Not that this relationship wasn't something I had wanted before. I had come halfway towards resolving the situation when I was married to Billie, but didn't follow it through. I had invited Alison and Jade to come down to London for the day and the three of us went to a restaurant together. Alison was understandably wary, while Jade was very sweet, but quiet. It went well enough, however, for us to agree on a follow-up visit, a weekend down at Hascombe Court with Billie and myself. Unfortunately this hadn't worked at all for me, but instead of putting my own emotions to one side and worrying about my daughter – and what she and her mum had been through for the last fifteen years – I buried my head in the sand and stopped any further contact.

This selfish action somehow became a double-page spread in one of the Sundays a couple of weeks later, under the headline, 'I Met My Dad Chris Evans and He Rejected Me – Again'. Not that Jade or her mum have ever courted such stories. I think it was more the bush telegraph where they lived that was responsible for informing the world that Disappointing Dad had failed miserably again.

The reality was that just as before, not a day passed by without me thinking about it; when and where my daughter and I might finally get properly back in touch.

But why is it that despite knowing exactly what we need to do to fix a situation we still allow it to keep us awake at night rather than sorting it out?

At thirteen I'd had my own dad taken away from me when he died. Knowing how painful that was, and how deeply his loss hurt, it killed me inside to think that Jade had been needlessly fatherless for her whole life. Yet I continued to drag my feet.

But maybe this was precisely the issue, maybe it was losing my dad that had caused me to fireproof myself against the devastating pain associated with the loss of real, unconditional love. This is the only reason that can possibly explain why I had put myself through years of illogical, irrational self-destruction when on the face of it, things were going so well. Every time I got close to anything or anyone that I might lose one day, I chose to leave before it – or they – left me. All the great jobs, all the great women. And most importantly, my daughter.

You can deny a truth to anyone except yourself but the more you try, the more that truth will consume you from the inside out. That's what the truth is for – it is there to make us do the right thing. I had been pretending for years that everything was alright, when the truth was that whilst Jade and I were still estranged nothing could ever be alright.

It's clear to me now that I had been hurting inside a lot more than I was prepared to accept or admit for most, if not all, of my adult life. This is also why my life had become one big exercise in diversion away from my emotions. Why I worked so hard, why I drank so hard and would rather pass out at night than go to bed sober and risk contemplation. All such things serve only to weaken the spirit and in doing so invite the demons in to feed on the core of your very being, quietly intent upon tearing you apart.

So what caused me to change?

Well, I can only guess, because I honestly don't know.

I suspect it was a combination of things brought together by Tash's pregnancy, with me having to accept responsibility being top of the list. Maybe this time I also felt I had more to offer, largely due to the fact that there was more of *me* present.

I can't tell you the relief as I slowly realised my days of denial were about to come to an end. It was time for the little boy who had lost his dad to grow up and accept the fact that the key to real and lasting happiness is to know, in your own mind, that you've done the right thing by everyone in your life that you love.

I wrote to Alison via my accountant. As strange as this may sound, it was Kirit and not I who'd had more contact with Jade and her mum over the years, via his various financial dealings with them concerning maintenance and other such issues.

Upon receiving Kirit's initial letter, Alison replied promptly, confirming that Jade was equally keen to sort out this hopeless situation once and for all. But I was warned, and quite rightly, 'He must not begin to promise something he cannot deliver, like the last time.'

After more correspondence, I arranged again to go for another meal with Jade and her mum, in London.

TAKE 2

As I sat at my favourite Italian restaurant in Soho awaiting their arrival, I was as prepared as I could be for whatever might happen in the next hour or so. I had rehearsed most scenarios and talked my way through various conversations over and over again. What I hadn't prepared myself for, however, was what Jade looked like.

Unrecognisable from her last visit, here in front of me stood a breathtakingly good-looking young woman. Where had this gorgeous creature sprung from? Her appearance totally nonplussed me; I was already on the back foot.

'Girls are so much better at this stuff than men,' I heard myself thinking.

After I had regained a modicum of composure we chatted for a while, we ordered and, with the niceties over, it became very much a 'cards on the table' affair. Unlike last time, Jade and her mum were in no mood to beat around the bush. They were happy to meet but I was left in no doubt that as far as this father-daughter relationship was concerned, it was now or never, do or die. I had one more chance and then that would be it.

When it was my turn to speak, I was mindful to be both concise and contrite. I told them in no uncertain terms that I was willing to do whatever it took to help, and get to know Jade in any way I could. If she wanted to see me then great and if not, so be it, I could hardly blame her – but even so, there might be something else I could do for her.

After I'd said my piece, Alison took over and ran the show – very efficiently too, I have to say – telling both Jade and me what we had to do to move the situation forward. She finished off by adding that we'd better get on with it sooner rather than later, seeing as we had twenty-one years to catch up on and now it was up to the two of us to prove to each other we wanted this to work.

It was time to arrange some dates with my daughter.

Slowly at first, we agreed to go to various shows and events, with Alison coming too, until she was sure Jade was OK on her own. There were plenty of awkward moments in those early days (but the more we became used to them, the less awkward they began to seem).

What do you do when you've been to all the tourist attractions in Berkshire and the restaurant doesn't open until seven? How do you act when you're on your own with your 20-year-old daughter for the first time? How do you say goodnight? How do you say hello? Do you swear less? Should you swear more???

I didn't know the answers to any of these questions, or a thousand others. But what I learned was that the most important thing is to just spend time together and let your relationship take its course. The important thing is just to keep talking.

I'm still miles behind Tash, of course. She has already had far more relevant exchanges with my daughter than I probably ever will but none more meaningful, and I suppose that is the point.

We've even been on holiday together and I – almost – had a father-daughter moment with her on the subject of boys.

And she's funny, she's really funny and cheeky too, a lot more I suspect than she lets on to me. She's also like her mum, inasmuch as she's sharp as a tack and doesn't suffer fools. She also of course now has a new little kid brother to hang out with. But before we introduce Noah Nicholas Martin into the equation, let's get 2008 out of the way first. It was not the year I thought it was going to be.

TOP 10
THINGS TO BEAR IN MIND IF YOU EVER GET YOUR OWN RADIO SHOW

10 Don't fish for freebies

9 Two great records are better than one poor link

8 Don't ignore research that says people don't like you

7 Listen to the listeners

6 How you end what you say is more important than how you begin

5 Empower your audience whenever you can

4 Real people are generally more interesting than celebrities

3 Always be positive

2 Preparation, preparation, preparation

1 Content, content, content

EVERYTHING WAS HEADING SMOOTHLY towards the proposed handover of the breakfast show to me from Sir Terry, who was still scheduled to make the big announcement during his Radio 2 programme on the Monday after the *Children in Need* weekend in November 2008. Everyone involved was still one hundred per cent on side and singing from the same songsheet.

But one thing that none of us could quite believe is how the news had remained a secret. With every passing day more and more people had to be told, due to their involvement in the ongoing process and, with a story this big, we almost expected a leak to happen. As a result, we had to be on constant stand-by in case the news broke prematurely and action stations were called.

Having said that, if someone had squealed, at least it would have meant we could finally start planning the new show. As it was, we were brimming with ideas and the general need to talk to people about them, yet were still unable to say a word to anyone.

However this was all before the arrival in Studio 6C one night of Messrs Jonathan Ross and Russell Brand.

What happened during this now infamous late-night radio broadcast has been well documented and if you don't know I can only presume you are an alien reading this book on another planet.

But alright – just in case.

Russell Brand, a very funny, deceptively intelligent comedian in his thirties, his career on the ascent. Good friends with TV chat-show host Jonathan Ross, approaching his fifties, not a comedian but quite funny – sometimes. Russell has a Saturday late-night radio show on Radio 2. Jonathan comes to play one evening and things get out of hand. They call up much-loved veteran actor Andrew Sachs, who played Manuel in *Fawlty Towers*. He's not in, so they proceed to leave a shockingly offensive message about his granddaughter on the sweet man's answerphone. Russell has been intimate with her, it is suggested, and Jonathan seems intent on pressing Russell further on the matter.

What either of them was thinking, few of us have any idea – but whatever the case, the fallout as a result of their ornate thinking in doing what they did was unimaginable.

Disapproval of their antics started with a whimper; just the one recorded complaint to the BBC. But after being picked up by the national press, this rapidly snowballed into a cacophony of discontent with complaints – some now being received from people who hadn't even heard the original broadcast – being counted in their tens of thousands.

Initially, neither of the two protagonists could see what all the fuss was about. Russell was pictured being 'cool' outside his London flat, whilst Jonathan began to lie very low indeed. The programme was pre-recorded, and as the authority to broadcast it didn't involve either of them, in a court of law they would have been absolved. This was obviously their route of moral defence but it wasn't washing with anyone. The people they worked with needed their help to deal with this situation; Russell and Jonathan were big personalities with a lot of sway and power, and their silence was deafening.

It was obvious to me what was happening, I'd been there before. When your image is hip and cool and outrageous, then to come out and say sorry for anything – even if you know you probably should – is almost like admitting what you do is not who you are. And when your career is based on the assumption that what you do is exactly who you are, it can leave you on quite a sticky wicket.

Should they have apologised?

Yes – absolutely and immediately, and if anyone close to them advised them not to, then they were even more misguided. But as I know only too well, the longer you leave the apology, the harder it is to make and the less effect it has. Every minute without word from the terrible twosome was now making the situation worse for everyone.

For the next fortnight Radio 2 became like a fortress under relentless attack. I came off air on the Monday evening at the end of my show, a week and two days after the incident was originally broadcast. It was 7 o'clock and I went straight downstairs from the sixth floor to the third floor to see Lesley in her office. She was huddled up on her sofa.

The moment she saw me she burst into tears.

'It's bad,' she said. 'They want a scalp and it has to be a big one.' By this, I presumed Lesley was referring to the scalp of either JR or RB but to be honest I couldn't care less at the time. I still thought the blame lay at their door no matter what the editorial guidelines may have said.

'I can't believe it – the world's gone crazy,' I replied. 'How on earth did this thing get so out of control?'

I sat down and we talked for ten minutes or so. Both of us were in shock. I had been in many strange situations in my life but this was off the scale. The quiet of Lesley's office was in stark contrast to the chaos waiting outside.

To see her so wounded made me angrier than I think I have ever been before. She lived and breathed Radio 2. Yet here she was, her world caving in around her, unable to go home, and all because of one stupid phone call that wasn't even funny.

I gave her a hug and asked if there was anything I could do to help.

'No, there's nothing,' she said. 'I'll be OK.'

I gave her a kiss, another hug and went on my way, my head still reeling at the unholy mess this had all turned into. But stupidly not for one second did it occur to me that the scalp to which Lesley was referring would be her own. If I had known that I would never have left her office that night – in fact, I would probably still be there now protesting the injustice of it all. I knew someone would have to fall on their sword, but I presumed it would be one of the two hosts of the show or at worst the senior executive – responsible for green-lighting the broadcast of the taped programme.

But therein lay the problem. Lesley had volunteered that the person in question was her and that although she hadn't heard the specific content contained within the show, she was aware something that might have been questionable made up part of it. She had indeed taken the advice of a senior executive who had heard the programme but nevertheless technically it was she who'd signed it off.

Her words to me later were, 'It happened on my watch, so I had to go.'

It's insane that a lady who did so many amazing things for the radio listeners of Great Britain, including turning around the biggest radio station in the country when it was heading for oblivion, was now going to lose her job as a result of two overblown egos who didn't know when to shut up.

I know that by the letter of the law this is the way it had to be, and ultimately I know Lesley did the right thing in her own mind by stepping down, but it all just seems so unfair.

When I went into work on Tuesday evening, the newspapers had spent another day killing the BBC but as yet they didn't have a body.

'Lesley's been at the TV centre all day,' a red-eyed Helen informed me. She just didn't know what to say next. As I surveyed the office, everyone was sombre and reluctant to look up. Something had happened, something big. 'What we need you to do tonight is go on air and be the best you've ever been,' Helen said, more serious than I'd seen her before.

'Why, what is the matter?' I asked, feeling like a child being protected from some awful truth.

'Just do that, please.'

Shit, I thought. I had no idea what Helen was not telling me or why, but I trusted her well enough to know she would have her reasons. All I could do for now was as she had requested.

Not only was it Lesley who'd had to resign but the announcement was being held back till the six o'clock news on Radio 2 that night.

The lead story was too ironic for words. The lady who had resurrected my career and then seen fit to give me the biggest job in radio, was now about to lose hers and have it announced on my show. When I was told what was going to happen, I felt I'd been hit by an express train. I was completely crushed, and worse, totally helpless. It seemed there was nothing I or anyone else could do to help our stricken boss.

The first hour of the show was a sickening blur; with absolute dread, I introduced the news.

'Good evening, this is Fran Godfrey. The controller of Radio 2, Lesley Douglas has resigned with immediate effect following the broadcasting of a telephone call to the actor Andrew Sachs during *The Russell Brand Show* ...'

And so the story went on, each word hitting all of us like a fresh punch to the stomach. Here we were on Lesley's own radio station, broadcasting her demise.

Of course we knew Lesley would be listening, which just about topped off the lunacy of the whole situation. How she was feeling we didn't dare imagine. We were in bits, so she must have been inconsolable.

We came out of the news with Bruce Springsteen, Lesley's favourite artist and his anthem 'Born to Run'. 'The Boss for the boss,' I just about managed to say, as the song ended, fighting back the tears. It sounds really cheesy now, but it's all I could think of at the time. I just wanted her to know we cared.

The rest of the show passed in a daze. When we came out of the studio our network boss, Tim Davie, was waiting for me outside. For the rest of the week Radio 2 would be under the media microscope and all the top brass would be on site in a show of solidarity, which was no bad thing. Tim and I went and had a chat, in Lesley's office of all places.

He wanted to know if I was alright, which I was and wasn't. I understood what had gone on and why but I was still in shock, sad and angry. Tim also wanted to gauge how I might react over the next few days. In the past I had had a tendency to air my grievances in public, a short-sighted philosophy that rarely if ever achieved its desired effect. This was the last thing the corporation needed right now.

I told him how I thought Lesley having to resign was a travesty, but I also assured him that my days as a loose cannon were over and I would do anything I could to help move the situation on. There had been enough irrational implosion over the last seven days and I was not about to add to it.

My ultimate responsibility was to the listeners and although they were aware of what had become the top news story of the last few hours on all media, come tomorrow teatime it would be no more than a fading memory to them and they would still want a bag of decent tunes and someone to keep them company on the way home.

I told Tim that there was absolutely no need to worry about me on any level. The only person that we needed to care about was Lesley.

'I'm going to talk to the news crews outside, though,' I said. 'I think it's important somebody says something,' which so far nobody had. This was such a big story and a lot of my colleagues had elected not to say anything, worried that one nervous word out of place could easily have fanned the flames. I appreciated their concerns for the station and no doubt their own self-preservation, but at the same time I felt now was the time someone needed to speak up.

'That's no problem,' said Tim respectfully. I think he could see that although I was in bits emotionally, I was very much aware that this was not the day for recriminations and finger-pointing.

I stepped outside the building to give several interviews. All the big news shows were represented and were ready to jump on me to get their soundbites. I think they were slightly taken aback when they realised that I was happy to stay and talk, as well as being surprised at how visibly upset I was.

I tried to convey what the atmosphere inside Radio 2 had been like. I said we were all aware that the phone call should never have happened in the first place, let alone gone out on air, and the fact that it had done so was completely unacceptable. Nobody was hiding from this, but we were all very saddened by the fact that this had resulted in our brilliant boss having to step down from the job she was born to do and loved so much. I went on to add that although few of our listeners would ever have heard Lesley's name before, I could assure them on behalf of all the staff that the reason their favourite radio station was in such fine fettle was largely down to her.

As a result of my willingness to talk I was asked to appear later that night as a studio guest on *Newsnight* and on ITV, but I had said all I needed to say.

Instead, I reverted to type and went for much-needed pints around the corner, an antidote to the craziest week I had ever experienced. A week that could have and should have been so easily avoided.

The pub was packed. It seemed that everyone who worked at Radio 2 had had the same idea and instinctively knew where to go. They were all at a loss at first but as the drinks flowed, the grieving process became more vocal and animated, as it so often does. To begin with there were more questions than answers. Would Lesley be the only one to have to resign or were there more heads yet to roll? What would happen to Jonathan and Russell? What would Lesley do next? And now that her quickly cooling controller's chair was vacant, who was going to replace her? Hers was one of the most powerful and prestigious jobs in British broadcasting and there was sure to be a hotly contested race to find a successor.

Once the main questions had been established, conjecture began to fly around the room. And as with all wakes, after the lull and initial sadness, some much-needed laughter began to filter through, as we raised a toast to our fabulous boss and agreed there would never be another like her.

While I was still in the pub, my phone started ringing and Lesley's number came up. Hastily I jostled my way outside to answer it. She wanted to meet the next morning, and asked me whether I knew somewhere we wouldn't be spotted. I said I did and arranged to hook up with her in a pal's office, no more than three minutes away from Radio 2.

I woke up the next day with the hangover from hell. It had been a long and emotional night. After stumbling around my flat for a while I suddenly looked at the clock and realised I was due to meet Lesley in half an hour. Get a move on Evans. You cannot be late.

The first tearful words spoken between us that day were, 'I'm so sorry, I'm just so sorry.' But it wasn't me saying them to my hard done-by boss. These were Lesley's words to me!

What the blazes was she apologising for?

'I've let you down,' she went on.

Had the woman lost her mind? The last thing she had done was let me, or anyone else for that matter, down. If anything, we had let her down, the system had let her down, two people in particular had definitely let her down, but Lesley, to my mind, had done nothing wrong. For the duration of our conversation Lesley was very upset. I could see there was much grieving that needed to be done and this was only the beginning.

'I feel I've let you down because there's no way Terry can walk away now, the BBC and especially Radio 2 will need to close ranks, to get over this madness.'

She was right, I could see that, but it really didn't matter. All I cared about at that moment was her well being.

'Lesley, nothing is important apart from the fact that you know how much people love you and I mean really bloody love you and care about you and want to do anything they can to help you.'

I think, to be honest, I was in denial, still hoping it might all blow over and suggested Lesley would be back in a month or so. But when I said as much, she left me in no doubt.

'That's never going to happen, Chris, not in a million years. You'll have a new boss soon enough, I promise you.'

'What are you going to do with yourself then?' I asked her.

I hasten to add that this entire conversation had to take place intermittently as Lesley's BlackBerry kept buzzing with messages from well-wishers, George Michael and Elton John being just two of the names I recognised as they flashed up on her screen.

'To tell you the truth, I've already been offered a job at Universal Music,' she said, modestly. 'What do you think?'

'Blimey,' is what I thought. They don't mess about do they? I was surprised at the alacrity of their offer. No time for tears with these guys. 'Lesley Douglas is available for work, shit – hire Lesley Douglas quick before someone else does.'

For what it was worth I told Lesley to take the job, although I think she was going to anyway. I said to her that the heat around a situation like this is so intense at the time that it's tempting to think it's going to last for longer than it actually does. To resign honourably from one big job and walk straight into another had to be the best option, in my opinion. Sure, there may have been more offers around the corner – lots of them perhaps. But why take the risk?

Having said that, the job Universal had in mind for Lesley was no small-fry part-time post sympathetically offered to make her feel better whilst buying her off the market. On the contrary, if she chose to take this new position, she would be exclusively accountable to the worldwide head of the organisation.

Lesley had arranged to see people all day, so we agreed that I would inform some of her now senior troops of a quiet drink session that evening and that she'd say goodbye to the rest of the staff at a bigger do a week or two down the line. Both these events subsequently took place and Lesley was left in no doubt how we all felt about her.

For the record, Lesley is still at Universal today and loving every second of her new life. She's even making movies in amongst her many music- and artist-related projects.

However, the fallout for the BBC continued long after Lesley had left and, as she had predicted, the handover of the breakfast show ground to a halt. Terry agreed to stay until everyone had screwed their heads back on and normal service was resumed.

In a nutshell, everything would have to be shelved for a year. It would be 'as you were' for the next twelve months but yes, Terry still intended to step down come Christmas 2009, and yes, I would still be the kid to replace him.

TOP 10 MOST PIVOTAL MESSAGES I HAVE EVER RECEIVED (IN CHRONOLOGICAL ORDER – NOT IN ORDER OF IMPORTANCE)

10 Tina (my first girlfriend)'s mum telling me it was over because of my affair with the captain of the netball team

9 'Dad's not going to make it' (Mum in the kitchen whilst I was fixing my bike when I was 13)

8 Letter from Tony Ingham (boss of Piccadilly Radio circa 1983) inviting me in for an interview to work on Timmy Mallett's show

7 Telephone call on Christmas Day from Sara the newsreader telling me our one-night stand was under review as perhaps the beginning of something more

6 Telephone call from my pal Andy in London offering me a job at satellite radio station Radio Radio when I was the most down-and-out I have ever been

5 Forty-seven messages on my answer phone after I returned from holiday telling me I had landed the job on *The Big Breakfast*

4 Matthew Bannister calling to offer me the Radio 1 *Breakfast Show*

3 Call from Michael (my agent) informing me I had lost on all counts in my case against SMG in the High Court

2 Call from Lesley Douglas telling me she needed to see me regarding a certain knight of the realm hanging up his headphones

1 Call from home telling me Tash was in labour

BACK AT THE HOMESTEAD, Tash was glowing brighter day by day with that beautiful bump of hers. Our baby was due in early February 2009 and we couldn't wait.

Thankfully, we had finally moved out of the caravan and into our new home, where the nappies, piles of babygros and cuddly toys were now threatening to take over.

Tash finally hit labour one chilly morning a whole two weeks after the predicted date. It was a forty-minute drive from our home to the Portland Hospital, where she was checked into her room by early afternoon. I made sure she was settled in, before getting the all-clear to nip off to Radio 2 – which was fortunately only a couple of minutes down the road – to do my show. There was nothing happening any time soon, our paediatrician said, so I was good to go.

When I returned just after 7 pm Tash was, well, bored really.

'Let's go out for some food,' I suggested.

'Can we do that?' asked Tash.

'I don't know, maybe it'll help,' I offered, having no idea what the heck I was talking about.

After discovering from our man Patrick that it would do no harm whatsoever to go for a meal, providing it was close by of course, Tash threw some comfys on and out we strolled for one of the most romantic and special evenings a couple could ever hope to have. Our destination? Locanda Locatelli – the finest Italian restaurant in the world, owned and run by our good friend Georgio.

What could be more apt than a *mamma mia* in labour going for dinner in an Italian restaurant? When we told the staff, which we couldn't resist doing, all the waitresses melted, whilst the waiters afforded me the kind of man-to-man respect that I knew was going to last for one night only and that I'd better make the most of.

Tash hadn't had an alcoholic drink for weeks, maybe even months – mostly because she was aware of the risks involved, but also because she just didn't fancy it which, considering what she'd been like when I first met her, was almost inconceivable. Not tonight though.

'May I have a glass of champagne, please?' she asked.

'Wow, look at you,' I remarked.

'What the hell,' she said. 'It's not every day you go to your favourite Italian restaurant when you're in labour. I think the occasion calls for it.'

She was beaming from ear to ear and I'm guessing this was the best night of her life – all Tash ever really wanted was a family and God willing she was about to get her wish.

The food at Georgio's was, as always, fabulous – we both had a starter, a main and a dessert. I'm not a dessert man, but whatever force had steered Tash towards her first glass of champers in ages, also steered me towards the sweet trolley.

All in all, after about two hours we were done and on our way back to base. As midnight passed I was pooped and it was the same old story: the man fighting to stay awake as his woman's greatest hour of need approached. It's so clichéd but so true. I must have eventually dropped off and I was woken up by the sound of Tash having a hot bath in an attempt to induce further dilation while I had been snoring happily along on her hospital bed.

Come 6 am on 10 February 2009, however, we had full-on main-engine start and it was time for Dad to wake the bloomin' hell up, as Mum was almost ready to drop.

With the baby's heartbeat monitored throughout, it was time for Tash to start pushing, blowing, breathing as she'd practised, and for me to realise how useless men would be in the same situation. My wife is a tough cookie, made of strong stuff, fit, healthy and all that goes with it, but she was struggling and sweating as I'd never seen her before.

'Shit,' I remember thinking. 'This is a really big deal going down here.'

The baby's heartbeat speeded up with every push but slowed down dramatically in between and Pat, our man on the inside – literally – began to look ever so slightly concerned.

'Alright Natasha,' he said. 'The baby's struggling a little bit and I want to get him or her out as soon as possible, so I'm going to have to employ a little extra help.'

It's at moments like this that you fall in love with people who are really good at what they do and this is the moment I fell in love with Pat. It was clear from the deliberate and calm way he had switched from suggesting what 'might' be going to happen to telling us what 'was' going to happen that there was something quite seriously wrong. Normally über-relaxed and laid back, in front of me now was a man earning every penny of what he was paid for.

He immediately deployed a ventouse, a simple but highly effective tool designed to stick to the baby's scalp, so the baby can then be more or less yanked out as quickly as possible. And thank the Lord he did, as our baby's umbilical cord was wrapped around his neck, not once but twice; a potentially fatal complication, with the baby increasingly struggling to breathe, as with each contraction the cord becomes tighter. This explained the rapid slowing of the heartbeat.

Pat performed his magic and had our baby boy out and the cord cut in seconds. How do you ever pay these people back?

Tash was a complete star throughout, and so brave. I, on the other hand, was a slightly predictable dithering wreck, though much less so than I thought I might be. I did have to step out of the delivery room for a few seconds earlier on but when it came to the crunch, or push and then pull as it turned out, I surprised myself by happily hanging out down the business end to see our little fella pop out.

I'm sure lots of people already know this, but when you've witnessed your wife, or partner, give birth, you gain a new and completely different respect for her and indeed for all women, especially your own mum. Jeez, it has been said before, but if men had to have babies the world would be a few billion people lighter.

We named our beautiful little baby boy Noah Nicholas Martin Evans. Noah because it's the coolest name on the planet, Nicholas because Tash had a kid brother named Nicholas who sadly didn't make it, and Martin after my dear dad – as a present for my mum. When we told her shortly after she arrived at the hospital that day, she instantly became glassy eyed.

Perfect.

As I held little Noah in my arms for the first time, so tiny and so dependent, I smiled a smile I never knew existed. It was as though my son had arrived to tell me it was all going to be alright.

The rule book had instantly been re-written, my priorities had changed for ever. Thank Christ for that. The biggest responsibility any human being can be entrusted with made me feel nothing but relaxed and calm. I thought about crying but there was no need.

Here in front of me was the best-looking little boy I'd ever seen. His eyes were such a steely blue, I couldn't stop looking at them. They had a quiet but confident mystery, fearless and enquiring, almost wise. Or was it that he was already giving me a look that said, 'Dad, don't try to be cool with me, we both know Mum's the real deal and you're lucky to be around, so drop it'?

Yep, maybe that was more like it.

Tash was due to come out of hospital within forty-eight hours, but the nurses encouraged her to stay in a few extra days. 'There are no medals for going home early,' said one of the lovely ladies looking after her. 'Stay in a couple more days and we'll give you a few lessons on this having-a-baby thing.'

It sounded like perfect sense to me, and Tash, having thought about it, agreed. The hospital was so close to Radio 2, it was no trouble at all for me to split my time between work and being with Tash and Noah for the duration of Operation New Kid on the Block. The staff even made up a bed for me in the next room and with the availability of 24-hour room service and even a wine list, this wasn't exactly going to be a hardship.

Please don't think my life has always been posh hospitals and preferential treatment, but whilst I can afford it, why not?

When home time finally arrived we appeared briefly at the door to give the press the shot they wanted – it's much easier that way – before returning inside and heading out the back way to our Land Rover.

Mother and baby were safely strapped in, in the back, whilst Dad was in the front, ready to drive his new family home – a happy man, a very happy man indeed.

TOP 10

THINGS THAT YOU LEARN TO ACCEPT AS YOU GROW OLDER

10 Turning up early and waiting makes a heart attack less likely than getting up late and rushing
9 When it comes to your body, maintenance is now all there is
8 Energy is no longer a God-given right but comes from a tank that must be filled with the correct fuel
7 Your digestive system now demands respect or else
6 Well-meant advice can easily sound like 'When I were a lad'
5 Your peers will begin to habitually moan – about everything
4 Fancying younger women equals dirty old man
3 Even looking at younger women equals dirty old man
2 Less is almost always more
1 Keeping it simple is the absolute key

I'VE BEEN ACCUSED BY MANY OF MY FRIENDS over the years of being unable to keep a secret, and they've been right. So it gives me great pleasure to respectfully say to you and them – how about that for two years of keeping my mouth buttoned up? While the outside world wondered about when Wo-gan would become Wo-gone, a small band of us, including the great man himself, knew exactly the schedule of events.

While the delay following Sachsgate was wholly necessary and appropriate, it meant that professionally 2009 threatened to turn into a bit of a damp squib for me. Not only were my services not yet required for the breakfast show, but in my head I had already said goodbye to *Drivetime*. This farewell could be put on ice for the time being.

The problem for me, however, was not refocusing on my tea-time show but rather what to do with the first half of my weekdays.

I need to be busy, I like being busy, I thrive on it. I'm better at home when I am busy, I suffer from terrible guilt if I'm not and I tend to be a nightmare to be around. The thought of 'relaxing' brings me out in a cold sweat. Who wants to relax? Sure – cook, garden, or go to the gym but 'relax'? No thank you.

I had been blessed with a whole year of unexpected mornings off, so what was I going to do? 'I know,' I thought, 'I'll get to work on that bloomin' book I've always said I would write one day.'

I called Michael.

'Can you get me a book deal, please?' I requested blithely.

Concluding a contractual deadline, and the threat of legal action if I failed to meet it, was the only surefire way of getting myself to commit to the loneliness of the keyboard.

Later that day Michael called back.

'Several publishing houses are interested in your story but they need to see some pages, i.e. whether or not you can actually write and exactly what it is you'll be writing about.'

'How many pages will they need?' I enquired.

'An intro, the first two chapters and a synopsis of the rest.'

'OK,' I replied. 'You'll get it before the end of the week.'

Three days later, I delivered forty pages to him, including what I thought was a fabulous intro contrasting Spiderman's uncle's philosophy to that of Frank Sinatra's 'My Way', which sadly never made the final draft. Never mind.

By the following week, we had a deal with my current publishers and ten weeks after that they had my book. I wrote voraciously from 6 am until 10 am every morning, no breaks except for wee wees and number twos. But again I was surprised by my own choice of subject matter. The obvious showbiz things I thought I would write a lot about I barely touched upon, whereas the things that I thought mattered least to my story ended up mattering the most, as well as being almost effortlessly therapeutic to put down on paper.

Sure, there were all sorts of fears involved in such a personal process, not to mention countless moments when I felt the butterflies of uncertainty and loves lost fluttering in my tummy. But the more I wrote, the more it felt right to keep on going.

So the book was finished – oh no it wasn't.

My publishers asked me to read it back.

My goodness it was clunky. There was plenty in there but it was full of glaring repetitions, blurred time lines, and pages upon pages of flowery irrelevance and flight of fancy that needed to be excised. 'The story has to march on,' I was told, 'the story is the thing!'

Three months after I had declared my book finished, my editor finally agreed that it might be and when I read it back again I completely understood what she had been after. I did write every word myself but I had a great 'sorter outer' who made it fly.

So why am I telling you all this?

I'm telling you because once I had written my book, it was time for me to go out on the road and sell it. This is the part of the process that a lot of writers are reluctant to do and will try anything to get out of. But in my mind, a book is not a book unless it is actually read and preferably by as many people as possible.

And so as the requests for interviews began to come in, a shortlist was compiled. And top of that list? *Friday Night with Jonathan Ross*. Here he was again.

Jonathan has featured in my story off and on over the last twenty years. When he had been up, I had often been down and vice versa. I had worked for him in my first job when I came down to London and he had also worked for me when I hired him at Virgin Radio. Here we were again, but this time the most equal we had ever been, scheduled to lock horns on his Friday-night talk show to discuss a book that would never have been written had he and Russell not made their naughty phone call to that nice actor chap.

Surely, my revealing this to Jonathan had to be the culmination of the interview.

I knew it was important, vitally important, in the interview with Jonathan that I got it right, so I prepared for my appearance with him like I had never prepared for anything before. I had seen some good, bad and downright ugly interviews that Jonathan had conducted over the years and I didn't want to be on the end of a roasting on national television. Plus, if I am being nakedly honest, I didn't want him to beat me.

The best way to avoid this, I concluded, was simply to be as interesting, intriguing and funny as possible from start to finish, and not even give him the pause for thought he might need to go anywhere below the belt. I was ready to fight dirty if he wanted to, but I hoped the story behind my story would be enough to hold his attention.

Every press, radio or TV interview I took part in leading up to Jonathan's show was a practice run for *Friday Night with Jonathan Ross*. Different interviewers want different things out of you, so they were all helping me prepare the ground for the big one.

I call it the big one because that's exactly what it felt like. While I had been in the wilderness, Jonathan was everything I wasn't. He was on television having fun, while I was out in the cold, pretending none of it mattered anymore.

So the countdown to our clash continued. I was due to appear on the Thursday of the week I had taken off to go on a nationwide book tour and I went to the gym almost every day, ate really well and drank loads of water. I also bought myself a new outfit in an attempt to look half decent. When it was time to record the programme, I couldn't have been more ready. I was determined to interest him to death, or at least die trying!

The main guest is usually on last, the slot I was scheduled to fill but earlier that day I had called the executive producer, who just happened to be my long-suffering ex-girlfriend Suzi Aplin. Suzi and I had long since been back on speaking terms. In fact it was Suzi who provided some of the photographs for this book and the first one. I was calling her to ask if she would consider putting me on not last but first.

This was for two reasons. Both Jonathan and I would have more energy if we didn't have to sit through the first two guests before I came on and, bearing in mind that Jonathan notoriously over-recorded – sometimes talking to a guest for almost an hour – I might well be half asleep by the time my intro was announced. Plus, I had been watching the show recently and had often found myself nodding off before the end, purely because it was so late. I reckoned I couldn't be the only one suffering from this affliction and reasoned that if I were on earlier rather than later, more people might get to see Jonathan and me sparring.

'I promise Suz, if you put me on first I will be on fire and help set the rest of the show up but I will be useless if I have to hang around,' I explained.

'Let me talk to JR,' she said. 'If he says OK, it's fine by me.'

The word came back. Jonathan understood where I was coming from and had agreed– already a good sign.

When I arrived at the studio I was shown to a lovely dressing room, with flowers, presents and a hand-written note of thanks from the man himself. He even popped in to say hello. His usual forthright self, chatting away – just another show for him, but a huge deal for me.

Not so, however.

'I think he's quite nervous,' said Suzy after he had left. Was she being kind to her anxious ex or did she mean it? 'No, I'm serious, you and he have a history and he's aware of that. He knows what you might think of him and I think he's ready to give you the interview you deserve. Don't get me wrong he's not going to give you an easy ride but prepare to be pleasantly surprised.'

Backstage, waiting to go on, I was calmer than I thought I would be but still on red alert, every sense one hundred per cent heightened. And all the time all I could think about was that if it weren't for Jonathan and Russell, I wouldn't even be here.

I was ... and Jonathan was about to introduce me. '... Please welcome Chris Evans' and a tap on my shoulder from the floor manager were my cues to walk out. Generous applause ...

I looked Jonathan in the eye and just waited for the questions to start coming. I knew I had all the answers, all I had to do was be honest and not go looking for laughs but let the laughs come. I had a great story to tell and all I had to do was tell it.

I made myself comfortable on his fancy black-leather sofa. After a couple of quips about my greying hair, Jonathan launched into his first real question. The audience hushed, we were off and running. Very quickly, Jonathan dropped all his banter, realising there was a whole heap of stuff that might be worth getting through here.

The laughs did come, interspersed with the applause. There were great moments of tension, a bit like a rally at Wimbledon when no one knows quite what might happen next and where the ball's going to end up. I had a feeling the audience also sensed something else going on here.

For instance, Jonathan asked, 'But when you were going mad – didn't anyone tell you that you might want to take a look at yourself?' It was a fair-enough question.

'But Jonathan,' I said, 'that's exactly what's happening to you. No one's told you either.'

As the interview continued, so many of the things I'd written about now applied to Jonathan. Were we going to swap places again? We sparred some more and in what seemed like no time we were done.

'What a fascinating interview, ladies and gentlemen,' Jonathan concluded, with obvious surprise. 'And there's more to come, Book 2 I believe.'

'That's right.' I confirmed.

'Well, please come back next year and tell us about it.'

'Alright, I will,' I said.

But as we now know, there would be no next year for Jonathan, at least not at the BBC. Two months after our 'chat', Jonathan would announce that he was upping sticks and walking away from his BBC contract after the cloud formed by his appearance on *The Russell Brand Show* simply refused to go away.

Do I think he made the right decision?

For the record, no – but it's not my career and it's not my life. It's up to Jonathan what he does and why he does it, and, let's face it, I don't exactly have the greatest track record in the world when it comes to making career decisions, do I?

TOP 10 BEST THINGS ABOUT THE MORNINGS

10 The birdsong
9 The shower
8 The chance to see Noah and his mum fast asleep
7 The first cup of coffee
6 Beth (our German shepherd) lazily raising an eyebrow in my direction
5 The lack of traffic
4 The weather making its mind up
3 The anticipation
2 The optimism
1 The possibility

BY THE AUTUMN OF 2009 Sir Terry was only two weeks away from announcing to his millions of loyal listeners that he felt the time was right to say, 'So long'. There were bound to be tears, perhaps even from the great stoic himself, but one year on from the debacle of Ross and Brand, the train was back on track and T-Day take 2 was once again looming.

We were so close now and, incredibly, after what was almost two years, the news still hadn't leaked. Would we make it to the finish line without being tripped up?

Answer: No, of course not.

Cue our good friends at the *Mail on Sunday*.

They printed the story almost word for word. Somebody just hadn't been able to help themselves. There were so many details they got spot on, their information had obviously come from a highly reliable source.

After a while, you can weed out the stories where the journalists are simply chancing their arm, hoping to flush something out of nothing, but all the other papers could tell this was a genuine scoop and were on to it like a flash.

Immediately our plans had to change, too. We waited to see what Terry wanted to do, it had to be his call. After giving it some serious thought and discussing the matter with his family, he decided he would say something the very next day on his show. There would be an announcement from the great man himself directly after the eight o'clock bulletin.

That Sunday evening, Terry sat down to say hello to his goodbye, to write the words of a statesman-like speech that would inform his loyal followers of the news they never wanted to hear.

Gulp. Terry announcing he was leaving was one thing, but me being presented as his replacement was entirely another. His abdication would be greeted with first sadness, then reflection and ultimately celebration, testament to an amazing career, but my anointment was bound to stir up a whole different subset of emotions – many of them perhaps not quite as favourable.

We had to wait until the following Wednesday for other contracts also affected by Sir Terry's departure to be signed before we could go public with the extent of the changes. It was a bit like a house-buying chain, as I was taking over *Breakfast*, Simon Mayo was taking over *Drivetime* and Richard Bacon was stepping into Simon's old slot on 5 Live.

Finally, the second half of the week's shock radio news was out there in black and white:

'Evans to replace Sir Tel'.

Now would you look at that, me sounding like a naughty schoolboy with just my surname up there alongside Sir Terry's noble prefix. This basically set the tone for the next month and kicked off straight away that night when I was the subject of another heated debate on *Newsnight*. I think this was my third to date; I must turn up for one of them one day.

I tuned in at home to see a man from commercial radio, who was extremely opinionated about me considering the lateness of the hour.

'Hang on a minute, mate', I thought to myself. 'Are you aware that I have actually been working for the BBC, and Radio 2, five times a week for the last four years. Not only that but I worked for BBC Radio for five years before that. In fact I have worked at the BBC for twice as long as I have ever worked in commercial radio, you numpty.'

I had completely bitten but of course that's what he was on there for. Thank God I didn't agree to appear. 'Only fight battles you know you are going to win,' says a very wise friend of mine.

Following this opening volley, I became the subject of countless other discussions on various talk shows, both on television and radio, featuring a stream of self-declared experts and spokespeople. Suddenly everyone professed to have an intimate knowledge of the inner workings of how to put a radio show together and what the listeners might want to hear.

'Give it a rest, for goodness sake.' I was still biting. I've been sneaking into studios at night coming up with ideas and practising with record players, CD players, tape-machines and now digital operating systems since I was a spotty teenager. Yet from a number of these comments anyone would think I'd won some kind of competition to be a DJ for a day.

The BBC message boards were also ablaze with many of the more colourful remarks and conjecture regarding my appointment. One could have been forgiven for thinking some of the things being posted there were in reference to the devil himself rather than a new breakfast show host who might not quite be their cup of tea.

All this and I hadn't even started the show yet!

Back on the radio, from the moment Terry declared he was off, his show seemed to me to take on a new energy, like a champion steeplechaser knowing this was his last outing.

His first week after the announcement was filled with almost continuous eulogies from his faithful listeners, many of whom were renowned for their ability to write almost perfect prose for their great leader to read out every morning. Now they too excelled, stepping up their efforts, knowing in many ways that this was goodbye for them too.

After an initial week of grieving, Terry declared it party time and insisted there would be no more tears, as well as going to great lengths to stress that amidst all the Wogan Woe and Tel Don't Go, he wasn't so much leaving, as merely scaling down his duties in order to host his new Sunday morning show – a live extravaganza from the BBC Radio Theatre.

The fuss, and there was lots of it – much more than any of us had anticipated – began to die down a little, and there was a brief hiatus in the first two weeks of December. Of course it was only the calm before the really big storm that was still to hit us, but it was a welcome relief all the same. As Terry's show moved into its last week, I braced myself for the bumps.

'Chris, Tel would love it if you came in on his penultimate show. Do you fancy it?' asked Alan 'Barrowlands' Boyd, Sir Tel's producer.

'Whatever I can do to help,' I replied, happy to oblige and appreciative of the chance to divert some of the fallout.

'Do we need a planning meeting Alan?'

'Dear boy, what a splendid idea. The Stag after your show?'

'It's a date.'

Alan, a very experienced old hand within Radio 2, sensed that Terry and I together was no bad idea – united we stand.

When I appeared with Tel on that Thursday morning, we both said how astonished we had been by the enormity of the reaction to the last month's events and equally what a relief it was that they were now almost over.

On air we tried to reassure each other, along with Terry's millions of listeners, that everything was going to be alright.

'We all have to leave sometime and if not now when?' was how Terry so aptly put it.

Somebody was always going to have to take over, and he was off and I was on.

Terry's last day on the show he had hosted for an astonishing twenty-seven years was all about the man and notably his music, something that came across as surprisingly important. Self-deprecating, witty and intelligent as ever, he held it together incredibly well in between the tunes that had meant the most to him, with his voice only faintly cracking right at the end.

After he stepped away from *Wake Up to Wogan* for the final time, Mr Radio stood on the steps of Broadcasting House, like an outgoing Prime Minister – but one who people actually liked. He was surrounded by photographers and television crews and, of course, hordes of his loyal TOGs, clutching their hankies, most of them all cried out.

'No blubbing allowed,' he insisted. 'I want to leave on a smile.'

A few more photographs, the last of the news interviews and fifteen minutes later he was gone.

I had been listening to the whole of Terry's show at home and as the reign of the most successful light-entertainment broadcaster British radio had ever witnessed came to an end, I said, 'Holy Mother of Mary', out loud as he signed off.

'The shit is about to hit the fan and it's all coming my way.'

I must have been learning because, for once, I was absolutely one hundred per cent correct.

TOP 10 THINGS A PRODUCER DOES FOR A DJ (WELL, MINE FOR ME, TO BE MORE PRECISE)

10 Gets up in the middle of the night to be in work for 5 am

9 Receives the script that I type on the way in, checks it and prints it out

8 Tasks up the team (Susie, Day and Joe) according to said script

7 Reads every email we are ever sent and selects the best

6 Receives, checks and adds additional changes to the music running order

5 Sets up the studio and briefs the studio manager

4 Shouts at me via talkback if I mess up or forget anything

3 Keeps any potential panic out of the studio and in the control room

2 Tells me I'm good when I think I stink

1 Does it all again the next day

CHRISTMAS 2009 CAME AND WENT like the popping of a light bulb. Noah saw his first Christmas tree and, along with our German shepherd Beth, tried to eat most of it, whilst Tash was intent on seeing how much food she could get into me before I exploded all over the living room.

It was all very homely and lovely but before I could ask, 'How about this for a New Year's Resolution?' I was back at a very Woganless Radio 2.

It was just coming up to 7:05 am, I was in Studio 6B on the sixth floor, the red microphone light had just become illuminated and I was about to welcome Britain to an all-new way of waking up.

Not that I was nervous – no one would be listening. Not because Terry's eight million listeners were unanimously covering their ears in mass protest, but because it was the week before we were due to go on air for real and this was the first day of our pilot week.

Hit the ground running, I had learned from my television days. In other words, don't let your first show be your first show. Pilots are worth their weight in gold, every minute another chance to make a mistake in private before messing up in front of the whole nation.

When it came to ideas for the pilots, Hells Bells (super producer and one of Hull's finest ever exports) and I had decided to throw it all at the wall and see what might stick, if any of it. It was always going to be too full. With a good radio show really being all about the flow – the cogs turning behind the scenes without the listener being aware of their existence – stripping back became an obsession.

With each pilot, our proposed new format became less cluttered but still way too busy. We had to come up with a more relaxed atmosphere for the listeners, especially after Terry's laid-back, sometimes almost horizontal style.

I was beginning to realise there was very little room for manoeuvre within a Radio 2 breakfast show. Keeping it simple was going to have to be the key. The biggest mistake we were in danger of making was, if anything, trying too hard.

By the time Monday 11 January – the morning of our first live show – arrived, I feared we might be so ideas-light that we risked leaving ourselves open to the criticism of not being creative enough, but we could only wait and see.

So, that first morning taking over from Terry was ridiculous in every way. It's the most important thing you can do to get some sleep the night before and yet the harder you try, the less chance there is of it ever happening – I did not sleep a wink on the Sunday evening. We've all been there. By the time I climbed into the car to head off to London at 5.30am, I felt like I was on drugs.

At least it'll calm my butterflies, I thought to myself. It's difficult to be both tired and scared to death at the same time.

Wrong! With no more than half an hour to go, our good old friend Mr. Adrenaline began to kick in, whereupon I proceeded to forget anything at all that might help me get through to 9.30. All cognitive thoughts of any semblance whatsoever left my head for fear of implication in any potential disaster that might be about to unfold. My brain shut down completely, my mouth was drier than the bottom of a budgie cage and the only thing I could still hear was the sound of my own heart pounding deafeningly somewhere in between my throat and my mouth.

Break it down, break it down, break it down – that had always been my mantra for confronting problems. All I had to do was get past the first link and into the first record. Ah now, my first record – that was another hot potato that had the commentators chattering. Some bookmakers had even started taking bets as to what it might be.

I was so close to 'Good Day Sunshine' by the Beatles but instead plumped for 'All You Need is Love', a positive if not entirely watertight affirmation by the greatest band in the world.

I scripted my opening two links. I had to, I was so nervous that I couldn't even be confident of recalling my own name, let alone anything mildly amusing or interesting to say on top. I was so dreadfully wooden for that first half hour that it makes me sweat just thinking about it.

I was also afraid to look up, in case the rest of the world was still there to tell me how terribly bad I sounded and ask what on earth had possessed me to even contemplate I was worthy of taking over from the King.

When the show was over, I felt as if I had been beaten up. The whole thing had been a blur, a complete panic from start to finish, and the worst thing was – we had to do it all again the next day.

The irony of all this worry, bother and everything else that might precipitate the onset of an early coronary was that, after the bun fight of the launch day, on the Tuesday there was barely a soul to be seen. When I arrived at the same place at the same time 24 hours later, Great Portland Street was like a ghost town. All the madness of the moment had moved on to find the next circus in town.

I was a mess for that first week and most of the country had witnessed my ordeal but by Friday, it was over. No one had died and it appeared that the good people in charge were prepared to let me carry on doing *The Breakfast Show* for at least a little while longer.

The media coverage of my debut was unending with pages and pages of critique and opinions dedicated to my oh-so-shaky start. Having said that, no one really went for us, not even the various characters we suspected might.

This spoke volumes to me. The press knew I was more than capable of hosting a popular national radio show and they also knew I had sailed through much rockier waters than enduring a bit of flack on the first day in a new job.

Plus, unlike a television show or a theatrical production, you can't really kill off a daily radio show with a few bad reviews. No matter what anyone had to say, they were well aware that I would be around for a good few years yet.

Helen, the rest of the team and I knew that quite a lot was wrong with those first few shows and I'd be lying if I said that some of the reviews didn't affect us.

The strangest and most frustrating aspect of all this for me was not being able to do a job that I'd been perfectly capable of doing a few weeks before, purely because of the intense external pressure and the huge weight of expectation.

I suddenly realised why perfectly accomplished sportsmen and women sometimes find it hard to perform at their best on the big occasions. It was almost like I had to relearn something I had been doing naturally for the last five years.

As the first ten, fifteen, twenty shows were notched up, with some deep breaths and a lot of praying – I'm not joking – all my necessary motor skills started to return and, along with more stripping back of features, the show began to sound a little more like we might actually know what we were doing, each one becoming a more successful date with our new audience than the last.

At the same time, complaints quickly began to dwindle. Soon they were no longer in even their hundreds and the begrudgers who were still bothering to make them almost sounded as if they were losing interest in their own point of view.

With the show now well and truly on the road, the next stage was to dig in and look for some consistency. To help achieve this, I had made the decision to stay on air for four months straight but Hells Bells had some late-breaking news.

'Christoff' – that's what people who vaguely like me, call me – 'you need to take a week off before April otherwise you're going to lose it,' she announced one morning, towards the end of February. This was by no means ideal, as there was also bound to be a mini rebellion of anti-Evans activists whenever I disappeared for my first week and the longer we put that off the better.

Helen, however, had other ideas.

'Those still out to get us are gearing themselves up for an assault in May. How about we take them by surprise, you take your week off in, say, a fortnight, we don't announce it until a couple of days before, they panic and say the first stupid thing they can think of and, before you know it, they've shot the last of their beans and you'll be back on air? You know, a bit like a Formula 1 car coming in for an early pit stop to flummox the opposition.'

This made a whole heap of sense and I loved the fact that Hells had tried to put it in motor-racing terms. Little did we know just how inspired her suggestion was.

Just as Hells had recommended, we decided to leave it until the Wednesday before to make any mention on the show that I would be on holiday the following week but, as it turned out, it wasn't so much *when* I revealed it rather than *how* I revealed it that caused such a stir.

Here's what I said:

'Oh, and by the way, we won't be here next week. I'm going to have a think.'

Why I said it like this and not in some other way, I have no idea, but my ad-libbed phrase, 'I'm going to have a think,' lit the touch-paper of another huge box of fireworks that was about to go off.

'Evans in Re-think to Breakfast Show,' screamed one headline the next day. Hang on a minute! Where did the 're' and 'breakfast show' bits of that phrase suddenly appear from? I know I hadn't used those words. What I meant by what I did say, was that I was going to have a think about life and my family and all the other things people think about when they go away.

But there was no stopping them now, they were off and running again.

The message boards lit up for a bonus session of Brekkie Boy-bashing, with one talk show now asking, 'Should the Beeb Sack Evans?' whilst other newspaper headlines shouted things like 'Evans Reconsiders Future' and 'Evans Breakfast Show Crisis'.

Hilarious, I mean really. I was on holiday. No more, no less.

People were stopping me in the street to ask if I was alright and reassuring me that, not only did they listen, but they had family and friends who listened too. One elderly lady jumped off her bike, threw it to the floor and rushed up to give me a kiss and a conciliatory hug. Even my next-door neighbours were not immune to the power of the printed word, intelligent sensible people texting me from their skiing holidays in Switzerland, 'Thinking about you at what must be a hard time.'

The great Sir Terry himself made contact, encouraging me 'Not to lose heart and just continue being you.' All this while

I was doing no more than catching up on some much-needed sleep, and having a few days downtime with my wife and son.

So, what to do?

Well, I have learnt that in many ways life is like golf – or perhaps it's the other way round, explaining golf's great popularity. Every golf shot presents you with the need to make a series of decisions; you walk up to the ball, assess the situation and decide what to do next. There are lots of different shots you can play but the most important thing is to play your own game and not get dragged into what other people want you to do.

It was important for me now, therefore, more than ever, to stay focused and not react by doing something silly. I had done that far too many times before and it was time to stop this pattern. I remembered to breathe – breathing gives you the space in which to think – and to relax. The more I considered what was going on, the more farcical it all seemed.

The amazing thing was that not one reporter actually bothered to contact me to check whether what they were saying was actually the case. There were literally pages and pages of conjecture with regard to my future, all based on nothing other than the misinterpretation of those six words, 'I'm going to have a think.'

But there was more to come, the nonsense factory was on a roll and was about to go into overdrive. I was still in the middle of my week's holiday when a new headline appeared: 'Evans Loses 800,000 Listeners in First Month'.

Now where on earth they plucked this figure from, I have not the faintest idea. I promise you, on the engine of my favourite car, that such figures categorically did not exist when the headline in question was written. The research simply had not yet been done. Yet people who really should have known better ran with this figure purely because it was now out there in black and white without a single one of them ever bothering to check or ask where it could possibly have come from.

One national newspaper columnist even wrote that I had gone to Terry to seek his advice, when all I had actually done was turn up for a posh lunch to give Sir Tel yet another award to add to his now burgeoning tally.

Whichever way I looked at it, I was plumb in the middle of a non-existent story and I could do nothing about it. If I'd dared to protest of course, it would look like I was jumping to my own defence and why would I do that if there was nothing to defend?

So, because I was at home, my happy happy home, and because I knew what was being said and written was one hundred per cent completely made up, I did nothing. I just sat there and resigned myself to the fact that for once it was they and not I who had lost the plot.

I did allow myself one other thought however.

What if, when the listening figures were issued, they turned out to be up and not down?

But surely that could never happen, could it?

It was time for another prayer. I was becoming very religious.

TOP 10

WHAT IFS ABOUT TAKING OVER EUROPE'S MOST POPULAR BREAKFAST RADIO SHOW

10 What if I can't get to sleep the night before the first show?
9   What if I can't get to sleep the month before?
8   What if I can't stop thinking about it the year before?
7   What if I can't talk about it for two years before?
6   What if Terry changes his mind and wants to stay?
5   What if they don't like my first record?
4   What if they don't like my first link?
3   What if Ken Bruce doesn't like me?
2   What if Lynn Travel doesn't like me?
1   What if the listeners don't like me?

THE TRUTH OF THE MATTER was that my bosses, my colleagues and I had privately accepted that the listening figures were more than likely to dip initially after Terry left, before hopefully stabilising and slowly beginning to recover. This was what *always* happened at Radio 2, when Jeremy Vine took over from Jimmy Young at lunchtimes, when I took over from Johnnie Walker on *Drivetime*, when Johnnie took over from John Dunne before him, when Steve Wright took over from Ed Stewart on weekday afternoons and when Jonathan took over from Steve Wright on Saturday mornings. My taking over from Terry would no doubt be the biggest test of this model thus far but from what history was telling us we'd better be prepared for bad news as opposed to good.

It was horrible in a way because it was like we knew we were going to get beaten up but had to sit and wait there for the fists and boots to start flying in anyway. It almost felt like we were wishing our lives away just to get over those first few months for the tanker to slow down, so we could finally get to turn it around.

But how low would the figures be, how many of Terry's old gals and geezers would have deserted us, that was what really worried us?

Anything fewer than a million, we had resigned ourselves to considering a minor victory, Terry was after all a giant who had been at the top of his game for close to four decades with an army of loyal followers and years of mutual good will.

Can you imagine, therefore, how we felt when the official listening figures for radio in the first quarter of 2010 were published, showing that Radio 2 had broken all records not for losing listeners but for increasing them?

We simply could not believe it. Like – really, really, not believe it. In a nutshell the results were as follows.

The Breakfast Show had added 1.5 million listeners – we were up to 9.5 million and not only that, but every other show had achieved record figures too. The gains were unprecedented. In fact, when the figures first came through, they were sent back to be checked. Nobody could believe it.

Ironically they were announced when I was taking my second week's scheduled holiday.

I was in Portugal, where we have a small place, and was playing golf – a four-ball with my best friend Paulo, along with two other pals, Donald and Michael, both of whom I have known for years. It was a game that had come about almost by chance, as none of us were aware that the others were around until the night before, when we'd bumped into each other in Paulo's restaurant.

We'd just had one of the most pleasant games you could ever wish for, laughing and chatting all the way round about the old times and where we were now compared with where we had been. We were all big drinkers back in the day and never tired of wondering how it was that we were all still here to tell the tale.

After finishing off our round and depositing our clubs back in the car, we ambled off to sit at a table overlooking the 18th green. It was time to tot up the various wagers and see who owed whom what.

'Drink, my good friend?' asked Paulo.

'Orange and soda please,' I replied.

'Same here,' said Donald.

'Me too,' added Michael.

Things really had changed.

As the three of us began to figure out who scored what, where, my phone started to vibrate and flash. There was a message, and then another, and another, each one interrupting the last.

'What the dickens is going on?' I said to myself. Finally, after it had calmed down, I went into my text messages.

'Chris, Bob at Radio 2 – call me asap,' read the first. Bob was the controller who had taken over after Lesley resigned. I suddenly remembered it was RAJAR day (they are the company who collate all listening figures for the UK radio industry). I excused myself from the boys and wandered off to stand under the shade of a palm tree. As I pressed the call-back button, I felt my mouth drying up.

'Hello.'

'Hello Bob, it's Chris, what is it?'

'It's good, Chris, that's what – it's very, very good.'

Now, as Bob is not a man prone to exaggeration, I had half an idea that I might like what he was about to tell me.

The figures had exceeded our wildest expectations. We would have been happy with a loss, provided it wasn't more than a million but over a million the other way – well, that was Christmas time! As Bob took me through the figures in a little more detail, he alternated between what sounded like a tone of mild disbelief and laughter. After he'd finished, I thanked him and immediately dialled Lesley's number, where I left a long and rambling message involving a lot of 'Thank you's and 'I love you's, followed by, 'Me, you, party, London, soon.'

My second call was to Helen, my faithful producer and partner in crime, the Batman to my Robin – or was it the other way round? I didn't care anymore, I was so relieved.

In many ways Helen is the opposite of Bob when it comes to displaying her emotions and I was therefore greeted with a deafening scream when she picked the phone up. Obviously euphoric and I suspect no more than a few minutes away from taking the team out for a rather large glass of something bubbly, Helen screamed a bit more, and for now we were done.

I would have loved to have been there to join in but at the same time I thought it was kind of apt that I wasn't. In many ways, celebrating had often been my downfall, come to think of it, and now here I was on the most successful day of my career, standing under a palm tree, with a soft drink waiting for me at the bar.

I took a moment to consider this. I was looking out over a fabulous golf course, the likes of which I could only have dreamed of playing on as a kid, when I had only a second-hand five-iron and a few old balls to play with on a field in Warrington. And now what?

I took a moment to let it sink in. I was a very lucky boy.

I called Tash next, who was thrilled, I texted Jade and then I called my mum. She was pleased but more interested in whether we were all safe and having a nice time. When I thought I was done, the phone began vibrating in my hand. It was my voicemail calling me back. There was another message. I clicked the answer button.

'Hello Chris, it's Terry here – what incredible news,' he said, chuckling. 'What the heck was I doing hanging around for so long putting all those people off?! Well done, really well done, I'm thrilled for you, I really am.'

Could the day get any better?

And was it really happening at all?

How on earth had my life ended up in such a good place when it had come so close on so many occasions to being an unmitigated disaster?

Still shaking my head in bewilderment and smiling, I wandered back to where the boys were sitting. They had finished working out the bets.

'Chris, my friend, you wanna know how it all ended?' Paulo asked.

'I think I've just found out but tell me anyway.'

'It finished all square.'

See you on the radio.

POSTSCRIPT

TOP
10 THINGS I STILL
WANT TO DO

10 Write and direct a movie
9 Go a year without a single alcoholic drink
8 'Acquire' some more hair
7 Get down to single figures in golf
6 Race a classic car
5 Buy a Hockney
4 Buy a house by the sea
3 Create *the* new TV quiz format
2 See my kids happy
1 Stay married to my beautiful wife

NOW HERE'S THE THING. The second I finished writing this book, more stuff started to happen to me and as usual, lots of it – all really rather fast.

There were the goings on surrounding my co-hosting *The One Show* on Friday nights. The former host had allegedly left because of my appointment. His female co-host also followed him out of the door. All my fault apparently (yawn!).

Then there was the second set of listening figures for the radio show which came out in July. They were down compared to the first lot but still the next highest ever recorded. Even so, we all felt a bit crestfallen for an hour or two after we found out until we remembered how lucky we were to be alive in the first place, let alone have our health, lovely families and a great job. Upon realising this, we all cheered up again immediately and went to the pub for a pint and a bag of peanuts.

There was also the small matter of me finally managing to buy my all time dream car – a Ferrari 250 GTO. Remember that for me buying something is entirely different to having the money to actually pay for it (Radio station, rock star mansion etc.). When it came to the GTO, once again, I would fall into the former camp as opposed to the latter. To raise the necessary funds for what was, in many ways, my most decadent purchase to date (and that's saying something), I had to sell my White Collection. This consisted of six other classic Ferraris I'd had painted white , all with matching blue leather interiors. As well as these six, I also had to sell the Coburn car that caused me so much grief in the first place. Seven cars for one! I know what you're thinking but it had to be done.

My plans for the future? Well, I'll have to do something drastic about my cholesterol first, or else there might not be one – it was over seven at the last count. But having said that, I want *The Breakfast Show* to be around for everyone that honours us with listening, until I'm at least 50 and I'd like it to always remain positive and relevant. I would like to stay on *The One Show* on Fridays and see it extend to an hour a week. I would like to write more books but to be honest, I have no idea about what exactly. I would also like to create a new television quiz format that was as good as, if not better than, *Who Wants To Be A Millionaire*. There is one particular idea I've been mulling over for a good while now that I think may have some real potential.

Most of all though, I want to be a good dad to Jade and Noah and whoever else might come along. Tash wants another baby and so do I. At the time of going to print this has not come any closer to happening, or at least not as far as I know about it. I'd also like to remain happily married. Those are the most important things for me. If I can achieve them, I will be a happy husband, a happy father and a happy man. Who could ask for more?

During the writing of this present volume, *Memoirs of a Fruitcake*, there were times when I shuddered at recalling how mad my life was. I remember thinking on more than one occasion, 'Alright it may have been fun now and again but by and large, thank heaven those days are over.'

I said this to my wife one night over dinner as the writing was coming to an end.

'You *are* joking, of course,' she said.

'No, why, what do you mean?'

'You are still completely insane. Have you forgotten the fact that you have since sold the black car you bought in Italy, along with all your other cars, to buy just the one GTO that we really can't afford?'

'Well ...'

'How about the fact that every day, you worry whether or not your radio show is any good, even though everyone you respect tells you it's fine?'

'Er ...'

'How about that you look at your belly in the mirror just before you go and pick up the Indian takeaway every Saturday night and then eat the lot, look at your belly some more and then hit the chocolate drawer?'

'Yes, but apart from that ...'

'And when you left the house the other day without anything on other than your trousers and you didn't realise until you were on the M25 and felt the seatbelt rubbing into your skin and the pedals hurting the bottom of your feet!'

She has a point of course, in fact as you can see, she has many.

Someone turn the oven back on, there's another fruitcake to bake.